More Praise for
RISK!

"Electric, daring, bold, ribald, terrifying. And that's just the first five stories."

　　　　—Dan Kennedy, host of *The Moth* storytelling podcast

"Powerful...The writers in *RISK!* are unafraid to bare their souls. These stories prove that when you take a chance—in storytelling and in life—anything can happen."

　　　　　　　—Lisa Lampanelli, comedian and playwright

"*RISK!* uncovers life at its most hilarious and terrifying. Each story leads readers over a tripwire and leaves you thinking, 'Wow...'"

　　　　—Glynn Washington, host of WNYC's *Snap Judgment*

RISK!

EDITED BY KEVIN ALLISON

RISK!

TRUE STORIES
PEOPLE NEVER THOUGHT
THEY'D DARE TO SHARE

EDITED BY KEVIN ALLISON

hachette
BOOKS

NEW YORK BOSTON

Compilation and Introduction copyright © 2018 by Kevin Allison
Cover design by Carlos Esparza
Cover photograph © Andrea Crisante/Shutterstock
Cover copyright © 2018 by Hachette Book Group, Inc.

Hachette Books
Hachette Book Group
1290 Avenue of the Americas
New York, NY 10104
hachettebookgroup.com
twitter.com/hachettebooks

First Edition: July 2018

Hachette Books is a division of Hachette Book Group, Inc.

The Hachette Books name and logo are trademarks of Hachette Book Group, Inc.

The publisher is not responsible for websites (or their content) that are not owned by the publisher.

The Hachette Speakers Bureau provides a wide range of authors for speaking events. To find out more, go to www.hachettespeakersbureau.com or call (866) 376-6591.

Library of Congress Control Number: 2018935481

ISBNs: 978-0-316-47828-1 (trade paperback), 978-0-316-47827-4 (ebook)

Printed in the United States of America

LSC-C

10 9 8 7 6 5 4 3 2 1

For those who dare to listen,
and those who dare to share.

CONTENTS

Introduction by Kevin Allison   xiii

Bad Samaritans

With Great Beauty by A. J. Jacobs   3

The Gift by Michele Carlo   12

The Riverside by Jan Scott-Frazier   18

Morning Shifts at the Horseshoe
by Hanna Brooks Olsen   26

Long Way Home by Jesse Thorn   35

Dressing the Wound by Jim Padar   42

Bitter Pills

The Power by Tori   53

Chasing the Sunset by Tom Coleman   62

Heart and Hands by Tracey Segarra   72

It's All Happening at the Zoo by Kitty Hailey   83

Man Up by Max   91

Uncle Louie by Roy Lazorwitz   100

Trauma and Transcendence

Always a Woman by Morgan   111

The Duel by Lili Taylor   120

Redemption by Pollo Corral   124

Another Saturday Night by Ts Madison   137

Surrender by Marcy Langlois   147

Dylan by Kyle Gest   157

A Bridge Too Far

Outside the Comfort Zone by Christopher Ryan   171

The Stranger by Dan Savage   182

Judgment Day by JJ   191

Ham and Samurai by Kevin Allison   198

An American Family by Nimisha Ladva   206

Slave by Mollena Williams-Haas   214

The Ring of Fire by Michael Ian Black   230

In Plain Sight

High Fidelity by Jonah Ray   239

Every Day Is Halloween by David Crabb   245

The Downward Spiral by JC Cassis   254

Like Mother, Like Me by Ames Beckerman   278

In the Shadows by Moloch Masters   285

Asking and Telling by Walter Zimmerman   292

Making the Best of It

OMG by Aisha Tyler   303

Unbreakable by Melanie Hamlett   312

Hookers 'n' Blow by Marc Maron   331

Doing Good by Chad Duncan   336

Who Talks Like That? by Paul F. Tompkins   346

Comfortable in the Water by Ray Christian   351

Afterword   359

Acknowledgments   361

About the Editor   366

Contributor Bios   367

Permissions   378

INTRODUCTION

You have a story you've never dared to share.

Maybe it's about that bewildering night you lost your virginity. Or the fistfight you hate to admit that you started. Or the week your dad died and you learned a creepy secret.

Maybe you have told a version of this story before—to your therapist or your spouse. But you cleaned it up a bit. You left one stone unturned. It could be you were tempted to spill the whole messy truth to your closest friend one night over drinks, but that scolding voice in your head said, "Hey now. Some things are better left unsaid."

But what if I told you there's an extraordinary place where you'd be *celebrated* for biting the bullet and sharing the whole damn truth—the good, the bad, and especially the ugly of it—with the world?

Hello kids, this is *RISK!* That's exactly what we're about.

If you're one of the millions of people who have heard the *RISK!* podcast or attended one of our live shows, you already know the motto we've lived by for more than eight years and 350 episodes. "*RISK!* is the show where people tell true stories they never thought they'd dare to share." We say that on *RISK!*, nothing is inappropriate until something just…is. But then we talk about it anyway! Because unlike other storytelling shows, *RISK!* doesn't censor our contributors' stories to suit the standards of family-friendly radio. Nothing is too emotional, too graphic, too strange.

I have collected in this book some of my favorite stories of unforgettable life experiences courageously shared on the podcast, as well as extraordinary new stories that have never been told anywhere. What ties them together is how surprising, gripping, and nakedly honest they all are. I tell people that *RISK!* is soul food, served spicy. Prepare for stories that will make you laugh and cry…and that may keep you up at night.

Our live show happens once a month in New York and LA, but I also take the show on the road. After each event, people line up to give the storytellers and me a hug and share something. A college kid in St. Louis had tears streaming down his face when he told me the podcast saved his life. A man once emailed to say getting his stepson to listen to a *RISK!* story helped the two of them to finally relate to each another and moved the boy to get help for his drug problem. A college student emailed to say the show helped her come to terms with her rape. After listening to *RISK!*, she knew how to get help. At a show in Austin, an older married couple told me they'd been on the verge of divorce, but then came out to each other as "kinky" after hearing an X-rated story on *RISK!*, and it saved their marriage.

These amazing shifts that happen to people—these transformations—are just as powerful on the page as on the podcast. They're what happens when we see true courage in action and are inspired to take a risk ourselves. All the brave storytellers in this collection bare not only their souls but also some of their darkest secrets.

I can attest to how unfiltered honesty saves lives. It saved mine.

Picture this. At five years old, I began to be terrified of myself.

I was a bucktoothed redhead, usually "bouncing off the walls," as my mom said. It was the messy mid-seventies, and we were as Catholic as they come in an oh-so-Republican part of Ohio. At that age, I'd never heard of "having a crush" on someone. But I realized that I felt something for Sammy Buchanan. He was born the same day I was, lived a few houses down, and we were the best of friends. Sammy had sandy hair, a sunny smile, and an amazing toy collection. One rainy afternoon, listening to the cartoon mice chirping on the Disney *Cinderella* LP, I blurted out, "Sammy! Wouldn't it be funny if we took off all our clothes?!"

I was right—it was hilarious! We ripped off our clothes and laughed up a storm. Romping around, some part of my little brain knew exactly why I'd made the suggestion—that for me this was more than just humorous. Suddenly, Sammy's eyes were wide as quarters and he said, "What's that?!"

He was pointing at my penis. I looked down and my jaw dropped. It was doing something both of us found bewildering—it had turned stiff and was pointing toward the ceiling. I instinctively knew this was an outward sign that I found this boy-and-boy nakedness *exciting*.

Sammy laughed it off, but I couldn't. I remembered something his older brother, Rick, had told the two of us just days earlier. "When people say *gay* or *fag*," he'd said, "they mean a boy who likes other boys the way that a boy is supposed to

like girls. That's why it also means 'disgusting' and 'lame.'"
I felt hot and cold with fear. "In one year, I have to go to
kindergarten," I thought. "I'm going to meet so many kids.
What if one of them finds out I'm a gay fag?"

Most gay kids aren't self-aware so soon, but I was a precocious (and horny) little guy. Because I forced myself not to be
honest with anyone around me, a black cloud of anxiety hung
over my head everywhere I went throughout my childhood.
I was obsessed with keeping my sexuality hidden.

But by my teens, I got gutsy, fascinated by the idea of coming out. A little over a decade after the Sammy Buchanan
incident, I finally mustered the courage to share about my
sexuality with friends and family members, one by one. I felt
a gush of relief and affirmation each time. Those relationships only deepened from my sharing the truth. I've spent my
whole life learning the essential lesson that each of the writers in this collection live out.

But it wasn't just my sexuality that was different. Family
members told me I was too expressive. Friends told me my
sense of humor was too strange. Teachers told me my voice
was too big. I felt like a freak most of the time. For a few
years after college, I was lucky enough to be in a sketch
comedy group called The State with a series on MTV, where
it was okay to be too much this or too much that. But
when I changed my focus to doing solo character monologues after The State broke up in '96, I was drowning in
self-consciousness about what Hollywood casting directors
might think of me. I did all I could to avoid seeming too
loud and gay, too Midwestern and polite, too goofy and
surreal, or too serious and spiritual. In an effort to not be

too much of anything, I had let myself become nothing. No one would hire me. I was a wreck, and I was starving.

Everything changed one January night in 2009. I was about to turn forty. I was twelve years away from my successful period on TV, and twelve years into drinking myself silly and thinking of jumping off the Williamsburg Bridge. I did not want to head into another decade in this rut, but on this January night, I did a solo show of character monologues at San Francisco Sketchfest, and everything that could go wrong did. The show was called *F*** Up* (about five guys who had f***ed up their careers!) and on that night, it lived up to its name.

A fellow State member, Michael Ian Black—whose amazing story "The Ring of Fire" I've included in this collection—was there. After the show, I asked him what he thought.

He paused, then said, "I think everyone in that audience tonight would have been more interested if you'd been sharing your real-life experiences. Why not just drop the mask and tell us the truth?"

I felt a sting of nervousness. I said, "Ugh. Putting myself out there like that, with all these odd contradictions that make up who I am, it feels too risky!"

He stopped walking and said, "If it feels like a risk, it's because you're opening up to the audience. But then they will open up to you."

It was one of the most important things anyone has ever said to me.

On the plane ride home, I promised myself I would tell the boldest true story I could think of onstage once I was back in New York. I'd heard of true storytelling shows but had never been to one. A friend told me that Margot Leitman and Giulia Rozzi hosted a show called *Stripped Stories* at the UCB Theatre in Chelsea featuring tales from people's sex lives, so I called them.

"I can tell the story," I told Margot, "about the first time I tried prostituting myself and failed, when I was twenty-three. It was a comedy of errors." She said, "Not only can you, *you must*!"

But when the day of the show came around, I felt like a frayed power line. Just a few hours before showtime, I called Margot to back out. "It feels too risky," I told her.

She said, "Oh wow! That's so great to hear!"

I was confused, but her laughter put me at ease. "Listen," she said, "there are still tons of taboos around talking about sex! So when one of my storytellers calls me the day of the show and tells me it feels too risky—and someone often does—I know that if I can just talk them into going through with it anyway, *that* will be the story that ends up meaning the most to the audience."

I had to do it.

That night, I told the story (later featured on *RISK!* Episode #451) called "The Hustler." As I was telling the story, I felt a voice in the back of my head saying, "Do I sound too gay?" and "Was that part too goofy?" and "Shit! I definitely sound too Midwestern here...." But eventually, I stopped focusing on that voice and started to notice something else. For the first time, I wasn't reciting a memorized monologue at the audience. I was conversing with them. Their eyes weren't just lighting up from the laugh lines; they shone with compassion and recognition. This flow of energy between myself and the audience was new to me. The more intimate I got with my revelations, the more they leaned forward. Afterward, people didn't just tell me I was funny; they offered their own truths and memories. I'd reached them, contradictions and all. I'd turned a corner.

I walked away from the UCB Theatre buzzing with excitement. What to do next clicked into place: I would create *RISK!*, a storytelling show where people could come out about anything, no matter how outrageous or emotional or scary, no matter how funny or strange. It would be a place where people could share the most meaningful moments from their lives with as much vulnerability as they'd show with their therapists.

In your hands, you hold the most stunning tales of adventure and wonder that emerged from this vision. These are stories about coming to terms with who we are, living our best lives and facing death, walking out of the house intending to murder a bully before your friend talks you out of it, being bitten by scorpions atop an isolated mountain, and getting a life-changing insight from the eccentric uncle from whom you least expect it.

Each of these stories will change you in a different way. If you let them, they might inspire you to come clean in ways you never imagined you would. Remember that story you thought you'd never dare to share? As I say at the end of the podcast each week, "Folks, today's the day. Take a risk!"

—Kevin Allison

BAD SAMARITANS

A. J. JACOBS

WITH GREAT BEAUTY

My wife and I have kids, and a few years ago we hired a babysitter. In our particular case, the babysitter happens to be crazy hot. Her name is Michelle, she's twenty-seven years old, and she looks like Angelina Jolie but without the freakish lips.

Beyond being a great babysitter and an unusually attractive person, Michelle is a lovely, kind woman. But since for some reason she's single, we wanted to see if we could find her a good boyfriend. So one day we sat her down and we said, "Listen, can we set you up on match.com? How about that?"

She was tentative. "It's a lot of creeps on there," she said, "and I'm not really a writer."

But I told her, "Listen, *I'm* a writer. I'll write the emails for you. No problem!" It seemed like a good idea. "I'll be sort of the gatekeeper," I said. "I'll email these guys and weed out the creeps and I'll help you, you know, just go out for a latte with the nice guys."

"Okay," she said. "I guess so…"

We set up an account. I put up some pictures of Michelle, and within a minute my computer goes "Bing!" I've got a page view! Then my computer goes "Bing, bing, bing, bing,

bing, bing!" Suddenly, I'm very excited. The emails start coming in. That first night, I get like a dozen. They look like you'd expect: "You are so beautiful"; "I love your smile"; etc. When I read those, I'm no longer just excited; I'm exhilarated. Because I've never had this much positive feedback in my life. And, yes, I realize it's technically not for me, but still, it's an incredible thrill.

I find that there are some potential good guys, but there are also a tremendous number of guys that I have to weed out. As I start to read through them, more emails come in, and I realize that there will soon be so many that I have to start coming up with a system. So I make a list of the deal breakers. If there's a guy who mentions the word *ladies* in his opening email, I figure that's not good. If he says that his best feature (the website asks you your best feature) is "Ass" or "Butt," even if it's ironic, that's a strong red flag. If the guy's head is tilted more than twenty degrees—to the right or the left; there's no right way to tilt as far as I'm concerned—then he's out.

There was one other deal breaker. If the guy mentions female anatomy in the first email—for example this one man opened with, "I'm not a professional gynecologist, but I'd be happy to take a look"—that's an easy no.

You'd be shocked by how many of these guys there are, and though I try to send notes to all of them to let them know I'm not interested, I find there are too many to write to them all. But I find this one guy, his user name was "Sexy Gentleman," and I said to myself, "Michelle should really respond to this guy." I thought this would be a nice thing for Michelle to do. So I sent him a note saying, "You seem nice. I don't think we're right for each other, but just FYI, you might wanna rethink 'Sexy Gentleman' as a screen name. It might be, for some women, a little too on the nose. You know?"

I felt like I was helping people. This incredible feeling rushed through me. I could help the creeps overcome their creepiness and also find some great dates for our hot babysitter. And there were certainly a few guys that I liked. There was this music teacher with long hair, and he was very humble and sweet, and he wrote these long, funny emails about xylophones. I took him to Michelle and said, "What do you think?"

"Alright," she said. "I'll meet him."

So they have a date at the Mexican restaurant. I don't go to spy, even though I really want to. When she comes back, I ask her to tell me everything, and she's like, "Yeah, I liked him. I think I liked him. He was cool, sweet. I'll go on a second date." And I'm like, "Yes!" Because I am living vicariously through her, and also through him—through both of them.

I was relieved, too, because this was her first date I'd set up and my personality—her online personality, that is—is a little bolder than her real personality, which I warned her about. But she told me that she changed her personality at the restaurant to try to fit into her online one. She tells me that when he walked in, she made him turn around to check out his butt.

I was learning quickly that it's very powerful—for me it's a rush—being a hot woman. For instance, I got this other email from this guy whose opening essay started, "When I was a child, I witnessed a clown jump to his death from a seven-story building, and it was the only time a clown has made me laugh." Obviously, I was disturbed, and so I wrote him back, saying, "You know, you seem nice. You're *very* funny. But you're a little dark for a sweet girl like me." Then when I look at his profile the next day he's changed his opening essay completely. Now it's all about Care Bears and snuggling and rainbows. He writes me that day saying, "I need a sweet girl. I like you." I felt a pang of compassion for this bizarre, creepy man. But I couldn't bear to reach back out and set something up—I couldn't do that to Michelle.

The sleazeballs continued apace, dozens of new ones every day. This one guy who looked like John Turturro opened with the line, "You seem like a handful." To that, my only response was silence.

A few months before all this, I had read in the course of my work for *Esquire* magazine a book about pickup artists, and one of the strategies they use as an opening line is to mildly insult the woman. The idea is to lower her self-esteem, and then she'll wonder if maybe this pickup guy talking to her *is* better than she is, and maybe she sort of sucks. The term for that is *negging*, as in saying something negative, and as the book about pickup artists came back to me, I realized this guy had just negged me. So I wrote him back, saying, "Hey, have you ever read the book *The Game* by Neil Strauss?" He writes back, "Why do you ask?" And I'm like, "I just busted your ass. I knew it." Because I knew that if he hadn't read *The Game*, he would have said, "No, I don't know what you're talking about."

After some back-and-forth I finally got him to confess that he's a part of this pickup artist community. He knew all these other guys who subscribed to the philosophy. When I find this out, I get quite angry. "This is not a game! I am looking for a boyfriend or a husband. Stop toying with my emotions!"

I was like Susan B. Anthony, and I just wasn't gonna take it.

Soon, I found another guy who I really liked, a scientist who seemed very sweet, though he had ears sort of like Prince Charles'. I asked Michelle, "What do you think?" And she said, "Yeah, let's try it."

We make a date. When Michelle comes back from it, I ask her about everything, and she tells me he never showed up. "He blew me off," she said. "I'm out. I can't do this anymore." I could tell she'd been crying. "You know," she said, "this is too…" but she didn't finish the thought.

I thought, "What the fuck is wrong with this guy?"

The next day, the guy emails me. He was at the Starbucks. He was outside and she was inside. "Sheesh," I think. "Kids today. They can't even find each other in a Starbucks!"

Next I get my favorite email yet. This guy whose screen name is "Watch Me on TV" and who doesn't have a picture reaches out. "Who is this?" I wonder. "Al Roker?" I open the email and it says this: "I'm married, but I'm looking for a girl on the side, and I wondered if you could be that girl? I love the forbidden fruit."

In retrospect, I should've just left it right there—that would've been the mature thing to do. But in the end I couldn't leave it. I've thought about why that was for some time, and partly it's because I think I'm a fourteen-year-old boy mentally, and I wanted to mess with him. Partly, though, it was also because this guy was my gender and he was out there ruining our reputation. He was a scumbag, and I wanted to punish him.

So naturally, I flirt with him. I say, "What's it like to be so famous?" And "Watch Me on TV" reveals that the reason he has that screen name is that he appears once every couple months on some CNBC show at something like three in the morning. I couldn't believe this guy. He's trying to leverage *that* into sex with hot women, on the side?

I keep going. "Hey, you're so famous," I write, "and I've always heard famous people can do some pretty crazy stuff. What's the craziest thing you've ever done?" He says, "I'm so crazy, I'm going to run for political office." Great, I think. This is what we need: more politicians who pick up women on the internet. Then he tells me that he has "some pretty wild fantasies."

"Do tell!" I say. I was starting to break a sweat.

"I don't know," he demurs, "they're a little risqué." I tell him not to worry. "I can take it. You can say anything to me." It was a total setup.

He emails me this two-page letter, a detailed description of how Michelle is wearing this fur coat in a strip bar, and she's got on a black bra and her nipples are hard. She's grinding her crotch into guys' faces. And it goes on and on, only getting more graphic. When I get this, I am, as you can imagine, very excited.

So I emailed him back. I decided to take a different tactic now. I wrote, "You disgust me! You want to treat me like trash. I can't believe you would consider me a piece of meat who would grind my crotch into guys!" Suddenly, he is all groveling and apologetic, saying, "Oh, I'm so sorry, I didn't know." That was when I decided I'd done my best to teach the guy a lesson, and it's time to move on. I wasn't Chris Hansen from *To Catch a Predator*. That guy gets to sit there all day doing this, but me, I've got to find Michelle a boyfriend.

She agreed to go out again with the guy with long hair, the music teacher. They meet for dinner. When she comes home afterward, I'm eager to discuss it all. "So, how was it?" I ask. "He's nice." She shrugged. I knew that was the death knell.

Although it broke my heart, she did not go on a third date with this guy. I did set her up with a bunch of other guys. It turned out that she didn't end up with any of them, but she did end up with an old friend of hers that she knew from a decade ago. So even though I can't take full credit, I do like to take a tiny bit of credit. The way I rationalize it is that Michelle hadn't dated in five years before I put us on match.com, so in a sense, I got her back into the dating mindset. Yes, it was probably delusional, but I didn't care—I felt good about that.

And for me, the online dating was one of the greatest experiences of my life. I loved it because I got all this positive feedback I wasn't used to, and I also loved how I got to see this side of men that other men typically don't. I got to see the sleazy guys that I kind of expected, as well as the guys I didn't expect—men who were very emotionally vulnerable and open and romantic.

Thinking about those men, I decided I'd do one more thing as Michelle. I searched the website for "lonely and depressed" and saw this guy with a profile that said, "I live at home with my sick mother. I take care of her. I have no life. I'm a loser. I go to work. I come home. I play video games. And I'm really depressed." I wrote to him as Michelle and said, "Listen, we can't date because you're in another state, but I just want you to know that I think it's wonderful that you take care of your mother. I think you're a rock star, and you're gonna meet some beautiful woman someday soon, and you're gonna make her very happy."

I felt that was important to do, because with great beauty comes great responsibility.

TAKING THE RISK!

A Q&A WITH A. J. JACOBS

You're used to writing for the page, but this story was originally spoken conversationally on the stage. How does that make you feel?

I try to make my writing as conversational as possible, so I think it's a good fit for me.

Are there any parts of the story that you feel need tweaking now? Why?

I wish I could redo the whole experiment now. In the age of Tinder, it might even be crazier.

MICHELE CARLO

THE GIFT

It was just a typical Tuesday a couple of weeks before Christmas. I came home from school and, as usual, went right into my bedroom, where instead of starting my homework, I opened up the window and went out on the fire escape, where I lit a cigarette, took out my mini boom box, and tried to get my favorite radio station's signal so I could finish a mixtape. That station's signal was weak in my part of the Bronx, so I had to wrap the boom box antenna in tin foil and point it toward the Whitestone Bridge.

In between making the tape and smoking the cigarette, it started to snow. So now I was trying to keep the snow off the boom box, too, so I didn't hear my mom at first when she came into the room and said she needed me to stop what I was doing and run to the store for her right now. And I thought, "Aw, man!" That was the last thing I wanted to do! When she told me what she wanted me to get for her, it was the last thing I wanted to get...Kotex. And not just any box of Kotex, but the "Super"-size box, which was big and purple with bright yellow letters. A box so tall it stuck out of any bag it was put in, so when you were carrying it down the street, anyone who looked at the bag (and you) knew you were the one that was bleeding…a lot. And when you're fifteen, you really don't want someone looking at you and knowing you are bleeding.

I growled to myself and stomped the five blocks to the drugstore, swearing that if I ever had a daughter, I'd never make her go out and buy my menstrual supplies. At the drugstore, the pimple-faced, four-eyed cashier gave me that weird, knowing look as he rang up the box. I stomped out of the store and started to walk home, when all of a sudden, I felt a gust of wind as two boys whizzed past me, grabbing the bag out of my hand as they slid down the block.

"Oh my God!" I screamed, because these weren't just any two boys; they were Dennis and Louie from the Overing Boys Crew, the two coolest boys in the neighborhood. Every boy in the neighborhood wanted to be them and every girl wanted to make out with them…except me. Which was a total lie because I had the biggest, my-first-ever crush on Dennis. But I knew, even before this, it would never be reciprocated, especially once he saw what was in that bag. And so my obsession turned into the type of hatred that only another teenager could understand.

I ran after them, trying to catch up, but when I got close, they started playing Salugi with me, which is the New York City version of Monkey in the Middle. I caught up to Louie, and he threw the bag to Dennis; I ran up to Dennis and he threw the bag back to Louie. Meanwhile, I was so terrified one of them would see what was in the bag and call me "Kotex Head" for the rest of my life, my fury and shame gave me superhuman speed. I jumped and yelled, "Fuck!" tackling Louie—and saw the box of Kotex fly out of the bag onto

Westchester Avenue, where a Number 4 bus immediately ran it over.

I started bawling. Louie's back was to the street, so he didn't see the maxi pads crushed down into the slush. He said, "Aw, c'mon, Shell, it's only a box of cookies!" And I thought, "Cookies?"

Then Dennis came over, looked in the street, looked back at me and said, "Shut up, Louie." I knew that he knew what was in the bag, but for some reason, he wasn't gonna tell. He helped me up and said, "Come on, Shell, we'll walk you home."

As we started walking back toward my building the snow was really coming down. We walked past all the neighborhood's holiday displays from people with small budgets and large imaginations, and somewhere between the talking Rudolphs, dancing Jesuses, and competing sounds of Donna Summer's and Andy Williams' Christmas albums, we started playing.

I remember twirling around, trying to catch those big, fat, wet snowflakes on my tongue. Dennis scooped up some snow from a car and threw it at Louie, and then Louie threw snow at me. We started climbing onto the cars to get more snow, which you could do before there were car alarms.

We pulled down all the snow from the car roofs and threw it at each other. Then we all started running, slipped and fell, and rolled down the street like giant teenage snowballs all the way to the end of the block, right up into a light post. When we hit it, a spell seemed to shatter. I remember standing up and seeing that the three of us were somehow holding hands. This freaked me out—you know, what with my crush on Dennis—so I dropped their hands. The sun was setting. The sky was a blazing purple-red, and in the halo of the streetlight, a snowflake was resting on one of Dennis' eyelashes. I remember thinking it was the most beautiful thing I had ever seen. Even though I knew I ought to stop looking at it, I couldn't, and so I saw Dennis was looking at me. "Shell, are you home?" he finally asked. I just nodded because I couldn't speak.

Dennis bent down and kissed me full on the lips, and Louie kissed me on the cheek. Then they both ran up the block saying, "Merry Christmas, Shell!" I had never been kissed on the lips by a boy before. I felt like Rudolph the Red-Nosed Reindeer, when Clarice, the reindeer he loved, kissed him and said he was cute, and I floated up the five flights of stairs to my family's apartment, saying, "I'm cute! I'm cuuuuute!"

When my mother asked, "Where's my box?" I told her a bus ran over it. She then made me pay her back out of my allowance, and when my father came home from work, he had to go out and buy it.

Not long after Christmas, Dennis and Louie were murdered. They were walking to a McDonald's when someone in a car driving past threw a beer can at them. Louie threw it back. The driver then looped around the block and someone from the back seat shot them both dead.

I don't know if you've ever been to a teenager's funeral, but it's not like when your grandfather died because he smoked for seventy-five years. Everyone from the neighborhood was at Dennis and Louie's funeral. Boys, girls, parents: comforting each other, crossing themselves, kneeling in front of the closed caskets because Dennis and Louie had both died from massive head wounds. I remember kneeling on the bench before Dennis' casket, shaking and crying, and out of the corner of my eye, I saw someone kneel down next to me. It was Dennis' mother. I looked at her. She was the grayest, saddest person I had ever seen in my life.

"Did you know Dennis well?" she asked.

I didn't know what to say, so I just said, "Yeah, kind of." She looked at me for a minute, and then went off to talk to somebody else.

Now, as I look back, I realize Dennis' mother was there alone in that huge room of people. I didn't see any brothers or sisters, no father, no grandparents, no aunts or cousins. She was probably about the same age then as I am now. And only now can I understand what a gift it would have been for me to tell her what a gentleman her son was. That he didn't betray my secret. That he played in the snow with me. And that his kiss was my first.

Many Christmases have come and gone since that day, but I will never forget what the wind and the snow and the colored lights gave to Dennis and Louie and me on the last pure night of our childhood.

TAKING THE RISK!

A Q&A WITH MICHELE CARLO

This story also appears in your memoir, *Fish Out of Agua*. What was different about sharing it as a radio-style story on *RISK!*?

Sharing "The Gift" for the *RISK!* podcast felt more intimate. In order for me to get at some of the more emotional stuff while writing the story for the book, I had needed to distance myself a bit from it. But when I told the story, I needed to be wholly connected to those emotions for the performance to have any impact.

How are stories about childhood different to craft than stories about things that have happened in recent years?

When you're writing a story from your childhood, you have to be aware of your perspective of those events as a child. You can use your grown-up experience to make sense of what things meant to you at the time, but you have to make sure you don't put your grown-up reasoning/reactions onto the child. When you're writing about your experiences as an adult, you don't have to worry about those two different planes of interpretation.

JAN SCOTT-FRAZIER

THE RIVERSIDE

In 1988, I was twenty-two years old and living in Japan. I had moved there the year before in order to study cartoon animation. I lived in a little apartment on the Tama River right at the edge of Tokyo. To earn money for rent and school, I worked at a restaurant, washing dishes and doing kitchen prep.

With the pressure of both animation school and work, both of which I was trying to complete with next to no grasp of the language, I found myself lonely and stressed all the time. One night, I decided that I would try something I used to do when I was anxious in my childhood: take a walk. There was no better place to stroll than along the Tama River, and since I had always walked south along it in order to get to school and work, I decided that this evening I would walk upriver.

The river was wide, and we were far enough from the city that there weren't very many people around, especially since I only started my walk at midnight. I wandered up this path, where the buildings got farther and farther apart. It got quieter and quieter until all I heard was the cool breeze, the frogs, and sometimes the ducks.

I kept walking up the river until I finally came to a place where the river widened, and there was a waterfall of sorts, a three-meter sloping drop. On the side of the river I was on—the north side—there was a big concrete platform, and at the edge of the platform was a waist-high railing. You could stand on that platform and study the river, which glistened in the moonlight as it streamed down the waterfall. Across the way, a small city, Noborito, threw lights into the sky.

I stood there for a long time that night, feeling the tension and stress flowing out of me.

After about an hour, I walked home. I slept so well that night that for the next few nights, I decided I should walk up there again. I would get off work at ten thirty or eleven, take the train home, then go for my little pilgrimage.

On the third consecutive night I went up there, I spotted someone ahead of me standing on the platform, a woman. I was startled at first, and then I felt invaded. I felt like my private little place had been taken.

On the other side of the platform were cattails and bull rushes, and on one side were huge concrete jacks meant to keep the area from eroding. I walked down into those jacks where the woman couldn't see me, and I sat there for a while, waiting for her to leave. But she wouldn't leave.

I wondered what she could possibly be doing. I crawled surreptitiously over these jacks until I could see her, standing against the railing. She was crying. Every so often the wind would blow the right way, and I could hear her sobbing.

After about half an hour, she finished and walked upriver. "How very sad," I thought, and then I realized I was doing much the same thing, which was even more depressing.

I spent my half-hour shift up there, and then I went home.
The next day, I got busy and couldn't go. But when I returned
the following week, I saw her there every day, standing at the
railing, crying. I went back down into the jacks, and every
time, I crawled a little closer to her.

I wondered if what I was doing would be considered stalking by some, though I didn't see it that way. I felt such empathy for her. On the final visit of the week, the moon was on its
way down, and because of the lack of light, I needed to climb
closer than ever in order to make her out. I could see that she
was a young woman, maybe in her very early twenties, and
she seemed inconsolable, just sobbing, sobbing.

After she went home, I was left standing there, looking
out over the river, listening to the frogs and the ducks. I kept
thinking about her and how very sad she seemed. Did she
not have friends? Did she have nobody who cared about her,
who could offer her some level of comfort that a solitary
river view couldn't? Somehow, I couldn't understand why she
would come here alone. I know I came here alone because I
was a foreigner struggling to live here for a year with almost
no knowledge of Japanese and no friends. How could she be
even more bereft?

I had to go back to get some sleep, but I couldn't stop
thinking about that woman. In fact, I started to feel a kind of
strong, warm feeling toward her—not a romantic feeling, but
one of deeply felt compassion.

I saw her again the next Wednesday, and I did my usual
thing, sitting in the jacks and waiting for her to leave. But this
time I had this strong drive to get up and say something. The
problem was that I'm about six-foot-one and she was about

five-foot-three, so if I tried to make an approach, I'd appear as this giant, tall, White person stumbling through curt sentences of misspoken Japanese. I would have been so nervous that I would have probably ended up saying something like, "Hello. I come to destroy you!"

So instead, I watched her leave again. The next week, I decided, I would say something.

But what could I say? "I wish I could help you," was something I wanted to tell her. Or, "How are you hurting?"

I was delayed at work, though, during my evenings the following week, and when I finally spotted her one day, she was just leaving. So I followed her up the river. I had never been beyond this point, and as I followed her I kept a good distance behind, since my white skin shines like a searchlight. She eventually left the river path to walk toward the KO train line, then she disappeared in this big group of apartments.

I continued to see her every week, and every time I did, I felt worse and worse. I just wanted to run up and embrace her, and tell her, "You know, there is somebody else out here. There is somebody who cares." I started to feel this love for her, strong love, not friendship and not romantic love, but something I had never experienced before. I could not get her out of my mind.

I decided that the next week, I needed to finally do something. I would set a trap, as it were. When I saw her, I would walk past the lookout up the river a ways to these other concrete cylinders that you could sit on, which were much closer to the lookout than the jacks were. "What I'm gonna do," I said, "is sit on these concrete cylinders and just kind of hang out, like I was casually reading a book outside alone at one o'clock in the morning."

I sat there, and luckily, there was this fat white cat nearby that was chasing bugs, so I got a weed, and I played with the cat. I looked for the woman out of the corner of my eye, wishing she would hurry up. I couldn't play with this cat forever.

Finally, she came, and I saw her, and did my best impression of someone who comes here to play with this cat at one o'clock in the morning every night. As she strolled past me, I turned and wanted to say something, but when I looked at her, I couldn't, because she had the saddest expression I'd ever seen on her face. I tried to put a thought together in Japanese, and by the time I did, she was long past me.

The trap had failed—I had failed at it—and so I looked to form my plans for the next week. I was beginning to form fanciful ideas about how our interactions could progress, probably owing to the dramatic stories I was writing in animation class. Nobody loved her, the story went. She was the saddest person in the world, to whom all these horrible things had happened. She didn't have anyone to talk to. The only person she would open up to about her problems was a mysterious foreigner who couldn't really speak Japanese. They met for coffee every evening, and they would talk and talk across their language divide.

On my way to my animation class, I walked by a toy store in which I spotted a cute white stuffed dog in the window. I decided I would buy her this dog.

The problem was that I didn't want to walk up to her and go, "Hey, dog!" using all the Japanese I knew, so I would need leave it there with a card explaining that it was a gift for her.

I bought the dog, and I wrapped this pretty red bow around its neck. The next Wednesday, it was raining, and I decided I would get to the platform before she would and leave the dog for her. I left work early so I could do this. I placed the dog on the platform, then went down to the jacks and sat there in the rain. As the water came down, I got colder and colder.

The woman never came, and the first thought in my mind was, "How dare you? I bought this dog. I've been waiting a month and a half to say something to you, and I finally get up the guts to do this, and now you don't come!" But the second thought I had was happy. Perhaps she no longer had anything to cry about. Maybe something wonderful had happened in her life.

It was a wonderful thought, but somehow I didn't really think that was the case. I retrieved the dog, which at this point was soaked, and I walked home to a very troubled sleep that night.

That was on Wednesday. The following Sunday, something happened at the restaurant where I worked. We had a dumbwaiter there—it was a two-level restaurant—and since it was wooden, I constantly had to put newspaper in it to keep it from rotting. As I put a layer of newsprint on the bottom of the dumbwaiter, I saw a picture in the newspaper that looked exactly like the woman. It was dead-on. By this point, I was confident I had memorized her face, having seen her from so many angles in the moonlight.

I spent the next two hours looking at the picture, thinking it had to be her. I tried to read the article, but my seven-month-old Japanese was not up to the task.

So I asked a couple coworkers to help me. They told me her name was Asuna Tsurukawa, and she had a difficult life. Right after high school, her father kicked her out of the house and said, "Go fend for yourself."

So she moved to Tokyo, the big city, to try to figure her life out. She wanted to go to school, but was unable to come up with the money. She took a job in a bakery instead, but she was very alienated from her coworkers there. She didn't have much in common with anyone, and didn't feel like she could have an honest conversation with people. In short, the article gave the impression that she didn't have any friends.

On the night when I was sitting out there on the jacks waiting for her, she had really wanted somebody to talk to, but her coworkers wanted to go out and drink, so they told her they were busy. She went home, and decided to take a bath, a nice, warm bath.

When I was sitting there in the rain with the dog, she opened her wrists with a razor blade. When I was walking back down the trail, freezing, the cold water dripping from me, her lifeblood was washing out into the tub. We went to sleep around the same time, both troubled and unhappy, only her sleep would last forever.

Years later, I would have the opportunity to travel more of the world. I stayed in many different countries, learned multiple languages, and vastly improved my Japanese. In all those lives I lived abroad, though, I don't think I met one other person on the planet who really cared that Asuna had lived or died. But I will always care. Now maybe you will, too.

TAKING THE RISK!

A Q&A WITH JAN SCOTT-FRAZIER

Considering that the *RISK!* podcast gets a million downloads around the world each month, did you ever suspect your story would be heard by so many?

I never thought my story would be heard by so many people. It's very exciting.

In what ways, if any, did you have to compress or expand on what you're absolutely sure is accurate?

I compressed a little, as happens with every story, but I did not exclude anything important.

HANNA BROOKS OLSEN

MORNING SHIFTS
AT THE HORSESHOE

When I was in college, I worked as a waitress at a twenty-four-hour diner in Bellingham, Washington, called the Horseshoe Café. Working there, I saw how twenty-four-hour diners are like the lightbulbs for the moths of society. At a certain time in the early morning, if you look closely, you'll find the oddballs around, the people who just don't have anywhere else to go.

I felt that way as an employee, too. I saw myself as one of these misfits and was at ease with them. I had made very few friends in college, in part because I was waiting so many shifts, but I made a ton of friends at the Horseshoe. At the Horseshoe, I felt at home.

One of the nights when I was working there, when I'd been there about a year and was coming up on graduation, I was going through a personally tumultuous time, as you do when you're about to graduate and you realize you have literally no job skills other than waiting tables. That night, this kid came in and he was like fourteen. He had that skin that fourteen-year-old boys have that's still really soft, and as a lady who values great skin, I wondered what cream I could apply to get mine to look like that.

MORNING SHIFTS AT THE HORSESHOE   27

The boy was wearing a flat 59FIFTY hat, skinny jeans, and a backpack. He was holding a paperback and $2 in his right hand. He asked me what he could get for two dollars. It was ten p.m. on a Tuesday, so I figured this kid was probably not supposed to be here, but as a waiter, it's not your place to tell people how to live their lives, how parents should raise their kids, or how kids should grow up. I said, "Oh, you can get coffee or a soda."

He nodded and said, "I don't drink coffee." And I thought, "Of course not, *because you're a literal child*."

I got him a soda, and the thing about the Horseshoe is that we have a policy that people need to spend a dollar an hour to keep their table, though I don't always stick to that because I'm not a monster.

It was a busy night, as the patrons from bars closing nearby were pouring in, and I forgot about the boy for some time. I probably would not have thought about him again for the rest of the shift if it weren't for the fact that he fell asleep. I was always on guard against sleeping. There aren't many rules at the Horseshoe, but one of them is that you can't sleep. The owner used to tell me it was some sort of a health code violation, but I'm fairly sure he was lying. I think the real reason is that at a twenty-four-hour diner, you're already providing food and a place to sit. You're so close to being a hotel at that point, that sleeping is a bridge too far.

It was probably around two o'clock in the morning when I noticed him sleeping, and it was obvious to me then that this kid did not have a place to stay for the night, so I went over to talk to him and asked him his name. He said it was Kyle.

Then I asked him how old he was, and he said he was four-teen. I asked where else he had to be.

"Nowhere," he said. "I don't have anywhere to go."

I have a lot of empathy for people in that situation. The thing with sleep is that, as animals, we require it to function. When you do not have a safe place to sleep, it amplifies every other problem you might be having. In fact, when people study homeless populations, they find sleeplessness is often the number one issue, and a big trigger of psychiatric issues such as paranoia or even schizophrenia, which are so hard on the homeless.

So this is the point where my twenty-two-year-old brain can't stop me from blurting out, "I'm off in a half an hour, so just come home with me. Just come, because I…I can't leave you here." I understood that maybe it was not the absolute best idea I'd ever had, but I would defy anybody else to look at that bleary-eyed fourteen-year-old and not be like, "Nah, kid. Come on." And for once, it was fortunate, I thought, that I didn't own a single thing worth stealing.

When I wrapped up my shift, he and I got in my car, and we went to the store and bought some food, because I had no food in my house. Then I brought him back to my place in the wee hours. I was gonna walk my dog and go to bed, and then, I figured, in the morning, before I went to class or whatever I had to do that day, we would both sit down and talk about his situation. We would figure it out. I'd contact a youth shelter and find him a safe place to go.

But as we were talking, I found out the reason that Kyle did not have anywhere to go was because he was on the run, not just from his parents (who did sound very shitty in his telling) but also from the law. Kyle had had a court date that he did not go to. So now, in my house, I had a teenage runaway—and I was harboring a fugitive. I was working through how I felt about it all, thinking, "I do not believe in the mass incarceration of youth. The way that we imprison children should be a crime." Yet it also seemed possible that jail might have been the best place for Kyle at that moment, because the kid had nowhere to go.

Thus began my campaign of trying to get Kyle to turn himself in, which lasted for the next four days that he stayed with me.

So we set up some house rules. He could not be in the house when I was not there. (I would text him when I was going home so that he'd have a heads-up to start making his way there.) He had to help me out around the house. And every day, I was permitted to harangue him to turn himself in, and he had to listen respectfully.

It turned out he was super-helpful. In fact, he was one of the best houseguests I've ever had. He helped with the laundry, walked my dog, and was very handy. When he wasn't doing chores, he read voraciously. This kid was so damn smart. He would read any paperback I would give him, and I would give him a lot, since I figured he didn't have anything to do all day and night while I was in classes and then working at the diner. I told him, "If you have a book, no one will stop you at the library and question you."

He and I had a lot of conversations. At the time, I was profoundly lonely, and I could tell that he was, too. And so we would sit up talking, and I learned from him one of the most interesting things I'd ever learned about how privileged

I was. I had believed I'd grown up pretty poor, and from a financial perspective I had. But I grew up poor with a model of what adulthood looks like. This kid grew up poor with no hope and no support, and that is a very different kind of poverty—an emotional poverty. He told me at one point, "If I could have a life that looks like yours, I'd be really happy."

I'd laughed that off. "I'm a diner waitress," I told him. "I'm living in a shithole apartment in a shithole town with no prospects."

"Yeah," he said, "but you have a job and you have a place to live."

That actually made me feel, more than I had in a long time, like maybe I did have my life together. Maybe I was on the right track, or at least not on the completely wrong one.

Kyle stayed with me for four days, and on the morning of the fifth day, I heard him get up, put a bunch of shit in his backpack, say goodbye to my dog, and then open and shut the door and leave. "He's probably just gonna go do some hood rat stuff," I assumed. "Perhaps that's what he does during the daytime when I'm gone."

When I got up later that day, I had a text from him saying that he'd found another friend he was gonna stay with, and thank you for letting him stay on my couch. I wished him the best. After that, I didn't hear from him, and I didn't see him around.

I always wondered what happened to him. In part, I wanted to make the connection again, because getting to know him had actually helped me pivot to living a happier life. I was hoping those days together had a similar effect on him.

Two years later, I felt I finally had my life together. Somebody had the audacity to hire me for a real job, and I moved to Seattle to work as a writer. That's when I got this phone call from a Bellingham area code. I assumed it was from my college, trying to hit me up for more money, and I was thinking, "Yeah, that's not gonna happen. You have literally all the money you are ever gonna get from me, and actually I would like some of it back when you have the chance."

But it was Kyle. "Oh, I'm so glad you have the same number," he said. He was calling me from juvie.

Which was for the best, he said. "You were right," he told me, which are the three greatest words you can ever say to another human being. He told me that he had gone to stay with a friend of his, and when her mom had found out what I had found out about the court date, she was not as forgiving as I was and threatened to call the police. That could have ended much worse, since getting pinched when you've missed a court date is often punished more severely than turning yourself in. So he turned himself in. On his intake, he was allowed to take a couple of paperback books, including one that had my number in it, and that's how he'd managed, years later, to call me. He told me that he had struggled at juvie for a couple years, and he wanted to call me when he knew things were starting to go right for him. He was calling today to let me know that he was getting his GED.

I started to cry, which I had done a lot when he was staying with me. I had felt profoundly lonely and fragile back then.

Then I told him what I had never gotten to tell him, which is that having him stay with me had been really great for me, too. I had been emotionally closed off at that point in my life. I was dealing with my bipolar disorder, and was on all kinds of weird prescriptions and self-medications. It was lucky for me to have someone to kind of take care of at that point, someone to have a conversation with, and someone to also show me that I actually wasn't fucking up as badly as I thought I was.

He made fun of me for crying, and then we said goodbye. I told him that if he ever needed anything again, he should call me. He'd need to be the one to reach out, because you can't just call back the juvie phone.

That was seven cell phones ago, but I still have the same number. So I hope Kyle reads this at some point, and I hope he gets back to me. I'd really like to tell him that I'm doing well, and that I hope he's doing well, too.

TAKING THE RISK!

A Q&A WITH HANNA BROOKS OLSEN

Looking at this story three years after you told it, are there any new feelings it brings up?

This story always gets me. It's a reminder of how much more open I was as a twenty-one-year-old. I'm not sure I'd let a strange teen into my house now! But as Seattle's homelessness crisis increases every year—and as I do more writing and research on the impacts of youth detention—I often think about Kyle and how he's doing, how many barriers there are for kids like him, and what we can do to help.

Did telling the story help you to better understand that part of your life?

Totally. I went back through a lot of my old journals to check the dates and timeline and found a lot of other hard stuff in there—different medications for mental illness that I was trying (but not telling anyone about), difficulties I was having balancing school and work and trying to make a life, and generally not knowing where I'd be in the next few years. This was a milestone in my

life, because it was one of the first times I was able to offer shelter to someone else, and it felt very adult.

**Is there anything that you hope will come of having the
story in this book?**

I'm glad that it will get out there, because I think it's
a really good reminder that a lot of the people we see
living outside as adults actually started doing that as
kids. One statistic I learned about after a Seattle report
on people living outside was that they had a dispro-
portionately high incidence of experience with the foster care or youth detention systems—meaning the kids
we encounter who are without shelter are not being
served, not being cared for. They don't have advocates
in schools or at home, and sometimes they find a
stranger who can help them, if only for a few days, but
most often, they don't.

JESSE THORN

LONG WAY HOME

My dad grew up in an abusive household, and in order to escape it, he volunteered for the Navy very early in the Vietnam War. I think he learned pretty quickly that he was ill-suited to the military. He ended up on an aircraft carrier in Southeast Asia, where, because he was ill-suited to the military, he constantly got in trouble. He ended up getting the worst jobs that you can get on an aircraft carrier, which are bomb loader, bathroom washer, and projectionist.

Being a bathroom washer is horrible for obvious reasons, and being a bomb loader is horrible because it's incredibly traumatic—even if you believe that the people you are fighting deserve to be bombed, you can make any number of mistakes that will kill a lot of other people. Being the projectionist was the worst job because he had to show the films from the tail cameras of the airplanes that were on the bomb carriers, so he would rewatch the carnage that he'd set off as a bomb loader earlier that day. Needless to say, he was traumatized, and he became something of an alcoholic, and eventually a leader in the Peace Movement.

He went into AA when I was three and worked through his addiction, but PTSD often never goes away. One of the ways

in which it continues to manifest itself is in his extreme suspicions. By the time he was a teenager, he had already been
doing speed and running away from home, and he was always
paranoid that I was going to start down that road and turn
into him. I went to an arts high school and didn't do drugs,
which he could never fully believe.

One time, he was yelling at me about something, and he
picked up a piece of turkey jerky off of my desk in my room
and said, "What is this?! You think I don't know what this is?"
And he named some drug that I have still never heard of.

"No, it's not," I said. I was crying, which isn't an easy thing
to get a fifteen-year-old boy to do.

"OK, I see," he said. I still don't know what drug looks like
turkey jerky.

When I was starting my sophomore year in college, my
dad was driving me to the dorms with all my stuff in the back.
We were listening to the radio, and a song by Sly and the
Family Stone, whom I loved, came on the radio. "Jesse," he
said to me. "What's up with Sly Stone? Is he dead?" This was
back when Sly Stone was still a recluse, before he made his
big comeback with a Mohawk.

"No, I think he's, like, a semi-vegetable," I said.

"Oh, is that so? Was it 'cause of drugs?" he said.

"Yeah. I mean, I think so."

"Was it, like, a drug-induced psychosis?"

I said I honestly didn't know. And he said, "Hey, did I ever
tell you about *my* drug-induced psychosis?"

I said, "No."

The story started when he was living in Hawaii after he
burned out on the Peace Movement in the early seventies. "I

was living on the Big Island," he said, "eating omelets made with magic mushrooms for a week. And I was nude, and I was in a sinkhole. I don't know if you've ever been to a volcanic beach, but there are these volcanic rocks with big huge holes. And I was standing in a sinkhole with water up to my waist, having this really powerful hallucination."

I said, "OK." I had said nothing to prompt this! But he went on.

"There were twelve huge men," he said. "Each of them twenty feet high, representing every race in the world. They were there, I was convinced, to decide whether I should live or die. At the time, I wasn't sure whether I should live or die, because I was still dealing with the trauma of being in the war, worried I hadn't done anything worthwhile with my life. It was difficult for me to even make the case for myself. I spent hours in this sinkhole, arguing with these twelve angry men, but I finally came to be able to tell them that my life was worth living. They delivered their verdict, and they'd decided that I should live, and it was one of the most powerful experiences of my life. But that was when the Hawaiian guys grabbed me."

He'd explained to me when I was much younger that Hawaii is this beautiful place, treasured by the native people who were conquered and subjected to American colonial rule. With that fraught history, a lot of Hawaiian guys are not crazy about White guys, especially naked ones tripping on mushrooms in sinkholes arguing with giant judges. So a group of local men pulled my dad out of the sinkhole and started kicking the shit out of him. My dad wasn't that long out of the Navy, and had remained in good shape, so he managed, despite the hallucinogens he had been taking for a week, to fight back hard enough that he was able to escape and run into the surf. The Hawaiian guys didn't want to get their clothes wet, so they didn't follow. Instead, they started picking up rocks from the beach and throwing them at him. My dad was so high that rather than dodge the rocks, he thought a good plan was to catch them. He was getting pelted.

Eventually, the Hawaiian guys got tired of even throwing rocks, and they said, "Hey! Haole! We decided we don't want to beat you up anymore. You can come back."

So my dad came back, and they started kicking the shit out of him again.

What was amazing was that this whole process repeated from beginning to end—my dad escaped into the water, again he thought he could catch the rocks but got bludgeoned by them, again the Hawaiians got bored and called him back, and he came back and they started pummeling him again.

The second time, he got so battered that a Hawaiian woman came to his rescue. She was the owner of the beach, it turned out, and she came out and started shooting rock salt at all the men, telling everyone to get off her land. But this lady was no big fan of tripping Americans, either, so she just left my father lying where he was until he found the strength to stumble away.

My dad said, "So I was naked and I was having all these crazy hallucinations and I was really badly beaten up. I figured the best thing to do would be to walk down the road until I got arrested." That walk lasted for two days.

In 1971, Hawaii was not that populous on that side of the

Big Island. When he finally did manage to get arrested, he ended up in the psych ward of the jail for a few months.

When he got out, he was still having symptoms, but he was offered a job in Minneapolis, and he got there in the winter. The way he finally got clean—the only way he could, he said— was that he knew no one there to buy drugs from, and it was too cold to go outside and ask.

My father turned to face me. "So I guess I never did tell you about my drug-induced psychosis, huh?"

He certainly hadn't. It occurred to me that, after what had felt like a lifetime of him telling me these stories about being a homeless alcoholic and painting the inside of his bathroom to look like the inside of a serviceman's coffin while listening to "Paint It Black" over and over on 45, he had finally told me this story, not as someone who was sure that I was going to become him or was him already, but as an adult to an adult. He finally trusted me to make different decisions than he'd made. I loved how he opened up to me that day. I felt as if twelve giant men were somewhere looking kindly upon me.

TAKING THE RISK!

A Q&A WITH JESSE THORN

Do you have any other thoughts you'd like to express about having this story on the podcast or in this book?

At the very least, we're all shaped by our parents and their experiences. I think for a lot of folks, their parents are kind of opaque—they are kind of a mysterious force in their lives. Not only were my parents' lives relatively open to me, but my parents had full lives before I was born. They'd traveled the world, been married and divorced, gone to war, and been to jail, all before they met each other and before I was even a cell in my mother's body. So I grew up with these stories and anecdotes. And I think I had a little perspective on my family, since I grew up in two homes—I always had a sort of sense of myself outside of my parents that other kids might not have. That can certainly be problematic in a lot of ways, but it did mean that to some extent I could make choices for myself based on the choices my parents had made.

It seems appropriate to me that, in part, this story

is someone else's story. I'm pretty circumspect in my life, very risk-averse. I've spent most of my adult life working very hard and very carefully, and now raising kids. I'm glad my folks did all the crazy stuff so I didn't have to.

JIM PADAR

DRESSING THE WOUND

It was the summer of 1975, and I was working homicide with my regular partner, Mike, out of the Maxwell Street station in Chicago. The call was a man stabbed at the play lot at the Henry Horner project on the West Side. That was exactly where we happened to be, so we pulled our squad car to the curb and got out.

We were dressed in what I call "summer homicide"—a short-sleeved dress shirt with a tie, and light trousers. We trotted toward the play lot and instinctively we slowed. There was a crowd there, and they were strangely quiet.

It was one of those situations that makes a cop's hair stand up on the back of his neck. "What's going on here?" you wonder. The answer could be anything. We unsnapped our holsters, put our hands on our snub-nosed revolvers, and slowed down. The crowd cleared a path for us and we walked in.

This was not a nice place for a cop to be. A couple months prior, a Chicago police officer had been shot and killed by a sniper firing from these very buildings. But tonight, we had been called for help.

In the middle of this crowd lay a muscular Black kid. He

was spread out on his back and was bleeding from what looked like a stab wound on the right side of his neck—his carotid artery, to be exact.

Every time his heart beat, he would send a stream of blood about ten or fifteen feet out, and that's what the crowd was watching in horror. Every once in a while he would rise a little bit or move, so the stream would change a bit and the crowd would murmur and step back.

My partner and I had the same instantaneous reaction, "Oh shit!" When you work homicide long enough, you see a lot of the human capacity to inflict and experience pain, but this wasn't your typical death. Mike and I had watched people bleed out from massive injuries—head and abdominal injuries, you name it—and there was typically nothing you could do to help the victims except to watch them bleed and try to comfort them. This was different, because there was one specific point where the blood was coming from.

"I'll get a compress," Mike said. He'd read my mind.

"Call an ambulance," I shouted, as he ran back to the car. Our radios were fixed to the dashboard in those days.

I bent down and felt the kid's neck for the wound. I put my hand right on the spot. He squirmed. I could feel his pulse, but the bleeding was slowing, so I just held my fingers there.

As I knelt there alongside this boy, he was wide-eyed and conscious, staring up at me. The only way I can describe the expression on his face is primal fear.

Sirens wailed in the distance. I prayed they were coming this way. It seemed like an infinite amount of time that I had been there, holding this boy's life in my fingers, though I suppose it might only have been a minute.

Suddenly, through the crowd came a uniformed officer from the Twelfth District, my partner, and two paramedics. They stopped, like they couldn't believe what they saw. They looked at these streams that had stained the concrete.

"Is that from the wound where your fingers are now?" a paramedic asked, pointing at the bloodstream stains.

"Yeah," I said.

"Don't move your fingers," the paramedic said. I wasn't planning on it.

They started unpacking their bags, pulling out yards and yards of Ace bandages, which they wrapped around my hand and the boy's neck. They barked commands at me the whole time. "Flatten your hand!" "Keep your fingers there!" "Pressure, pressure, maintain pressure!"

My hand was all wrapped up in the bandage around this boy's neck. Then one of them finished wrapping the bandage and told me, "You're going with us."

The other paramedic had gone back to the ambulance and was returning with a stretcher. In a few minutes, we were gliding up onto the back of the ambulance. When we entered, it was obvious that I was bandaged onto the kid in the wrong direction for conventional transport. "You're going to have to kneel on the floor," the paramedic said.

I saw the corrugated steel on the floor, thinking about my summer pants. "Not without a pillow," I said.

"Give the pussy a pillow," the medic said to his partner.

"Don't fuck with me," I said, "or I'll move my fingers."

They dialed into the county hospital, and soon they were

getting directions from a doctor. The medic was trying valiantly to start an IV—this young man had lost *a lot* of blood. In fact, somewhere during the wrapping of the Ace bandages and the transport to the car, he had gone unconscious.

The crowd had followed us to the ambulance, and they started pounding on it. "What are you doing? Aren't you going?"

A cop emerged from the crowd and warned us we had to move. "They're getting restless," he said.

"Shit," the paramedic muttered, jumping into the driver's seat. We drove a few blocks to the far side of the parking lot at the Chicago Stadium. He stopped there and notified the hospital he was trying to start an IV.

The doctor said, "Negative. Move him now. Get him here."

"If I can't get this IV started, we're going to lose him," the paramedic said to himself. He ignored the instructions, and the IV probably only took him another five seconds. Then we were off to the county hospital, snaking our way through the corridors, up to the second-floor trauma unit.

They took his vital signs. "Is that where your hand is now?" one of the doctors asked me. I nodded, and he said, "Don't move your hand." I said I'd heard that before.

I stood there and watched one of the most miraculous performances, as perfectly choreographed as a ballet.

At any given moment, there were six or eight people working on this boy. They were calling out his blood pressure with a single figure rather than the ratio we normally hear. "Eighty," they said, and then in a few minutes, "Seventy-five." There were no breathing sounds in the victim's right lung. The doctors thought the internal bleeding had drained down into the pleural cavity and collapsed the lung.

I had to move farther from him so that they could get this tap into his chest to start draining it out. The boy moaned when they pushed it into his chest without any anesthetic—an encouraging sign. The tube immediately filled with a gush of blood.

"Clamp it!" a doctor shouted. "Clamp it!" They couldn't allow more blood to escape from his cavity, or he'd bleed to death.

After the doctors worked for some time, they started paying attention to me and my hand. "When we tell you," one of them said, "take your hand away and step straight back out of the way."

I turned. I saw I had a clear path behind me, and they started unwrapping and cutting away the blood-soaked Ace bandages. When it got to where it was just my hand and his neck, they told me, "Now!"

I stepped away and never looked back. I knew from their talk that they had a vascular surgery team assembled and he was going to head up to the OR.

I went to the back of the trauma unit, where there was a wash station. In those days—it was 1975—they had these hexachloride-impregnated sponges. I was scrubbing with one of those sponges when my partner, Mike, showed up at my side.

"Where's that four-inch compress I sent you for?" I asked.

He said, "Go fuck yourself. Can we go now, Doctor?" The trauma unit people glanced back at us.

I sighed, thinking about everything that had happened that day. "Do we have any idea who this guy is?" I said.

"Larry Wiggins," Mike said. "He lives in the Henry Horner homes, and we're looking for Pookie."

"Let's go back to the station," I said.

By the time we got there, it was the end of our tour of duty. After rehashing the events for a few minutes and pondering what we had ahead of us, we agreed to go home and pick up on the case tomorrow. I had blood on my shirt and trousers and was happy to be able to peel those clothes off and try to forget about it all, if only for the night.

When we came back to work the next day, Larry was in intensive care in extremely critical condition. We tried looking for Pookie and quickly discovered that there were four dozen Pookies in every housing project on the West Side. We weren't getting anywhere.

After the second night of looking, we stopped by the hospital to visit Larry and found that his condition had improved. He was now critical, no longer extremely critical. The case dropped down on the priority list a few notches because, as is always the case on homicide, bodies continued to come in, and as bad a shape as Larry was in, as horrible as the attempted murder of him was, he was alive.

On the third day we came back to the station from the afternoon shift, our boss told us that Larry had died that morning. He had suffered a stroke, apparently from a blood clot at the site of the original stab wound. It was awful to hear.

Right after roll call, we went over to the Henry Horner Homes, and this time we went right up to the apartment where Larry lived with his sisters and his mother. We knocked on the door, and they let us in. It was a quiet, somber atmosphere.

One sister—I learned later that it was Larry's younger sister—leaned over toward her mother and said, "Mama, this is the detective I told you about." His mother took three steps forward and grabbed me in a bear hug. "Sweet Jesus," she said. "Sweet Jesus. You saved my baby. You saved my baby!"

"Good Lord," I was thinking. "Doesn't she know that he died?"

Her child had been dead for twelve hours. Someone needed to tell her. I hugged her back and I put my mouth close to her ear and I said, "Mrs. Wiggins, Larry died this morning."

She took a step back and looked at me and took both of my elbows in her hands and she said, "Jesus put you there so we could say goodbye to him. You gave us that chance. Don't you understand? So we could tell him we loved him one last time and say goodbye."

There was a moment of silence. I didn't know what to say.

Finally, Mike said, "We're looking for Pookie."

Mrs. Wiggins straightened up. This was a strong woman.

"We know Pookie," she said. "We'll bring him to you."

"That's our job, Mrs. Wiggins," I said. "We don't want you to get hurt, and we don't want Pookie to get hurt."

She stared firmly into my eyes. "We will bring him to you. Nothing bad will happen."

We went back to our station, and by God, about an hour later, Mrs. Wiggins showed up with some witnesses, Pookie's mom, and Pookie. He was a big guy, but only eighteen or nineteen years old. Pookie told us everything that had happened. We called the state's attorney, got approved for murder charges, and a few hours later, everything was taken care of. Pookie's mom, Mrs. Wiggins, the sisters, and the witnesses all walked out.

I watched them from the second floor as they walked across the street. They had both just lost a son to violence, but they marched arm in arm to their car. I have never seen two more resolute mothers.

TAKING THE RISK!

A Q&A WITH JIM PADAR

Are there some stories from your history you're still wondering if you should share?

Well, my content advisor (read "my wife") has nixed a few of my stories as being in poor taste. She's probably right.

Have you ever been in a similar situation at another point in your career? Did anything in your experience in this story lead you to act differently at all?

No, this was indeed the most bizarre experience of my police career.

The most common reaction from fellow officers is a shake of the head and a "You can't make this shit up!"

BITTER PILLS

TORI

THE POWER

Six days before my thirteenth birthday, I remember lying in bed and suddenly feeling something cold, first against my toes, and then my legs. At first I thought I must have kicked off the covers, but then, when I opened my eyes, I felt the linen from my nightgown over my face. There was something heavy on top of me. I could feel that my underwear was off. I felt hands between my legs and hot breath against my neck. Then I realized it was my stepfather.

He whispered in my ear, "This is what happens to girls who think that they know everything." I was in shock. I don't know how long it lasted. I only remember that while it was happening, I kept on thinking about the dinner we had just had, where we had talked about my thirteenth birthday party and what kind of cake I wanted. I needed to think about that dinner instead of what was happening.

It had started out with hugs that lasted a little bit too long. Then my stepfather started pretending that he had to go to the bathroom every time I undressed to take a shower. Noticing the repetition of these things, I started casually bringing them up to my mom, saying, "Well, don't you think that's weird?"

"You know, everyone has a busy schedule," she would say.

But at the same time, she started saying things to my sisters and me like, "You guys are getting older, so make sure you cover yourself up when you leave the bathroom."

I hadn't really thought much about any of it until, one day, I came home from field hockey practice with a huge knot in my calf from getting hit with the stick. As I was icing it, my stepfather offered to take a look and reached his hand way past where I had a bruise.

But on that night six days before my thirteenth birthday, I had no doubt about what had happened. I remember getting up really early the following morning and waiting for him to leave for work. When he left, I got into my mom's bed.

I don't think my mom thought anything of me crawling into bed with her. At first, I just told her I had had a nightmare. For a few days, we went through our regular routines, me getting ready for school and my mom leaving for work, and I spent my school days just trying to figure out, "How am I supposed to tell her what happened? What do I say?"

I remember one day at the grocery store, not long after the incident, when my mom was looking at me, not knowing what to say but clearly sensing that something was wrong. She grabbed what we needed to get, and right when she pulled the food stamps out of her purse, I said, "Daddy is molesting me." The cashier heard it. I wasn't sure if my mom had, though, because she seemed to have ignored it, putting things in the bag and leading us out of the store. Our walk home was quiet. I was crying, trying to tell her what had happened, but she was walking with purpose, trying to get back to our house.

My mom opened the door, and I remember looking at my

stepfather eye to eye—I had sprouted up over the past two years and was about his height. When my stepfather would get upset, he would clench his fists, and you could see the veins in his arm. He had a vein that would go up his neck that would pop out, and when it did, I would become nervous about what would happen next.

I remember my mom sending me and my siblings upstairs, and telling us to wait up there until she told us to come down. She and my stepfather argued, yelling back and forth. Then there was a pause, and I heard my stepfather run up the stairs, grab some things out of his room, and then leave, slamming the door hard enough that the house shook.

We didn't talk about what had happened—there was no "Everything's going to be okay"—but I knew things were going to change. "You guys need to eat," my mother told us. "Let's hurry up and get you to bed."

My stepfather had checked himself into a mental hospital. It was good not having him in the house, but at the same time, it was hard to answer questions from my younger siblings. Not knowing what was going on, they would ask, "What did you do to make him go away?" I didn't know what to say to them or anybody else. Every now and then, we had a phone call with him. He'd want to talk to me, and since I wouldn't want to talk to him, I would just pass the phone off. I remember one phone call my mom got was not from him, but from someone at the hospital saying that he had tried to kill himself.

When he returned home to us, he had a scar across his neck, and that shifted all of the focus for the family from what he had done to me to what he might do to himself.

I wasn't sure how to process it. The idea was that we all

had to work hard to make sure that he was comfortable, but nobody seemed to be checking in on me to see if I was comfortable.

Then one day about a month after the molestation, I came home from school and my mom was sitting at the kitchen table when she was supposed to be at work. She was talking with a man, a social worker. I was told that there was a report made of me being abused but he couldn't disclose who reported it. I was asked a whole bunch of questions, and the social worker insisted that we drive to the emergency room for me to get checked out.

The exam was inconclusive. I overheard nurses talking about how I was probably lying about the abuse. After the exam, my mother asked the social worker, "Well, what was going to happen?" He said that if there had been any evidence of abuse, they would have taken all four of us kids out of the home and into separate foster families and teen shelters. She asked how that would be safer for us. He didn't have an answer.

Then I met a girl at school who was in a teen shelter. She said, "You're gonna have to lie. If you end up in the group home, you'll have to watch your back with the staff." So I called the social worker and told him I had lied.

I remember the pastor of our church doing a family consultation and a special prayer later on. My mom imagined that the only counseling that I would need from then on would be from the pastor. I was thirteen years old. I couldn't explain all this to this strange man at this point.

My stepfather eventually moved back into our house, and my mom felt that it was the perfect time to renew our faith and our dedication to God. Instead of just going to church on Sundays and going to Sunday school, we began going to prayer meetings and Bible study. My stepfather, who before all of this had never gone to church, started joining us. He started testifying to the whole congregation about how the devil had tried to break his family apart and how sinful it is to break up a Black family.

That's when I just stopped participating—in church and in everything else I could. I stopped saying yes to things and no longer felt comfortable volunteering. I remember my mother yelling at me, saying, "You're making people talk. Why don't you want to do these things?" Saving face in the church was the priority.

The only thing in my life at this point that felt like a glimmer of hope was how my grandmother protected us. She made sure that my siblings and I were never alone with him. I remember my grandmother telling me how much she didn't really like him, and she never said, "I believe what happened to you," or anything that direct, but she told me, "He's not right." After school, we would go to her house—she lived right next door—and we would wait until my mom got home before making our way over to our house.

The one time aside from church when we would all need to see each other was Sunday night, when my mom demanded that we have a family dinner. On one particular Sunday, my mom served my favorite meal, chicken parmesan, and my little sister kept on talking about hula-hooping at school and how she could hula-hoop the longest. I was trying to just make it through the dinner, because the only seat that had been available at the table by the time I got there was next to him. I was trying to position myself in my chair so that I didn't have to look at him.

"Tori, you say the prayer," my mother said, but I didn't want to talk. I didn't really want to say anything to anybody, and so I just remember kind of mumbling grace into the plate. Soon, everyone was grabbing food and putting it on their plates. Whenever my stepfather ate, he would shovel food into his mouth like he hadn't eaten for months.

At one point as we were eating, he jolted straight up, and his nostrils were flared. It looked like he was trying to say something, but nothing was coming out of his mouth. I looked at the rest of the table, and no one had noticed it. No one had seen what was happening except for me. Everyone was talking about their day at full volume. I realized that my stepfather was struggling to breathe. He was choking. And he saw that I was the only one who knew. All I could think about was this terrible year that I'd had to live in this house and how everyone felt sorry for him because he acted like a family man battling to keep us together, and how I was never able to get to sleep at night because this man who molested me was on the other side of the wall.

I thought to myself, "If I just sit here and let him die, then I won't have to sit up late at night with my field hockey stick in my hand, making sure he doesn't come in." Finally, I would not be afraid every time I would hear footsteps to the bathroom. Then I thought about what might happen if he died, how people would make him a martyr—*Oh, he was such a good man who died in front of his family, trying to keep them all together*—when it was really my lie that had kept us together.

I pushed my chair back and walked over to him,

wrapping my arms around him and trying to find that spot beneath his chest to put my fist in. I was thinking about the video that we had watched in health class about the Heimlich maneuver. I had all this hate for the man in my hands, wanting to crush him. I was not even thinking about saving his life, but about how I wanted him to feel all of the hurt that I had been feeling. I wanted him to at least have some sort of scar from me doing this, for making me feel so unsafe.

I remember his head falling forward and the food just kind of plopping out of his mouth onto the plate, and that's when everyone else at the table finally noticed that he'd been choking. The first sounds I heard were my siblings. "Oh, my God! That's so gross. He just threw up in his plate."

My mom jumped from her chair and ran over to pull her arms around him. She didn't ask if I was okay, too, and somehow, watching just how lovingly she'd come to comfort him, I realized, finally that the line between us was drawn. Her priority had always been her husband, not her child. I saw how I would have to navigate all of this, and the rest of puberty, on my own.

Then I looked down at him, limp in her arms. He was gasping for air. He looked up at me, and just for a moment, I felt like God. I had the power to give life, I had the power to take it. I had the power to love, and I had the power to hate. And I knew in that moment, and for the first time that year, that this man was never going to fuck with me again.

TAKING THE RISK!

A Q&A WITH TORI

Was it emotionally challenging to re-create the scenes of abusive behavior?

At the time I submitted my pitch to *RISK!*, I'd spent several years working on an essay collection about the abuse and the aftermath of it. I was at a point where I could talk about the abuse, but I was surprised about how emotional I was when talking about my mom. The two of us have come a long way since the time period of my story, but for the first time, in the *RISK!* story I was able to connect with my anger toward her that I'd harbored growing up. I wasn't expecting that.

What were some of your hopes or fears about putting this out there?

My hope was that someone who is going through something similar will know that they are not alone. Also, I wanted to give perspective on why it's so hard to come forward about sexual abuse. Even though there are systems in place to protect children against abuse, they can sometimes put a child in even greater danger.

My only fear in telling this story was about my mom

being upset with my sharing it. We are still working on repairing our relationship, and I know there isn't a day that goes by that she doesn't wish she had made different choices back then.

How have you grown since you first shared this story?
Since then, I've been able to talk to one of my sisters about it all. Before the story was on the podcast, I didn't talk about that time period with her. After listening to my story on the podcast, my sister shared with me how she felt. It made me realize that even though she wasn't abused, it hurt her to see my spirit disappear. In some way, the podcast gave us permission to talk about the abuse and what was going on with our family.

TOM COLEMAN

CHASING THE SUNSET

When my wife told me to come into the bedroom and sit down, I knew exactly what she was going to say, because she told me the exact same thing the exact same way seven years before: "We're pregnant!" Like it was a surprise.

She was a devout little Catholic girl playing Russian Roulette with natural birth control, so it was only a matter of time.

Cathy was the baby of eight and spoiled rotten. I was the oldest of six, wanting to spoil her for the rest of her life. She was five feet of smile, a pure smile that was like a magnet, and I was stuck. We married when we were both too young to know what we were doing, settled down in her hometown, and had a couple of kids. We were a perfect couple, but dirt-poor, as her parents would say. They helped us out a lot, probably too much.

So when I received a real job offer out of state, I knew she was going to veto it, but she surprised me and said, "Let's go!"

We uprooted our small family from South Louisiana and moved up north. And something interesting happened. We became Mr. and Mrs. Coleman, no longer Amy and Cliff's daughter and her husband. Cathy became the matriarch. It was kind of cool. This little teenager became a mama and a house maker, and every house we had, she made into a home. And we had a lot of houses, because we kept moving.

Our fifth house found me in the corporate office in Atlanta, and Cathy made a home there, too, but she did more than that—she made a community. I loved to watch her do that. I was even envious of it, because her smile, her personality, had a gravitational pull that you couldn't escape. I used to get this voyeuristic thrill from watching a complete stranger encounter Cathy for the first time. It was mesmerizing and amusing. I wanted to be able to have that effect on people.

Now, before you think this is a story about Saint Cathy, let me explain something. That little dark-haired Cajun girl was as stubborn as a cat and had a temper that I could make her lose in a heartbeat. I could wipe that cute little smile off of her face in a flash, like I had some sort of useless superpower. And I may have overused it at times.

Baby number three arrived in Atlanta, the first child born on non-Cajun soil. Even as our house filled, Cathy missed her hometown. She used to tell me, "I'm homesick," and she and the kids would make that ten-hour car trip back to Mama's five or six times a year to recharge that smile.

Remember how I said I wanted to spoil her? I put in for a job transfer to one of our offices in south Louisiana. It wasn't home, but close to it. Seven years later, there we were, living in Thibodaux, Louisiana, on an Atlanta salary. You could say we were comfortable. Maybe a little too comfortable. Then we were pregnant.

Now, all three of her other pregnancies were great, but this one started off rough, and it got rougher. The doctors put her on immediate and complete bed rest—she couldn't get up. Which meant that I was Mr. Mom, and I was pathetic.

I'm a Delta elite member, a frequent flyer, and the furthest thing from someone who knows how to do simple domestic chores like laundry.

About three months before she was due, a tragedy struck my family: I lost one of my younger brothers. It really shook me, because he was the first one in my generation to go. Cathy was sad she couldn't make the funeral; she kept asking me, "Are you okay?" I said, "I'm okay, I'm fine." I had to share with her a phrase that someone told me when my mother died many years before: "If you should die today, your family will eat supper tomorrow," which means you can't die with the dead. Just because they can't go on living is no reason for you not to. We can only keep them alive in our memory.

Cathy's condition never got much better, so the doctors wanted to do a stress test—put her in the hospital, keep her under observation for a few days. She went in on Thursday and passed with flying colors. Friday was a celebration! I mean, she granted so many audiences in that room—family, friends coming to congratulate her—that by the end of that day she was exhausted. I told her I was going to take the kids home and feed them dinner, and after I put them to bed I was going to come back and visit for a while. I wasn't home very long when she called and asked if I could come back early because she wasn't feeling right.

When I got to her hospital room, she was in a lot of pain. All I could do was hold her hand. The nurses were trying to take care of "stuff." I didn't know what to do. Finally, an alarm went off, and I looked, and it was a blood pressure monitor. The nurse asked her, "Do you have a headache?" and she said, "It's excruciating!" "Do you see flashes of light in your eye?" And then she squeezed my hand and said, "I can't see anything."

The nurse tried to ask her some more questions. She couldn't answer. It was gibberish, nonsense. And then her hand went limp. A whole bunch of doctors and nurses grabbed the bed and the alarm, and rushed everything down the hall, leaving me sitting alone in a hospital room trying to figure out what I was going to do next.

A few minutes later, a nurse came in and said, "You better call some people. You're having a baby tonight."

Soon the kids arrived with our neighbors, who are our closest friends there, and we waited and waited and waited until a pediatrician finally came out and said, "It's a boy! But we got a lot of work to do." I said, "Hello, Graham," and we watched through a window as a whole team was around this little table, working real fast, and over at the nurses' station I overheard somebody calling and saying, "We need a helicopter transport for a mother and a newborn to New Orleans." Just a few minutes later, they canceled that order and said, "We need air transport for a premature infant to the neonatal unit in Baton Rouge." I didn't know if that was better or worse.

In a little while, they wheeled Graham out in what looked like a fish tank, with so many wires and tubes on him you couldn't even see the three pounds of baby that was underneath. They opened a little porthole, let me touch him, and then, zoom, shot him off into the night. We waited there for a long time, until the doctor came out and said, "Cathy's in a lot of trouble. Her liver ruptured, and there's nothing we can do

about it. We're going to put her in ICU." Well, I told everybody, "Go home, I'll call y'all if there's any news."

Now, an ICU waiting room is a bright and cold and uncomfortable place. And there's only one thought that kept
coming into my head: "Cathy's going to be stuck in this hospital for God knows how long, and her baby is sixty-five
miles away. She is going to be hysterical." I didn't know how I
was going to manage that.

It was just past midnight when a doctor came out, introduced himself as a neurologist, and said, "Scans show there's
blood on Cathy's brain." He told me he'd keep me updated.
Half an hour later, the news was the same. Half an hour after
that, the same—until many half hours later, when two doctors
came out and told me they couldn't detect any brain activity
at all. "You might want to call your family."

Soon, that waiting room was filled with faces that I knew,
and all in a state of shock. The doctors came to me and asked
me, "What do you want to do?" I told them I didn't know.
That was a lie. If there's one thing that Cathy and I talked
about, it was that if everything seems hopeless, we don't want
to be kept alive by a machine. It looked hopeless.

Just then, the priest came, went into Cathy's room, and
I saw him talk to the doctors afterward. Then he came and
spoke to me. He held my hand, looked me in the eye and said,
"Cathy's not there, you know." I said, "I know." If I was honest with myself, I'd say I knew that last night. I'm just very
grateful to the doctors that they gave Graham a birthday all
to himself and let the dark anniversary follow the next day.

I made my decision. Then I had to tell my kids. And that is
the hardest damn thing I have ever done in my life. How do

you tell a six-year-old how to say goodbye to his mama? They took us into her room, and I reached under the sheet to touch her. Every night when we'd go to bed together, I needed what I called a "skin fix." I needed to touch her shoulder, her arm, her thigh, her hip, something. I just needed that connection, needed to connect with that smile. That day, I got my final skin fix. I felt her warmth for the last time. The doctor asked me if I wanted to stay. I said, "No, no, no, no, no. I've already said my goodbyes. I can't stand to watch her go."

Remember that crap I was talking about, "not dying with the dead"? That's exactly what it was: crap. Because at that moment when I left that room, I had no desire to go on living. Every hope, every dream, every plan that I have ever had involved that woman lying right there.

I remember crying myself to sleep that night, dreaming of chasing the sunset, to never let that day end. But I knew I just had to sit still and let that dark night overtake me and pray to God that there would be a sunrise.

My days were full of Graham and the kids. We made that three-hour round trip to the Baton Rouge hospital every single day—we were his little cheerleaders—until he came home four weeks later, on our twenty-third wedding anniversary. We had a brand-new celebration.

The town of Thibodaux saved my life. Everybody pitched in to help us, though at night it was just me and Graham, touching our fingers together, looking into each other's eyes. One night, he woke up at about two a.m. for his feeding, and I reached over to an empty spot in the bed and I said, "It's your turn." And for a split second, I forgot. And it hurt all over again. It was always my turn.

I finally had to go back to work. I had a real job, and I was kind of excited, too, because my twenty-year anniversary with the company was coming up and I was wondering, "What do you get for twenty years?" Apparently, it's a pink slip. I got laid off. You know what I told them? "Okay, see you later." They were shocked. I guess they had been expecting that I'd be angry. I said, "Hey, I have just endured one of the worst tragedies that anybody could, and I'm still standing. I'm a changed man. I've learned not only to expect change but to embrace it."

I really did want to change—I wanted to change more than I wanted anything. All those fantastic qualities that Cathy had, I didn't want them to be lost. I was going to take them and make them my own. I wanted to learn how to say yes all the time. I never wanted to leave a stranger in my wake, but a friend along my path. And I wanted to do it all with a smile. And while I was changing, why not go whole hog? I got a job offer from Dallas, Texas. That meant I was giving up my Thibodaux support network, and we were gonna try out this new family without training wheels.

Single parenting sucks. But it's also the most rewarding damn thing I have ever done in my life. Quite often, we made that same trip to Granny's that Cathy had made so many times before, but now it was for *me* to recharge.

And then, one day, without any warning, any plans that I thought I might have became toast. Because I met her.

Pamela is a loser, just like me. We both lost something very precious to us, and empathy among widows and widowers is tremendous. But you've got to believe that this invitation to coffee was as innocent as could be, I swear to God.

All I wanted to do was commiserate, to talk to someone who understood what life after death really meant. She was tall, blonde, very young, and beautiful.

She wasn't my type, I told myself. Bull! The truth was, I couldn't imagine I was her type. But as we talked, we found out I went to college ten miles from where she was born and raised. She asked me, "What do think would have happened if we had met when you were at school?" I said, "Nothing. You were twelve!"

When you quit playing the game and your defensive walls are down, there's a chance that someone might sneak into that very personal and private place you have, and things can get very serious. That is what happened with Pamela.

Next, I had a big task: I had to tell Cathy's mom.

She cried. She told me I must have really been in love with her daughter, because only someone so in love could miss it so much that they would want it back. And she was right.

Pamela is the only mother that Graham has ever known. He knows all the stories about Mama Cathy, but to him they're just stories, and by the way, he's an Eagle Scout and graduates high school in May. He survived me. I find that pretty impressive.

Pamela didn't marry Cathy's husband. Pamela married the man that Cathy changed. And both of us know all too well that, sooner or later, one of us is going to experience another sunset. But right now, that couldn't be further from our minds. We are smiling, celebrating the hell out of all this sunshine.

TAKING THE RISK!

A Q&A WITH TOM COLEMAN

What do you hope readers take away from this story?
Sadly, widows and widowers are not special or unique. Our numbers grow daily. Losing a spouse feels like the end of the world, and the wound is extremely deep. In time, I learned that there are new worlds to explore and that this exploration does not in any way disrespect or diminish the world one shared with their lost spouse. Time may eventually heal the wound, but there will always be a scar and a limp that reminds you of it.

How was sharing the story on *RISK!* a somewhat different an experience than you originally anticipated?
I am a professional storyteller, but my stories are mostly fictional and humorous. This baring of my soul in front of an audience without an artificial persona was difficult for me, because I am constantly striving to put an audience at ease. I knew this could be a difficult ride

for some. The feedback I received after the show was so warm and genuine that I appreciated everyone's company on this journey. If anything, sharing the story has actually caused me to be bolder and more genuine since then.

TRACEY SEGARRA

HEART AND HANDS

After two miscarriages, I'm pregnant again for the third time, and I want to be happy about it, but all I feel is scared. When I go for my first appointment with my obstetrician, my first sonogram is internal. She's poking around in there, and all I can think is, "Please let it be good news. Please let it be good news." I'm afraid that there's gonna be nothing.

Then all of a sudden, she turns a knob on the machine, and I hear it. "Whoosh, whoosh, whoosh." My baby's heartbeat. Finally, I breathe. But apparently the exam is not over, because my obstetrician continues poking around. I wonder what she could be doing.

Then she says, "Huh."

"Huh?" I ask.

She turns the knob up again, and I hear, "Whoosh, whoosh, whoosh." She turns to me and she says, "Congratulations, Tracey. You're having twins." I just start laughing hysterically.

After the exam, I run out to my car and I punch in my husband's number. "Hey, how'd it go?" he asks.

"Honey, are you sitting down?" He says no. "Well, please," I say. "Sit down. Right now. Because we're having twins!"

For a second he thinks I'm kidding. Neither of us can believe it, because we're older parents and we've been trying for so long. The craziest part is that, just a week earlier, when we first got the positive pregnancy test, we'd said, "Wow, wouldn't it be great if we were having twins, so we could just be done, and poof, instant family?"

The first few months of my pregnancy go great, and I start wearing maternity clothes before I'm even showing, just because I'm so excited to be pregnant and that things are going well. I'm so proud of this belly of mine that's starting to get round.

Then the complications start. I get gestational diabetes, which means that all of those milkshakes and hamburgers I've been eating have to go, and in their place, I have the privilege of pricking my finger every day. And then I start getting these Braxton-Hicks contractions, which are not real contractions, but could lead to them. The doctors tell me to slow down.

At thirty-two weeks, I go in for a routine exam. Since it's a high-risk pregnancy because of my age and history with miscarriages, they do sonograms and everything. The nurse is taking my vital signs, and as soon as she's done, the doctor comes in and he gives me a quick exam. Then he says, "Go to the ER right now."

"What?" I say. "But I have a haircut appointment and a pedicure."

None of it makes sense. I feel fine. But apparently my blood pressure is really high, I'm having real contractions, and they need to get me to the hospital.

When I get to the hospital, I realize the doctor must've

called ahead, because the nurse is practically ripping my clothes off, and they quickly pump me full of magnesium sulfate to stop the contractions. They give me something else to bring my blood pressure down, then they put these two baby bracelets on my wrist, just in case none of this works and they have to do an emergency C-section right then. It is not until I see the baby bracelets on my wrist that I realize how serious this is. I start freaking out because it is much too soon for these babies to be born.

Thankfully, the drugs work. Now, however, I am considered an ultra-high-risk pregnancy, which earns me a hospital stay on strict bed rest for the rest of this pregnancy. I spend my days lying in this bed, so bored that the highlight of each day is when I see those ladies wheeling around the crafts cart. I make every damn craft on that cart. I make a mosaic-tiled trivet that spells out "Dad." I work for like a week on this gorgeous painting of a horse. My obstetrician comes by one day, and he is so impressed, until I confess that it's paint-by-numbers.

Finally, the day arrives for my babies to be born. It has to be a C-section, because Baby B has her foot squarely wedged under Baby A's head, blocking the runway, as it were. As they wheel me into the operating room, I am suddenly consumed with this horrible fear that something terrible is going to happen to my babies. When I see my doctor, I think to myself, "This is elective surgery. It's not an emergency." I ask him, "Can we elect to do this another day?" He looks at me and laughs a big, booming laugh, and he says, "No, Tracey. It is time to meet your babies."

So the operation begins. I'm numb below the waist.

There's this big tent, and my arms are outstretched, like I'm getting crucified. My husband is sitting at my head and making idle chitchat with me. A C-section is the most bizarre experience when it's not an emergency.

At one point, my husband gets bored waiting for this to happen, so he stands up and starts to peek over the tent. A nurse looks at him and she says, "Mr. Segarra, would you like to sit down?"

"No, no," he says, "I kind of want to see what's—"

"Mr. Segarra," she says. "Would you like to sit down?!" He gets it: this is an order. In retrospect, I think we're both very glad that he did not see what was going on down there. Marriages have ended for much less.

Within an hour, although it feels much longer, my daughters, Jessica Rose and Lily Anne, are born.

When I hear their dueling banjo cries from opposite sides of the OR, I feel like I can finally relax and just be a mom.

But the next morning, they detect a murmur in Lily's heart, and further tests show that she has a very serious congenital heart defect called tetralogy of Fallot. She's gonna need open-heart surgery in the next few months in order to survive. As I'm listening to this cardiologist who I've never met before explain to me what's wrong with my baby's heart, I am horrified. She's only four pounds, and he's telling me about obstructions and holes, and when he describes the surgery, what they have to do sounds awful. I begin to feel angry—at God, mostly—for giving me this broken baby.

The next few weeks are just a blur of learning how to take

care of infant twins, checking to make sure that Lily's blood oxygen level doesn't go lower, thus turning her blue, and interviewing heart surgeons.

Now, I don't know anyone less qualified than I am to interview heart surgeons. Medicine and science and I do not mix. The closest I've come to heart surgery is in seventh grade, when I dissected a frog, and that frog was already dead. But I know that it's my job right now to find the best surgeon for my baby, so I'm going to have to figure out how.

The first surgeon we interview tells us that he wants to use Kevlar to patch the holes in Lily's heart. I know what Kevlar is—they use it in bulletproof vests—and I am nauseous at the idea of him putting that in my tiny baby's body.

The next surgeon is this really handsome, sandy-haired guy, and he's so confident. He tells us there is absolutely no reason to have this surgery until she's a year old, when she'll weigh more and have a stronger heart that's safer to operate on.

The third surgeon we meet is Dr. Q, who, even though he's only five-foot-six with these bushy eyebrows and dirty brown hair, intimidates the hell out of me. It doesn't help that he's got the bedside manner of Vladimir Putin. I can tell within a minute of speaking with him that he cannot wait to get my husband and me out of his office. I almost catch him rolling his eyes. He says, "I do three hundred surgeries a year" in his thick Belgian accent, "and I have better statistics than most."

I'm still asking questions, because that's what I need to do, about how long she'll need to be on the bypass machine, what the risks of the surgery are, what those statistics for the number of babies who have complications from this kind of surgery are, and on, and on. Finally, he just stops answering my questions with more than a couple words, and his gaze drifts toward the door, as if to say that he's done with us.

When we get out of that office, I practically hate this man, but in the end, when we weigh all the different surgeons, we decide to go with Dr. Q. Because in the end, the only question we asked that really mattered was, "How many of your babies don't die?" And Dr. Q has the best stats.

On the day of her surgery, Lily is five months old, weighs just ten pounds, and has a heart the size of a walnut. I wonder how you can even operate on a heart that small. When we go to the hospital, I can't even hold Lily because I'd been nursing a cold and we can't run the risk of me getting her sick. So Fred, my husband, is holding her.

We get to the OR and have to hand Lily to the doctors at these big steel doors—we can't go in. I see one of the doctors with her hands outstretched for us to give her our baby, and I think, "No. No, we need more time!" But Fred gently hands Lily over to this doctor, and she disappears behind those doors.

That's when I lose it. I am her mother. I'm there to protect her—how can I let them cut her open? I calm myself as best as I can, reminding myself that we have to do this. I think, "What can I do to be productive, even if in the smallest way, while I'm waiting?" I decide to go to the lactation room because I am still breastfeeding.

When I start pumping the milk, a sense of calm envelops me.

A few hours later, the surgery is over and Lily is wheeled into the pediatric ICU. Dr. Q tells us it went great; everything was fine. And that's the last we see of him.

But during the night, there are complications. Her lungs have filled with fluid, and she has to be intubated and sedated. Until her lungs clear, they can't wake her up. We sit there every day and we watch this machine breathe for our baby. Every day, I ask the doctor who is in charge of the ICU, "Can you wake her up today?" And every day he says, "No, not today." They just don't know when it's gonna happen.

Every night, I go to my mother's apartment, where she's watching my other twin daughter, Jessica, and I take care of her while Fred keeps vigil in the hospital by Lily's bedside.

One morning, I come back to the hospital and Fred looks at me and says, "It was a bad night." I look at Lily, frantic, but he puts an arm around me.

"No, no. Lily's okay." He starts to cry and he says, "One of the babies didn't make it, and all of the doctors were running around trying to do whatever they could. It was pandemonium. The parents weren't even there."

On the fifth day, we ask the doctors, "Can you wake Lily up today?" They say, "Not today, but maybe tomorrow." On the sixth day, they can finally wake her up. I can bathe her, and I can feed her for the first time. As you can imagine, she smells like antiseptic and sour metal, the perfumes of our health care system. I can't wait to get that smell off of her. I gently rub her down with baby wipes, and I put her in her teddy bear cotton onesie. I hold her for the first time in a week, and when I hold her, I'm just so happy.

A few days later, we get to take her home. I am still incredibly nervous. She's got this Frankenstein scar up and down the length of her chest, and I can tell that she's dealing with residual pain. About a week later, I go to pick her up from her crib one morning, and she turns to me and gives me this crooked little Lily smile. It's the first time she's smiled since the surgery, and it's only in that moment that I finally know in my heart that she's gonna be okay.

Well, thirteen years later, we go to a hospital gala. It's honoring Dr. Q.

Lily's there with my husband and me and her sister, Jessica. During the night, I say, "Lily, we have to go meet Dr. Q." I'm a little nervous, but I don't tell her about him, about his personality.

"Okay," she says after some convincing. "But you have to do the talking." She's a little shy at thirteen. I tell her, no, she should say hello to him.

We find him in the party, and I tap him on the shoulder, and I say, "Dr. Q, there's someone I'd like you to meet." Lily goes up to him very bravely and she shakes his hand. She says, "Thank you for fixing my heart." A hospital photographer sees the moment and takes a picture of Lily and Dr. Q. As we were coming home from the party, I remember thinking about how all of these surgeons were so arrogant and so sure of themselves, how they had so little patient/parent interaction. And even though I'm grateful to Dr. Q, I get the sense that surgeons probably go into the field because of the intellectual and the physical challenge of the surgery, not so much because they really care about their patients.

A couple of weeks later, though, I come across a profile of Dr. Q in a magazine—he's a very famous surgeon—so, of course, I read it. I find one particular paragraph in the article that really sticks out: a paragraph in which Dr. Q talks about how, in order to do what he does every day, he has to keep a certain distance from the families.

After I read that, I go back and I look at the picture of Lily and Dr. Q. Lily is grinning ear to ear, her curly hair flowing down around her shoulders. Dr. Q is stoic as usual, not even cracking a smile. But then, when I look closer, I see that his arm is tightly gripped around her shoulder, and that one of her curls is wound around his finger, and I think to myself, "You know, maybe we're not so different, Dr. Q and I." I'm a writer, and when I'm writing, I block out everything, so I can focus—my family, my kids, everything. It doesn't mean that I love them any less.

Now, when I look at the photo of Lily and Dr. Q, I focus in on his hands, because these are the hands that reached into my broken baby's walnut-sized heart and returned it to me whole. And here they are wrapped around my child, in what maybe, just possibly, is a hug.

TAKING THE RISK!

A Q&A WITH TRACEY SEGARRA

I remember your daughter Lily giving you feedback the night you told this story at a *RISK!* show. Have your family members heard most of your stories?

Yes, they've heard most of them, but the *RISK!* show in Philly was the first time I'd performed this story, which is one of my most personal, in front of my daughter. I never tell my family my stories before I perform them at least once in front of an audience. I'm almost superstitious about it. Once they do hear them, though, I am open to constructive criticism, or to get their perspective on the story. Lily, for instance, reminded me after the show that she was the one who tapped Dr. Q on the shoulder at the hospital gala, when I was sure it was me.

How has your life changed since you got into story-telling?

It sounds very kumbaya, but I honestly feel that, in my fifties, I've finally discovered what I'm meant to do with my life: to tell and listen to compelling, true stories. The joy I get out of telling stories, hosting my own story-telling show, and helping other people learn how to tell their own stories is off the charts. Standing on a stage and taking the audience along for a ride through a pivotal moment in my life is indescribably wonderful. Thank goodness I've led a colorful life—I don't think I'll ever run out of stories to tell.

KITTY HAILEY

IT'S ALL HAPPENING AT THE ZOO

I married my child when he was still a man. I didn't plan it that way. But that's how it happened.

I met John on South Street in Philadelphia at a coffee shop, and it was love at first sight. Who wouldn't fall in love with a guy who looked like a tall Willie Nelson? He had a motorcycle helmet next to him, his BMW K1100 was resting outside at the curb, and he was reading the *New York Times*. It was strange to find myself in love again, because I had already had two failed marriages—the first because I was too young, the second because that husband was by no means a monogamist and…I was! So I had promised myself I was never going to fall in love again. Probably would never bother dating again. Might even never have sex again.

But there I was, unable to stop myself from falling for John. We went on one date, and we fell for each other so hard that I gave him the key to my house. We were inseparable from that moment on.

I had two and a half of the best years of my life with him. We were both solidly in middle age, but together, everything felt somehow special. I did things I never thought I would do again. I had sex like I'd never dreamed of.

Unfortunately, after two and a half wonderful years, something happened. On his fiftieth birthday, things started to change.

John started to forget things. At first, it was little things from the store. But no worry, it was only three blocks away. Then he couldn't dial the telephone. He couldn't remember how to buckle his belt. He was an architect, but soon he'd find he couldn't remember why a line started here and ended there. It was difficult for us to wrap our heads around what was going on.

We had him diagnosed, and he had a very strange form of dementia. Unlike Alzheimer's, which deals mainly with memory of the past, the Frontal Temporal Dementia that John had made him forget the present. He was like a videotape of life that was rolling backward in time, but it wasn't rolling slowly—it was rapid.

Within the first six months, he lost ten, twenty years of his life, and he started forgetting how to do everything.

His palate changed. He went from the man who loved gourmet and ethnic food—from pâté to pad thai—to a man who liked peanut butter and jelly, macaroni and cheese, hot dogs, and ice cream.

I wondered when this might ease up—what form of stability we could possibly find—but the changes in him only seemed to accelerate. Eventually, he more or less forgot how to speak.

Instead of being my love and my husband, he became my little boy, and I became Mommy. I tried to be positive. We could deal with this, I thought. I loved being Mommy. In fact, up until I'd met John, being a mommy had been the best part of my life. And John was the best little boy in the whole world.

Except the problem was John was six-foot-three, and it was a little difficult to deal with a six-foot-three-inch-tall little boy who was frustrated and often could not find the words to communicate what he wanted.

We tried to make the best of it. We drew pictures together. He colored them in and painted them. We loved life.

Then one morning in October, I realized that if I had to watch *Finding Nemo* one more time, I was going to shoot myself. "What would I do with my kids?" I thought. I calculated where John's mind was in its backward journey and figured he was about seven now.

"Johnny," I said. "Forget *Finding Nemo*—let's go to the zoo!"

Though he had lost most of his ability to talk, he still spoke when he could remember the words. That morning, he walked around the house chanting, "Zoo. Zoo. Zoo."

I was thrilled. I was going to make him happy, and I didn't have to watch that damn movie anymore.

"Johnny, let's make sandwiches together," I said. We made peanut butter and jelly sandwiches, and he spread the jelly all over the place.

"How do you want to cut them today?" I asked. "Do you want triangles?"

"No. No."

"Do you want squares?"

"No."

"Okay, fingers. You want four fingers?"

"Yes. Fingers!"

So I held his hand, and we cut finger shapes. We wrapped

each little finger in plastic wrap, and we put it in a paper bag. I had drawn a picture of a fish on the paper bag. He liked fish, and he colored it in. I wrote "John" on it. He held his lunch bag with a big smile.

We got into the car, and I helped my little boy put on his seat belt. Then I talked to him, saying things like, "John, when we go to the zoo, don't walk away from me. I need you to hold my hand. If we get separated, you just stand still, and because you're so big, I'll find you."

"OK," he said. "OK. Zoo."

As we pulled into the parking lot, I realized there were nine hundred yellow school buses lined up, with children pouring out of them. My John didn't take sensory input too well, so I tensed up, but it was too late to turn back. He was far too excited.

"It'll be okay, John," I said. "It'll be fine."

Before I knew it, he was outside of the car, running across the parking lot. I locked the door and ran after him.

Inside, John's six-foot-three-inch legs were pulling me forward to the first animal, a rhinoceros.

There were all these little schoolchildren looking at the rhinoceros and pointing. "Look," one said, "he's got five legs."

Well, it wasn't a leg they were looking at. John stared at where they were pointing, and when he saw it, he reached down, looking for his own "other leg." It was nice, in a way, to see him remember that he had one. His return to childhood had robbed us both of an important part of our lives.

Then I realized the situation wasn't stable—this big man fondling himself in front of a group of children. I needed to distract him. "John, let's go see the next animal," I said, and I started dragging him toward a zebra.

There was a group of children around the zebra, and I was very disappointed to find that the zebra also had five legs.

Some of the children were gaping at the zebra. "Look at that," one of them said. "He's peeing through his leg." The little boys giggled, and the girls joined in, whispering to each other.

I stood beside it all, holding John's hand, and I realized that he was lost in thought, wondering, no doubt, about this whole fifth-leg thing. His hand went down to himself again, and he was feeling his manhood. As the children shrieked happily, I was starting to get worried, especially when I felt an electrical charge pass from John's body to mine.

He started to rock, and I worried he was upset by the noise of the kids. I knew this was my time to move. We needed to get out of there.

I dragged John across the path, and I remembered there were giant turtles there. "Come on," I said. "We're gonna go see the turtles. Big ones."

There was this group of grade school students gathered around the turtles, and with them, a young teacher about twenty-five years old. As we got close, I heard these little voices saying, "Oh, he's going to hurt him! He's gonna hurt him! Don't let him climb on top of him. Miss Thompson, he's gonna crush him! The big one is too big!"

By then, my John was really getting it. His eyes were glued to the scene in front of him, those synapses made brittle by his illness starting to connect. I was holding his hand, and I felt him shake.

And at the top of his fifty-three-year-old lungs, he yelled, "*No!*"

Everybody jumped back. The teacher looked at us, bewildered. But John was elated.

"NO!" John said. "He's not hurting him! THEY'RE FUCKING!"

Miss Thompson's eyes shot daggers at us, as if to ask why I couldn't control this perverse man.

The children started yelling. "Did you hear what he said?!" "Fucking!" they said.

I was about ready to bust a gut. I grabbed John's hand, and I said, "Johnny, let's run!"

That's exactly what we did. We ran all the way to the other end of the zoo, away from these people who were pointing at us now. Safely out of their sight, I caught my breath, laughing and gasping for air. Johnny was so thrilled, so proud of himself, because he had put together a thought, a word, perhaps even a memory.

We sat on a bench together in this peaceful contentment.

We unwrapped each little finger of peanut butter and jelly sandwich, each little soldier, I called them. We nibbled our sandwiches, watching the lions, who were—what else?—fucking.

And John knew exactly what it was.

TAKING THE RISK!

A Q&A WITH KITTY HAILEY

This story has it all. Laughs, tears, love, and loss. Might you tell more stories from that time in your life?

I have probably thirty more from the awful years of dealing with my husband's disease. But the funny ones are helpful, because you need a sense of humor to get through this sort of thing. I wrote the story while in the thick of it, instead of checking into an insane asylum or at least seeing a shrink. It was an amazing four years of watching my love become my child. And the story was written from the heart, totally true, and captures my emotions at the time.

Where do you fall on the spectrum of the "Some things are better left unsaid" and "Live without filters" philosophies?

I am a considerate person. Taking away filters may be fun for the teller, but I don't want anyone else to be hurt.

What was it like sharing this story for *RISK!*?

Though I tell stories to groups with regularity, most of what I talk about is my investigative life (I'm a private investigator). Before this one, I had never told a "John" story. I didn't know if I could do it. It was too raw—even eight years later. It was the hardest thing I ever did in my life. I had lived his illness in private, and written about it in private. Telling it out loud was liberating. I wanted to respect him and also discuss the impact of the disease.

MAX

MAN UP

I used to belong to a secret society, an underground organization that came out of the men's movement in the nineties. I'd gotten introduced to the group by a couple guys from Wall Street whom I'd met in a program in which we were all trying to get sober. They'd taken me under their wing and said, "Max, we have just the thing for you. We belong to this club, a secret society, and we want to let you in on it."

"Sure!" I told them. It sounded cool.

They told me there was a weekend initiation process in upstate New York, and it would cost $1,300 to go. The money made me hesitate, but they really felt this club was the lifeline I needed. "Trust us, Max," they said. "It's gonna be good for you."

I was down. I was on the lookout for a sense of purpose in my life, a sense of belonging, and I thought that maybe this would be it. They took me up to the meeting place on a Friday night. It turned out they had rented out the Poughkeepsie state armory. The initiation would be a thirty-six-hour marathon, starting at six o'clock in the morning on Saturday and ending at six o'clock on Sunday night. My Wall Street friends prepped me on Friday, giving me this big feast in a hotel room we'd rented for the night near the armory. We bought tons of food, and they fattened me up like a big pig and they said, "You're gonna need it, Max." I was beyond curious about what they could possibly have been preparing me for.

They dropped me off at the armory at five the next morning, and I got in line with 150 other guys who were there to be initiated. The people who ran the group introduced themselves to us, the leader and about fifteen other men who were facilitators. One of the first rules they gave us was that there could be no eating and no drinking, not for thirty-six hours. They were going to give us water at controlled intervals, a cup every twelve hours. We also were not allowed to go to the bathroom. Instead, there were buckets circled around the perimeter of the room, and at twelve-hour intervals the buckets would become available, and everyone would have one chance to piss in one, after which you'd need to wait another twelve hours if you missed your opportunity.

I remember for the first twelve hours there were these seminars they put us through about how our society was poisoned by modern culture and how men had lost their way. They mentioned the advent of feminism and equality as an example. I was surprised by that, having wholeheartedly believed in the good that feminism and equality had done for everyone in our society, men included, but these guys insisted that men were being emasculated, and this seminar was for us to take back our dignity and our birthright as men to be like rulers and powerful businessmen. Looking around this room I was trapped in, I could see that we weren't the CEOs that our leader was telling us we were. We were broken men, desperate for someone to tell us how we could belong to something bigger than ourselves.

The leader lectured us on different struggles that men go through—rites of passage, he called them. He began to invite people to share their experiences, and men were coming up and talking about how they had been abused by their parents or how they were beat up by bullies or by authority figures. They had become insecure as a result of these rites of passage, the leader said, and insecurity stopped them from being able to develop the full pride and joy of being a man. I remembered, in the heavy air of that crowded room, how I was beat up a lot by bullies growing up. I remembered the street gangs that I ended up joining as a teenager for protection.

The initiation processes for the street gangs had been rough. I'd had to pledge for eight weeks straight, and I would go to a meeting once a week where the guys would bind my arms behind my back and everybody in the club would take a shot at me, punching me in the stomach, kicking me in the face, or socking me in the jaw. Then, at the end of the meeting, you'd have to sit still for ten swings with a baseball bat. People were breaking baseball bats over your ass.

What got to me about the leader's lecture at *this* initiation was how he was telling me that everything I endured was something I *had* to go through. It was my journey to being a man. "No," I thought. "That's wrong." We didn't need to be subjected to that shit.

After twelve hours of not eating and not drinking, the weekend was starting to get to me. I knew what they were doing, giving us these doses of energy and then teardowns so we'd buckle. There was a lot of running around and swinging fists in the air, going, "Whoo! Whoo! Whoo! Whoo!" But then there were guys like me, who just weren't buying it.

After about thirty hours, the leader said, "Some of you guys seem skeptical. Who here doesn't feel like this is right, and they're not getting their money's worth? I want you to raise your hand right now." Mine was one of the first hands to go up, and when I turned, I saw about twenty other men around me raising their hands. I'm sure there were another twenty or thirty other guys who wanted to raise their hands but were intimidated.

He asked us skeptics to stand up. "I want you to follow this facilitator toward the end of the room over there," he said, pointing. We followed this guy, and when they let us out into the hallway, they put blindfolds on us. Some people started panicking. They led us down these stairs into a basement. At first, we were okay with it, thinking this was some sort of joke. But after about an hour of standing blindfolded in silence, people started to get impatient.

I went to lift up my bandana to see what was going on, and somebody slapped my hand away. "If you lift that bandana," I heard, "you're getting kicked out."

They had us like that for the next four hours. I almost felt like I was being held hostage by the Taliban. People started melting down out of boredom or despair, crying even. One or two guys had to be excused. Even I started getting worried.

Then, all of the sudden, we heard Indian war chants from above. I started to realize how a lot of the philosophy the leader had been talking about was grounded, at least supposedly, in Native American culture. He was always talking about Indian warriors. And the chanting went on for about forty-five minutes.

Then, we heard a door open, and someone said, "We're ready for them." The facilitators who were with us told us to stand up and, still blindfolded, walk back out into the giant auditorium. We were hit by a wave of heat and smoke and energy. They told us to take off our blindfolds.

There was a giant, fifty-gallon drum with flames shooting out of the top. There were around fifty men running around us in a circle, like possessed warlords. Paint was smeared on their faces, and they were completely naked, screaming and howling and grunting.

The leader emerged in a cape, like Dracula or something. He strides over to the fire, saying he was talking to the fire gods. "Who wants to face the fire demon first?" he yelled. At this point, I'd had enough of this, and I either wanted out, or I wanted someone to show me, quickly, that this wasn't a complete waste.

I raised my hand again.

Two facilitators grab me and walk me out to the fire. One stands on one side of it, and the other stands on the other side. "So, Max," the leader says, reading my name tag, as the flames are licking all around us. "What are you so insecure about that you don't feel like we fixed you while you were here this weekend?"

I took a moment, but I let it out. I said, "I'm really ashamed to say this, but I was sexually abused when I was growing up by an older guy, and it really freaked me out."

He said, "Why is it still bothering you?"

"I don't know," I said. "It just does."

Then, one of his facilitators comes over and taps him on the shoulder, asking if he could take over with me. So the leader nods and backs away.

"I think you're a *faggot*!" the facilitator says.

At that point, I just fucking lose it and I spit right in his face. I bash him in the chest and he goes flying back. This guy was a lot bigger than me, though, so when he gets his bearings, he lunges at me. But he doesn't realize I was a street fighter growing up. I know how to fight. I had no problem.

So we were beating the shit out of each other, and everybody started jumping on us, trying to break us up. But the leader waved them off, saying, "No, let them fight!" And since the guy was so much bigger than I was, I knew I was only going to be able to beat him if I got him on the floor, so I wrapped myself around him and threw him to the ground. All the naked, painted warlords are circling around us, screaming and jumping up and down, going nuts.

After about ten minutes, out of complete exhaustion, the facilitator and I were just done. "Okay," the leader said, pulling us apart. He got in my face and said, "Are you ready to join us now?"

I looked at him and I said, "Yes." These guys came over and they took all my fucking clothes off and they painted my face. "Join the men in the circle," the leader told me, and I ran to the outer circle. Then we started running around screaming our heads off. Then the leader said, "Who's ready to go next?" Nobody would volunteer. And the next thing I knew, the weekend, was over, and we could all now start paying membership dues to this secret society.

The truth was, I didn't need these crazy motherfuckers to tell me what it means to be a man. I wasn't more of a man because of the bad things or even the good things that had happened to me. I was a stronger person because, good or bad, I'd always come through. So I quit.

TAKING THE RISK!

A Q&A WITH MAX

How did telling stories on shows like *RISK!* affect your life?

I could go on and on, but suffice to say that it was liberating and cathartic. It helped me take pride in my bohemian side and place that at the forefront of my persona, as opposed to continuing to hide it at the back end. I also had stage fright and hated public speaking. Telling my stories at the shows gave me confidence and helped me develop stage presence, to the point that I was hosting and performing onstage for a career. It was awesome!

When you heard your story on the episode, did you think, "If only I could change this or that part"?

I'm of the mind that I ought to neither regret the past nor wish to shut the door on it, so no. I accept that what I said was what went down, and it's what got me to where I am today. My life is (and usually has been) beyond my wildest dreams. Through all the difficulties I've been through, I've learned to be tough, to the point where, sometimes, I practically feel like a superhero. I'm still fighting the fight and working through things, but I have no regrets about what I've shared. In my neck of the woods, there's an old saying that "you're only as sick as your secrets."

If a younger version of yourself heard someone else share a story like this, do you think you would have been less likely to try to join the secret fraternity in the first place?

Probably, yes. I would've thought that leader was a freak and would've left sooner if I'd gone in the first place. In many respects, I've had a fucking tough life and wouldn't wish it upon anyone. A lot of my friends who went through similar things are dead. Miraculously, I survived. I need to own this precious life and be the best I can be in everything I do, and I hope this story helps others do that with their lives.

ROY LAZORWITZ

UNCLE LOUIE

It's December 23, 2014, and I'm in my childhood bedroom. In two weeks I'm going to move to Austin, Texas. After college, I had lived in New York for a few years, and that clearly wasn't working, so I had decided Austin was the place to go.

When I decided to make that move, I outwardly told people I'd made up my mind—I was making a bold decision, and it was done. Austin is the place for me. Inwardly, though, I didn't feel that way. I didn't know anyone in Austin. So when I decided to make the move, I also decided to spend as much quality time as I could with my family. My mother had told me that my uncle Louie was visiting from California and he wanted to see New York. Uncle Louie hadn't been to the East Coast in fifty years, and he wanted to know what had changed.

A few days later, I'm sitting there in my bed, recounting the failures of my life to this point, as if I've lived seventy hard years. My mother calls me, saying my uncle is here, and immediately I hear someone yelling outside, saying, "GET DOWN HERE, SMART-ASS!" I haven't spoken to this man in maybe my entire life—at least in my entire conscious life—and he's already calling me a smart-ass.

I go downstairs, and what stands before me is a six-foot-five, 250-pound man who's wearing a collared shirt, slacks, brown shoes, and a yarmulke, because, as I had learned from my mother, he had recently rediscovered his Judaism.

Also, he has crutches attached to each one of his wrists, because he was in the Vietnam War, where they used Agent Orange. What they didn't know when they were using it is that soldiers who got exposed to it would suffer untold negative effects on their insides, and if they were lucky enough to survive the war, their bodies would years later begin crumbling.

It's December 23, 2014, seven p.m., and it's starting to snow, and I'm taking a man who needs crutches to walk into New York City for the first time in fifty years. We get on a train, and I discover that Uncle Louie doesn't know how to control his voice. The poor guy is mostly deaf. We're sitting there, crammed between everyone looking at their phones, and he's like, "I HAVEN'T BEEN HERE IN FIFTY YEARS. CAN YOU BELIEVE THAT?"

I said, "The whole train can't believe you, Uncle Louie. The whole train." Eventually, we get off the train, and I'm looking for escalators, I'm looking for elevators, whatever I can do so he doesn't have to walk that much.

We take an escalator up to the street. And for those of you who have not been to Penn Station, it is not a pleasant place. As we weave and bump our way through the hordes of people streaming through the city, it starts to sleet, and we step out onto the sidewalk. Uncle Louie starts to cry.

He looks up at the sky, and his glasses are covered in sleet and tears. He's ignoring the neon signs, as well as all the people who are giving him dirty looks because he's standing right in the middle of one of the busiest sidewalks in the city.

He starts asking people who are walking by to take his picture. "Excuse me, sir!" He gestures. I interrupt and say, "Uncle Louie, I can take your picture!"

I take his picture and I say, "Okay, here we are. What do you want to do now, bud?" He says, "I want Italian food. They don't have real Italian food in California."

I said, "Great." I took him to a place, that, to him, was a five-star restaurant, but it was just a hole-in-the-wall pizza place, to be fair.

I got a slice of pizza, and he got a slice of pizza. And then he got baked ziti. It was enough baked ziti for three people, and he happily ate the entire thing. He kept saying, "Oh, this is so good! The cheese, the pasta…it's all so bad for me. My diabetes."

I said, "Uncle Louie! I didn't know you had diabetes! I wouldn't have taken you here if I had known that."

"I'm with my nephew. Fuck it."

So we walk around a little bit more, and he's telling me some stories. He's telling me about my cousins, whom I've only met once, and my aunt, whom I've only met once. Then we get on the train to go back home at about eleven o'clock. If you think walking around New York City by yourself is tiring, I learned that day that walking around the city with someone else who hasn't been there in decades and can't really walk very well, who you're constantly watching for fear he's going to fall, is so much more tiring. I'm dozing off on the train when Louie starts to talk to me more. He's talking at a whisper now, which is very nice of him to do.

He says, "Roy, have you ever been in love?"

"Let's not talk about that, Uncle Louie," I say. I was going through a breakup at the time, and thinking about it bummed me out.

"I've been in love, you know," he says.

I say, "I know that! You have kids, you have a wife."

He says, "But it wasn't with my wife."

Alright.

He says, "It was with a man in the army, and his name was Oscar Willis."

"Oh, boy—I think this is our stop," I say. And it was.

We got off the train, and my dad picked us up. I didn't say another word about it. We just talked about the trip. We talked about going to get ziti. And my dad said, "Louie, you got diabetes!"

Louie shrugs and says, "I'm with my nephew."

We all go to my parents' house that night, and I go upstairs to my childhood bedroom and I think about what he had said to me. I tell myself not to worry about it, but I can't.

The next morning, I'm woken up at five-thirty by my mother patting me on the shoulder. She says, "Uncle Louie wants to go to breakfast with you." I tell her I need two hours.

But I can see in her face that I won't have them. "He's been up for an hour," she whispered, "and he *won't stop talking*! Please, please take him to breakfast."

At the diner, he gets eggs, and I get pancakes. He plays a few rounds of peek-a-boo with this baby behind him, who seems to hate it, probably in part because Uncle Louie is so loud.

As we pay, he's asking about my life and he's talking about me. I'm wondering if this is the time I should bring up what he told me, or if I should just let it slide. We get in the car and it starts to rain, then it starts to pour.

Louie turns to me and says that he's lived so long in California, where they don't know how to drive in rain. "Do you mind if we sit here for a little bit?"

I tell him that's fine.

He starts to talk to me about the war, and about being in Amsterdam. He was a naval officer there. He described these buildings over there. "They've got all these floors and each floor is dedicated to the thing that you like—first floor, drugs; second floor, S&M; third floor, ménage à trois; fourth floor, any homosexual acts that you want to partake in."

I said, "Uncle Louie, did you partake in any of this?"

And he said, "No. I was policing the people who were partaking in these things. I could never."

I finally asked him, "What about Oscar Willis?"

He paused. "Oscar and I—I called him Willy. And it wasn't about lust. It was just two guys who happened to find each other at an interesting point in their lives. We just knew how to talk to each other and we had an instant connection."

I said, "Did anything happen between the two of you?"

And he said, "Absolutely not. I never wanted to risk my career. I didn't want to risk Willy's, either."

"Uncle Louie," I said, "why didn't you pursue the feelings that you had after you got out of the war?" The drops were coming down harder now—it almost sounded like a marching band.

"Risk my family? I could never. But I got a bucket list. I

want to know what it feels like to kiss another man. I want to know what it feels like to hold the hand of another man. And if I don't complete this before my life is over, I'll consider my life a failure."

That's when the wheels started turning in my brain. Realistically speaking, here's a guy who's sixty-seven years old. He can't use the lower half of his body. There's a good chance these things aren't going to happen for him.

As the rain pours, he asks about my life.

I tell him that I've kissed a man once or twice. Haven't we all? But his response is, "Tell me about it."

"Uncle Louie, it's pretty much the same thing as with a woman. It's not that big of a deal." But that's a stupid thing to say. To him, it's everything in the world. Soon, I start telling him about my trip and my plans to move to Austin and what I'm going to do. I tell him about how I was feeling weird about it, and I don't know if I really should do it. I wasn't going there with prospects. I was going because I felt like I had nothing left in New York.

He leans over to me, and he says, "Roy, if I can tell you one thing, if I can leave you with one message, it would be that if there's something you want to do, if there's a weird feeling that you have, go for it. If there's something you want to do that you don't want to tell your mom and dad about, do it. Because we only live one life, and there's nothing worse than sitting down in a chair fifty years later and thinking about what could have been."

The rain starts to let up. He says, "I'll take you home now. I'm sorry that this is how your Christmas Eve started."

I say, "Don't worry, bud. This is an adventure."

We drive back to my house. It is then that I know for sure that I need to make this move. He brings me back home, and I go up to my room to continue packing, which I have been putting off because I've been so unsure.

That was the last time I spoke to Uncle Louie.

He left an hour later, and he spent Christmas with my other uncle and then drove back to California. But since that day, I've had a recurring dream about once every couple months. In the dream, I get an email from Uncle Louie, and in its subject line it says, "Wish you were here." The email is a picture of his feet buried in the sand. His feet are swollen and not looking great, but on his face is a gigantic smile like I've never seen on him before.

In every dream, I call my parents and I say, "I just got this weird email from Uncle Louie." And my mother always says, "You'll never believe what happened. Uncle Louie left his wife for a man." And then I wake up and I remember that I am where I'm supposed to be. And it's because of him.

TAKING THE RISK!

A Q&A WITH ROY LAZORWITZ

What was it like to share something so intimate with strangers?

It was exhilarating. When I was stuck in this car with Louie and he was telling me all of these secrets and desires, I thought that it was really a shame that what he was telling me might live and die in that car, because it was so inspiring. Two years later when I first started working on this story, I was torn because I wasn't sure if I should share all of this. The factor that pushed me over was that I realized he'll never get to have any of these experiences that he wants so badly, because at this point in his life, it's just not physically possible, so if I can share his story, hopefully it inspires others to get out in the world and act on their dreams and desires, when they're pure, whatever they may be.

Have any relatives or close friends from when you were younger heard the story and reacted?

I'm very close with my brother, Mike. When this first happened, I shared the story with him, and he was in shock. He laughed, because he thought it was a joke, a very inappropriate joke. I sat him down, looked him in the eye, and told him that our uncle was being completely honest and that he felt like, for most of his life, he'd lived a lie. It affected him in a similar way it did me—we both felt the need to go out and make our lives what we wanted them to be, so far with mixed results.

TRAUMA AND TRANSCENDENCE

MORGAN

ALWAYS A WOMAN

I've known my whole life that I was in the wrong body. I can remember asking my mother, "When do I get to carry the purse? How about some frilly stuff for me?" Being a child of the fifties, that got me a smack in the head from my mother, the one person I should have been able to tell my truth to. It was very hard to figure out why—why it was wrong, why my desires were so unacceptable. And they never went away.

By the time adolescence hit, I had been swiping and trying on my mother's clothes for quite a while. She had begun to catch on—asking me questions about whether I'd been going through her stuff—and so I realized I needed a new place to shop. I couldn't just go to a store and say, "Hey, I want, you know, I want ladies' stuff," because I was told this was wrong. Instead, I found Salvation Army dropboxes. They were all over town. Any big department store or chain store had one of these receptacles in the parking lot where people would put clothes in. And if you were agile and adventurous enough, you could climb right in there and find outfits. So that's what I used to do. I used to pilfer Salvation Army boxes for my ladies' clothes. I would take the outfits that I con- cocted in the dark from these boxes out to the woods and pretty much dress up just for the squirrels. The nice thing about squirrels is they don't judge.

And again, it never went away, not for a second. A big part of being transgender for me was that I was bent on overcompensating, just because I didn't want anyone to know. Early on, I started anesthetizing myself. I figured out how to drink and do drugs because that made my inconvenient truth a little bit easier to bear. I learned how to act, pulling off the boy thing for years.

I didn't really do a lot of high school. I actually stopped going to school around seventh grade, because kids are so nosy, and I thought they'd find out. I felt like a secret agent.

I was good with my hands, and took on blue-collar work to take the heat off, to better conceal my secret. I did auto-body work for a while. I paved roads. I worked with carpenters. I did all sorts of stuff. I hitchhiked from coast to coast for the first time when I was thirteen years old. I know the God of my understanding has a sense of humor because the God of my understanding decided, "Let's give the trans girl a ten-inch cock!" Really, God? Do you have any idea what this shit is doing to my panty lines?

That overcompensating thing carried on, too. I figured, I've been given this ten-inch cock; I might as well play with it. I tried to marry a woman and hide my feelings, and it was during one of my marriages that I had a friend who was a union ironworker who told me, "I got a job for you, Joe."

I had been doing iron work on the waterfront in Jersey City for ten years. I worked on a bunch of different buildings. Hanging out with the boys, right before lunch, I remember how we'd be looking over the side of the building from like the twentieth floor or something, and seeing girls. They'd be thinking, "We could do those girls." I'd be looking at the pumps, thinking, "I could do that outfit."

The story of my transition starts at like four-thirty in the morning in Island Heights, New Jersey. I'm up at four-thirty because I got a seventy-one-mile ride to work. I get there and I tell the boss that I have to leave at twelve because my wife and I are going to a convention or something. He tells me, "Fine. Take an apprentice and go to twenty-eight and start cleaning up. There's a floor gonna be poured tomorrow." So I go up in what we called a buck hoist, that screened-in elevator that rides the outside of buildings. I ride to twenty-eight with Benny, the apprentice I've been given for the day. Benny is a great guy to have on your crew if you have dope that needs smoking, or if you want to play hide-and-seek instead of working. When we get to twenty-eight, he disappears.

I start looking around at what the job's gonna entail. I'm supposed to be cleaning up. I see a piece of plywood that needs to be moved. A full sheet of plywood. I'm little. I've never been big enough to just pick up a piece of plywood and move it. So what I would do is pick up one end of it waist high, and go to push it out of my way. I did that. My first step was great. My second was into a two-story fall. I went from the twenty-eighth floor to the twenty-sixth floor, and I broke all the shit you could, twenty-nine bones in all.

I was in and out of consciousness, and the first time I came to, the ironworkers had me leaned up against a column. I looked out in front of me and I knew it was bad, because the whole working gang was there. Even the guys from the ground that had been sending iron up were there, too. They were in a half circle, all eyes on me. They were looking at me like little boys that had just shit their pants. I thought, "Oh, this is bad." Then I looked down and saw there was bone sticking out of my arm. I thought, "Oh damn, this is real bad."

Then I realize there are two EMS guys working on me. One of them is cutting my pant leg off, and the other one is cutting my boot off. The only thing I could think of was, "These guys are gonna see my legs are shaved and my toes are painted." Not, "I just fell two floors and I'm probably gonna die," but "These guys are gonna see Jungle Red on my toes." I'd never be able to talk to them again—I'd be as good as dead. In Jersey, cross-dressing is practically a hangable offense.

The next time I came to, I was in intensive care, where I realized that morphine is a wonderful drug for when you fall two floors and break twenty-nine bones. Not so much for Friday nights, as I had thought earlier on in my life, when I was first trying to run from who I was. The next thing I realized was, I've lived fifty years without ever being able to tell my truth. And I also got a real grip on just how precarious life is. You know how many pieces of plywood I moved before I moved that one? You know how many buildings I worked on before I worked on that one that day?

Lying there in that hospital bed, I thought that if I could come to grips with who I was, I'd never be out of place. There's plenty of ugly women out there. I'd made my decision, and anyone who wanted to stop me needed to get out of the way. I told my wife two months after I fell what I'd been hiding from her. We had been married for twenty years before I fell, and we loved each other. Strangely enough, I'd always felt like I was in a lesbian relationship. She thought she was in love with a well-hung man. She listened with compassion, but when I asked about the possibility of trying what we had with my new identity, she was not receptive at all.

I decided it still had to be covert. I wasn't ready to obliterate my old life yet. For a few months after I recovered, I snuck some items from her side of our closet. And she knew. We really tried to address it, to make it work, but it just couldn't for her. She was just repulsed by it.

But I knew my heart. It had been female all along. If you fall off a building as a union ironworker and live, it turns out that can be pretty lucrative, so I had the money for my transition. I did the research, found the best clinic, and on the days of my endocrinologist appointments, I would drive to Jersey City, where I'd done all that iron work.

One day, I drove to Jersey City, parked my vehicle, and walked down the sidewalk. Out in front of me were two ironworkers who were on the same building I was on when I fell. Except they didn't recognize me because I had begun my transition. It was early on in what I call my "clown hooker stage." It was hard to tell what it was that I was going for when I first started dressing up and going out—I didn't have any practice trying different looks on in public. And since my wife wasn't really in my corner, I don't know that I got the best information from her about how I looked or about whether this went with that. The two ironworkers in front of me were part of that half circle that had surrounded me after I fell. They were guys I saw every day, and they didn't recognize me now.

I couldn't let the moment go by. I'm like, "Hi. I'm Morgan. I used to be Joe." They looked me right in the face and said, "Damn, you really did bang your fucking head, didn't you?"

I get a lot of that, but I learned how to take it. This is my truth, and I'm not going to hide. I don't know what tomorrow's gonna bring. I don't know what later today's gonna be like. But I know this is my truth, and I know it's not wrong. I know I'm a good woman.

There's a lot of shit I'm still learning. Until a few years ago, it hadn't occurred to me that bringing a ten-inch cock to a lesbian relationship could be a good thing! How would I know? The closest I ever came to not getting the surgery was when I met someone new, the woman that I'm in a relationship with now. I met Sharon when I was pre-op. She's a confirmed lesbian, has been forever. She saw my heart. But she was also quite enthused with the penis! Eventually, I did more thinking and more research and decided that I still had to go through with the surgery. I had to believe somebody could love me for who I am.

I told my mother I was going to Trinidad to have the surgery, and she was mortified. I was like, "No, Mother, Trinidad, Colorado." We tried to laugh, but the conversation was tense. My mother had a son for fifty years, and she's from that place where if you don't talk about stuff, it goes away. Well, it really doesn't go away.

One of the questions that still hangs with me, something that the psychiatrist asked me in this final evaluation in order to qualify for the surgery, was if I was ready to give up the power. And I was like, "Oh my God, what power? I'm getting a pussy. I thought *that* was the power." And she was like, "No, the power of being a male in this society. Are you ready to give that up?" I understand now what she was talking about, how it's a male-driven world, even if I do get better service at Home Depot with my little push-up bra.

Since I transitioned, I've thought that part of being responsible was letting everybody know. There was a spot where I used to fish for striped bass on the other coast, so one place I wanted to come out was at the store where I would go and buy sandworms. The first time I went there after my transition, I pulled into the parking lot, grabbed the door handle, and for a while there, I couldn't bring myself to get out of the truck. It was genuinely scary. I finally got the courage to open the door, and I went in, presenting as the other gender. And Dennis, who worked behind the counter, was in there, and I was like, "Dennis, I want a dozen sandworms." He turns around, goes over to the cooler, gets a cup, and starts counting the sandworms out and putting them in the cup. I'm talking the whole time— "Dennis, this is what's going on with me. I've known my whole life." Blah blah blah. And I'm telling him and telling him. He finally gets up to twelve and he turns to me and he goes, "Well, do you have the money for the fucking worms?" And I'm just like, "Yeah, Dennis, I have the money for the worms. I wanted to tell you about—"

"Yeah yeah, it's fine," he says. "Now go fish!"

If you had told me that the man from the bait-and-tackle shop was gonna be so on my side, I would have said, "Bullshit." But he was. He was my friend.

One thing I learned that day is that your real friends, the people who really care about you, are going to be there always, no matter what. They want to see you happy. And that's all you want for yourself.

Since coming to San Francisco six years ago, I don't know if it's the fact that I'm in this little bubble, or that this is how San Francisco is, or that I'm of a certain age and at peace with my truth. Whatever the case, my life has been unbelievable. I've been doing stand-up as a way of saying stuff out loud and making people laugh. I've always been a storyteller, and apparently I have an interesting story. I want to keep telling my story and getting it out there, because it's not wrong. I am a good woman.

I feel like my mission is to clear a path for the people who come behind me. A lot of the people who do transition do it later in life, when their parents have died, when their children have married and gone away, when this or that make it easier to live the life they're destined to. The God of my under-standing, with her sense of humor and all, knew it was going to take a two-story fall to give me the strength to do what I'd always wanted to do. When I get discouraged, I think about the new parents who are my heroes, the mothers who, when their kids tug on their purse and ask, "When do I get to carry this?" are finally listening, and ready to show them how to hold it.

TAKING THE RISK!

A Q&A WITH MORGAN

If you'd heard someone else tell this story when you were younger, what might it have meant to you?

I may not have had to live the lie I did for as many years as I did. I might not have needed something as dramatic as a two-story fall to convince me that my truth was bearable.

How do you think this story might affect a reader who is not trans?

I think my story might be very meaningful to someone who is unlikely to ever live through a similar experience. Knowing what I felt, they may be able to find some compassion for someone else going through what I did. If I get to help smooth some of the bumps out of someone else's path, if I can do just a bit of that for anyone, I'm happy.

LILI TAYLOR

THE DUEL

My dad suffered from severe manic depression, and as I was growing up he was in and out of hospitals. There was one particular time when I was sixteen that he had an especially intense manic episode. There was a feeling of dread in the house because we could all feel where things were going. There were six kids—the two youngest being my brother Duffy and me; he was fifteen, a year younger than I was. We came home from high school one day, and my dad was sitting there in his big, black chair, in a pink slip. His hair was up in bobby pins, lipstick smeared across his lips.

He had a big smile on his face. He said he was just so happy that we were home. "Would you please sit down on the couch?" He asked what he could get for us to drink.

We sat down. In front of us we saw every knife from the kitchen, about twenty-five of them, all lined up on the table, starting with the small knives and going to the biggest, sharpest knife.

"Listen," my dad said, "I can see you've seen these knives, and here's what I want to talk to you about. Duffy, this is for you." He paused. "You see, there's been a problem, which I think we can all sense. There's just, unfortunately, too many men in the house, and not enough room for the both of us." He frowned. "One of us has to go, and it's not going to be me, I can tell you that much!"

Duffy and I glanced at each other.

"So," Dad said, "I would like to challenge you to a duel. I would like you to take any knife you want, and we'll go down in the basement, and have it out like two gentlemen, and one of us will come back up. Please, Duffy, chose whichever knife you'd like." He gestured to the table.

Duffy said, "I don't want to duel."

"Come on!" Dad said. He was inspired. "I mean, you've gotta say it's a brilliant plan, Duff!"

Duffy kept saying he didn't want to. I saw how far gone my dad was, but I didn't know what to do to try to reach him.

I was panicking. He had been a writer at one point in his life, so I reached for a ridiculous metaphor. I said, "The pen is mightier than the sword, Dad! Why don't you write it out with Duffy?"

Dad wasn't listening. He looked away from me, and back at the glimmering knives. He was getting more and more agitated.

I said, "Oh, you know what, Dad? I'm going to get you a Dr Pepper!" He loved Dr Peppers. "We'll just drink a little Dr Pepper, and, you know, get our bearings."

I snuck away and, scrambling, called my mom at work. She was the one who could always get Dad back. "Get home fast—he's gone!" I whispered.

Back in the dining room, my brother kept stalling for time and Dad was getting impatient to pick up those knives.

Then, my mom sprinted through the front door. She saw the knives laid out.

"What the hell is going on here?!" she said. She scooped them all up, went into the kitchen, came back out, took my dad by the hand, and went into the bedroom with him. They closed the door behind them. We sidled up to the door to listen, but could only hear whispering. After about forty-five minutes, Mom and Dad came out. He now had his hair combed over and a suit jacket and pants on. He had slapped on some cologne.

We heard the sirens of the ambulance outside. Dad just looked down at his feet and walked past Duffy and me. He mumbled that he was sorry, and then went off to the hospital with our mom, where he stayed for about a month and got calibrated.

He came back home one day, tired, but somewhat restored to sanity.

TAKING THE RISK!

A Q&A WITH LILI TAYLOR

What do you hope this story does for those who hear or read it?

Even though the story is intense and unusual, I hope others find something inspiring for them in the "every unhappy family is unhappy in its own way" theme.

What were you most concerned about in sharing this story?

Exposing my wounded family to others. I have held nothing back in this story, and it's frightening to think about describing the worst parts of my childhood to people in a public way.

POLLO CORRAL

REDEMPTION

I found myself being called into a meeting on a dark Saturday evening, and I knew the news was not good. The meeting was at a park in Juarez, Mexico. It was the regular meet-up spot for my contacts and me, but this time they asked me to get in their vehicle and come along with them, which they had never done before.

I saw their van pull up, and a hand reached out and waved me toward them. At that moment, my contact, who I knew by the name of Z-20, told me to sit in the front seat. He told me to hand him my cell phone and asked *what the hell* had happened. I knew exactly what he was talking about. He was talking about the last shipment of drugs that had gone missing. The bosses wanted to speak with me, and I had no choice but to do as they said.

I heard voices coming from the back seats, voices of men I didn't know. I was forcefully told to put a blindfold on, and somebody quickly moved to tighten it across my face. Next, they shoved my head down, stuck a gun in the back of my head, and the van began to move.

I wondered how I was going to explain what had occurred. This shipment was valued in their eyes at approximately

$700,000. I'd worked with these people for years, and I knew from experience that they didn't mess around. This was serious shit!

The error was my fault. See, even though our operation was going well, I got greedy. No big surprise—this business is all about greed. Somebody had introduced me to another group of transporters, and I had jumped at the chance to expand my operation. Long story short, the new crew saw a weakness and devised a plan to rip off the load of drugs.

The next thing you know, the van pulled into a garage. I could hear the door squeaking as the gears lifted it, then squeaking as it fell behind us. My door was opened, and I was told to keep my head down. At this point, my hands were handcuffed behind me.

I heard lots of voices. There was yelling, cuss words, and some sort of scary, euphoric energy. I was dragged into another room, where all of a sudden it was eerily silent. My heart was beating hard and fast, and cold sweat was coming from every pore in my body. My mind was going a hundred miles an hour as I considered that the worst was yet to come.

What was just a few minutes seemed liked hours of waiting in that room. Then the door was kicked open and an authoritative voice said, "Where's our shit?"

"I don't know!" I went on to offer the few details I had—that I ventured out with a new group, that the shipment was apparently ripped off, and that these folks weren't returning my calls—but I was cut off. They didn't want an explanation.

"You fucked with the wrong people," the guy said.

In my mind, there was only one option of what could happen here. The people I worked for were the kind of people who are concerned with two main things: their reputation (which equates to their power) and getting their money.

Before I knew it, I heard more voices rushing into the room, and I was being kicked all over. I was being tossed around like a soccer ball. I was trying to at least cover my head by tucking it as far between my legs as I could. There was screaming, cuss words, and more kicks to my abdomen, head, and legs. Evil, cold laughter filled the room. "This is what you get for fucking with us!" one man said.

I slowed down my breathing, trying to bear the pain. One of the guys in the room told me I was about to "feel" his belt. That's when I heard him yanking it out through the belt loops. Swish! A cold metal object struck my back. It turned out to be the belt buckle. They were going at me like crazy, whipping and screaming, "Where is our shit?" The pain was so intense I couldn't talk.

A voice in the room wickedly said, "Let's let him take a little break." I guessed that he wanted to hold these lunatics off so that they could come back and interrogate me again before they lost me completely. Hours went by, and I eventually passed out on the floor. I felt weak, sore, fearful, and desperate.

I grew up in El Paso, which is a border town with Juarez. Because my parents wanted the best for me, they enrolled me in a private, all-boys Catholic school there, the school of choice for elites in the city. Ironically, it was there that I had met the people who had led me to make the detrimental decisions that had led to this moment.

As a freshman, I hung out with a group of friends who lived across the Mexican border in Juarez, and there was something that I really liked about them, something about their lifestyle that seduced me. They seemed to ooze power and money. I remember seeing them being driven up to the school by bodyguards in their bulletproof cars. I wanted all of that.

So, as my relationship grew with these guys, I started to learn ways to make money from dealing drugs. It started by dealing a couple of dime bags, and after a time of doing that, it went to selling pounds of pot, and from that, I started to connect with people who had been in this business for years. I got to a point where I was really good at what I was doing, and it wasn't about pounds of pot, it was about shipments of it.

As years went by, I started to get deeper and deeper. People knew my work ethic was good and they wanted to do business with me, and when business is good, the money flows. When I turned seventeen, I had a conversation with my parents, saying, "I'm moving out," and they said, "Where are you going?"

"Business is pretty good," I said. I of course had never told them what kind of business I meant, but my dad had long been an entrepreneur opening up car lots, and I helped him manage the deals, which allowed me to launder my money. My parents were proud. They thought I was a successful young businessman. It was a perfect front for my illicit lifestyle.

Business got so good that I didn't know where to put the cash. I was seventeen years old, moving out of my parents' house and getting my own place that I'd bought in cash for $48,000. There was more cash than I knew what to do with.

As the money was rolling in, my reputation was growing in the Juarez drug world.

A safe wasn't cutting it anymore, so I got creative and, looking at my closet door in my bedroom, I realized I could take out one of the thin layers of wood, and inside I could stash the packs of twenty-dollar bills that were coming in on a regular basis. I bought another home, more vehicles, fancy clothes, all the jewelry you can think of, trips to anyplace you could name. The next purchase on my radar was going to be an old helicopter. I didn't wind up buying it, but that was the extravagance that I lived in.

And now, I was passed out and blindfolded in an empty room. After some time, I finally came to. I could feel a tingling sensation all over my body. Eventually, I heard people shuffling into the room who asked, "Are you ready to talk?" I didn't respond, which was not a good thing, because they took it as me being defiant. I got kicked again. More voices came into the room. "Get the other shit!" I heard, and it turned out that the next level of torture was to stick me with electric shocks.

One of the guys took the handcuff off of one of my hands while stretching my arm back. "Point out your middle finger." I did so and felt him wrap a wire around my finger while the two other guys were holding me down. Another guy went to connect the electrical cord into the socket. In and out, in and out. The pain was excruciating. The shocks continued until I passed out again.

The next time I woke up, one of my hands was handcuffed to a metal desk that was close to the floor. I felt like I had a hangover mixed with a seizure. Bones in my body that I didn't know I had, hurt. My vision was blurry and my instinct to live was weakening.

This went on for days. I remember a guy would come in, feed me ramen noodle soup, allow me to pull my blindfold up, and tell me that this would never end. A couple of weeks into the agony, I started to wonder how I could get out of this. I had money, properties, and influence, and I was good at doing what I did. "Just one more deal and I can make it right," I thought. I was only fooling myself, though—I was completely under my captors' power. I was nothing.

A couple weeks into being at the safe house in Juarez, they allowed me to make one phone call. I decided I would call my family. They hadn't heard from me for weeks, but that wasn't an anomaly. I would often disappear for periods of time while out on vacation or for my deals.

"Pollo," my dad said, picking up the phone, "your mom and I are worried about you. Where are you?"

I told him the news wasn't good. "I can't give you details," I said as I was looking into the face of one of the torturers. "I owe a lot of money and I need to pay it now," I said.

At that point the phone that they had lent me was ripped out of my hand, and my abductors told my father that they would be in contact with him again soon. They hung up. "What have I gotten myself into?" I wondered. This was no longer just affecting me. Now, my decisions, my selfishness, my pride, my arrogance, my plan, my greed had become my family's nightmare.

These guys continued communicating with my father, who offered to step in to cover the debt in a way that I never thought anybody would. My father wound up selling everything he owned—property, including the home that my mother and he lived in, his retirement account, jewelry that had been in the family for years. Businesses were signed over to them—my family was left with nothing. Even after all that, the full debt was never fully covered, but we got to a point to where these people were, in a way, satisfied.

I remember the day when they came in and they said, "You're going home." I didn't believe it. "You're going home," in my mind, could mean something completely different— like being thrown into a ditch with a bullet in the back of my head. Regardless, I wanted all of this to come to an end in one way or another.

For almost forty days I was treated like an animal, tied up, fed once a day, forced to pee in a milk carton that had had the top cut out and tortured whenever they got an urge to do so. There was no shower, no splash of water on the face, no teeth brushing, nothing. I remember looking down at my long fingernails and wanting to peel them off, but a voice in my head said, "Well, if I am going to wind up dead, at least the forensics people will be able to identify me from the DNA from my nails." I wound up peeling all my nails off and putting them in the pocket of my jeans.

My parents had been involved in a local church and I remember my mom inviting me to join them. I played the part, though I never believed. In my deepest moment of despair, however, I tried to pull myself up by my bootstraps and remind myself of what I'd heard at that church, about how there was something bigger than us. One night, I got on my knees in that empty room and said, "God, if you do exist, I ask that you either save me from this horror (because I can't live one more day like this), or that you let them kill me." I just wanted closure, one way or another, and it turned out that God did save me.

When they told me I was going home, they helped me stand up. I remember being shoved into a car, blindfold still on. A gun was shoved into the back of my head and they said, "This isn't over. We're gonna give you instructions for how we want you to do this. We're gonna take you to a corner, push you out of the car, and you need to count to sixty." They didn't want me to see the vehicles they were in. "We've got a follow car," they said, "and that follow car will make sure that you do count to sixty. Don't fuck up, Pollo!"

The drive with the gun pointed to the back of my head seemed to take forever. I tried to count the turns and stops to figure out where we were, but I couldn't.

We eventually came to a stop. They handed me a phone card that I could use at a pay phone in Mexico. "Here," they said. "Call whoever you want to call and have a nice life." He laughed.

I was pushed out of the vehicle and all my brain could think to do was to count slowly. *One…two…three…* I finally got to sixty.

It must have been minutes before I pulled off the blindfold. I looked up and realized I had no idea where I had been dropped off. It was dark and humid, as if it had just rained. I couldn't process what had just happened. Was I really free?

"I don't know if I've got five seconds to live or five minutes," I thought. My reaction was to stand up and run, but my legs would not respond to what my brain was saying. It was probably because my muscles has atrophied after hardly moving for forty days. I spotted an elderly couple walking down the street, and they must have thought I was crazy or on drugs, because I remember looking at them and yelling, "Where are we?" They glanced at each other and walked the other way without answering.

I took a few steps, then galloped a little bit, until I got to a corner with a pay phone. I pulled out the card that they had given me, stuck it in the pay phone, and called one of the only numbers that I could remember, which was my dad's cell phone. I said, "Dad!"

"Pollo!" he said, "I'm on my way. Tell me where you're at." I told him the street signs I could see.

"Give me ten minutes," he said. I was shaking, wondering if I was still being followed, and if my father could get to me without putting my whole family's safety at risk.

My dad pulled up in a white Chevy pickup, and the window rolled down. "Dad, it's me," I said. He literally did not recognize me. My beard had grown out, and I must have lost at least fifteen pounds.

He got out of the truck, ran to me, and we hugged. It was the most memorable hug I've ever had in my life. At this point, I still didn't know he had sacrificed everything to ransom me from my selfish, horrific, greed-driven decisions. "Let's go home, son," he said.

Next thing you know, we're riding in the truck, and I'm just staring at him, and I can't really even believe that I'm alive. I felt like I had smoked some kind of weird shit and that I was in a slow-motion dream. I looked over at my dad and put my hand on his shoulder. "Thank you," I told him. "Thank you for loving me so well."

My family knew that I was going to be released that night, so we got home to find a couple of close family members and my favorite meal, pepperoni pizza. I remember being able to see my mom's face for the first time in forty days and weeping, tears running down my face. All I could do was apologize over and over. My dad was standing next to her, while looking at me. "Our love for you is not tied to anything," he said. "It's unconditional."

It was in those minutes that I started to taste, perhaps for the first time ever, how the grace and love and unconditional acceptance that my parents relayed to me was the same love and unconditional acceptance that God relays to His children. He never gives up on us.

I eventually wound up in Dallas. It's been eighteen years since I was kidnapped by the cartel, and everything is so different now. I've got a beautiful family and I feel like I'm writing a new chapter. It turns out that even the darkest moments in my life were redeemed by somebody who was looking out for me the entire time. That is a story of redemption.

TAKING THE RISK!

A Q&A WITH POLLO CORRAL

What do you for a living now, Pollo?
I work at a nonprofit that has a focus on giving back to the community via appreciation projects for some of our city's most dedicated and hardest-working public servants, such as teachers, police officers, and firefighters. My colleagues and I started the nonprofit because we wanted to teach our kids to give back. We're a faith-based, but not a faith-required, group. We're trying to create an environment where people can come, be real, share their fears, doubts, and pain. And in the midst of having a place to share, they can learn that there is hope, no matter where we're at in life. We tell stories, we listen. Mic dropping is not allowed. Nobody fully gets this thing called life—we need each other because we're better together.

When did you first start telling stories?
I began telling stories while I was volunteering at a church. One day, they put me onstage to help act out a story. The kids were engaged, and I had a blast and

felt like I was instilling something good in these little lives. The opportunities I found to tell stories grew from that moment on.

Your life is so different now than it was during the era you describe in your story. Was retelling it like going back into that other lifetime?

Retelling my story always creates multifaceted feelings. I cannot believe that I am alive and that a selfish fool like me got a second chance on life. Parts of my story foster feelings of fear while other parts stir up great joy. Overall, I think it is healthy—for me, anyway—to often hit rewind and remember who and where I once was. Reliving that part of my life by telling the story definitely helps me stay in touch with a state of humility.

Have your kids heard this story? Or maybe just parts of it? If so, how do they react?

Discerning when and how to share it with our children, who are now ten and twelve, was a difficult process for my wife and me. On one side of the coin, I didn't want them to hear it from somewhere or someone else. The internet keeps no secrets. On the flip side, when would be the appropriate time to share a story that involves so many adult themes (drugs, power, money, greed, anger, pain, eventual joy, etc.)? After much deliberation, my wife and I decided when we were on a family vacation at a lake that it was time. There were no interruptions, and the timing felt right. We all sat around a table after a day out on the water, and I prepared them by telling them I had something very intimate that I wanted to share and trust them with. I warned them that there were many parts of my story that would be difficult for me to share, and that I was not proud of who I was in my "past life." I remember that, as I began to share, my voice cracked. I attempted to hold back tears, but eventually, I just let it all out. We talked and cried. We hugged. I asked if they had questions. Our son had technical questions that boys tend to ponder. "Were you handcuffed, Dad?" "Did they put a bag over your face?" "Was it scary to have a gun shoved in the back of your head?" He was in awe. My daughter quietly asked, "Daddy, do you think you would be who you are now and that we would be the family we are today if you wouldn't have lived through all of that?" My wife and I stared at each other. I took a deep breath. I had to really think about it. This was not a moment for BS. Tears began flowing again, I grabbed her soft hand, pulled her close to me, sat her on my lap and said, "Sweetie, I know for sure that I wouldn't be who I am today without having gone through all of that." She threw her arms around my neck and said, "Then I'm glad you did, because I love exactly who we are today!" There's my mic drop!

ANOTHER SATURDAY NIGHT

These days, people know me as an entertainer and a viral vlogger, but I also happen to have some adult entertainment on my résumé, and it's the first thing to pop up when you Google me. There was a time when I was just plain old Madison, trying to survive on the streets of Miami, Florida, and being a queen, a trans woman, and African American, it was very difficult for me to obtain money for my transitioning. I had to work the street. Prostitution has its ups and downs—some nights you get all kind of good dick, other nights you get bad ding-a-ling, and then other nights you get robbed.

It was November 22, 2001, and I was in the midst of trying to decide whether I was gonna continue to live in Miami. It was a couple of days before Thanksgiving, and I had come to the conclusion that I was going to focus solely on my escorting work off of the internet. I was going to only use a website called Eros and maybe the upscale magazines. But when you're working out of the more established channels like those, you don't get the good dick that you can get from the sidewalk, honey. So I said, "Madison, I'm just gonna tiptoe a little bit out here, and just tiptoe a little bit

out there on the sidewalk, and, you know, have a little fun
and make a couple dollars before I go back to my upscale
whoring."

Well! A guy picked me up on the corner of Northwest
Seventy-Ninth Street and Twelfth Avenue. I think it was
about midnight because, you know, the freaks come out after
twelve. He had to be about twenty-nine years old, with a
pudgy stomach and a cute face. He had a nice caramel skin
tone, and I could tell he had a small cock. But, you know, I'm
the "Big Dick Bitch," honey, so of course he wanted a big-
dick bitch in his mouth.

And he says, "Hey baby, you wanna blow?"

I said, "Oh, but of course! But that's gonna cost you." A
blow job back then was sixty bucks.

He said, "Well, I don't have sixty, all I have is twenty." But
who was gonna turn down $20 and a good blow job at the
same time? I know it wasn't me.

Still, the guy had all this jewelry on, and I was thinking,
"You got on all this jewelry, and all you have is twenty
bucks?"

But I climbed my ass over into the car, this little Toyota
stick shift. I called out to all my queens on the street, "See
y'all in about ten minutes! I'm just gonna get some fellatio!"
In his car, we turned the corner, and there was a vacant house
with a lot of shrubbery. "Baby, don't park here," I said. "I
have a bad feeling about this area." And being that I'm a Libra
baby, I know these things.

He said, "It's OK, baby, I give good head." Well, when they
start talking about head, it just puts a spell over me and I
gotta get it on.

So I said, "OK, then, just back up a little."

But he says, "No, baby, I'm gonna pull over right here!" And he parked there right in front of the damn bushes. He said, "OK, baby, lean the seat back."

So I leaned the seat back, you know, pushed my boobs up to the top and pulled one titty out of the bra so he could suck my nipple. So he sucked my nipple, and it got me aroused, and I got an erection, and he was like, "Whoa, yes!"

So I said, "Baby, give me the money." I said, "I know you've seen the goods, so give me the money." He gave me the twenty bucks, and I slid it under the back of the Afro wig I was wearing.

So I laid back in the seat, and he was performing. Going, "Mmm mmm mmm," like a bobblehead. But I still have this uneasy feeling about these bushes right beside us. I'm looking at them and I saw thFby the timey began to shake. So I tapped his head. I said, "Baby, look up! I think there's something moving."

But he said, "It's okay. Mmm mmm mmmm." And by this time, my erection is shriveling down to nothing.

I said, "Baby, there's something *crawling* in these bushes!"

Well, by the time this fool finally looked up, there was a double-barrel sawed-off shotgun poking through the window at us right there in the car. It was a guy with a ski mask on, and he said, "You motherfuckers don't move!" I lay there frozen in my Afro wig, my panties around my ankles, and my dick now dead asleep.

The guy with the gun said, "Give me all y'all's fucking money and jewelry!"

Would you believe this disgusting fool pulling his head

up from my lap had the audacity to say, "I just gave her all the money!"

I said, "You dumb bitch!" Then I said to the man with the gun, "Baby, listen, I don't have any money, but *he* has all this jewelry!"

The guy leaned into the car and said, "Don't you fucking run then, just give me all this jewelry."

My customer, he just starts crying and blubbering, "Don't kill me! Don't kill me, man!" Then, all of a sudden, he had opened the door and shot off running.

So he leaves me alone in his car, panties around my ankles, dick soft as cotton. The robber is looking at how fast the man has run away, like Speed Racer, and both of us are shocked. The dude jumps in the car, turns it on, and throws it in reverse. He turns around and hits a hundred going up the street.

I said, "Baby, are you serious?" He put the gun to my ear, and he said, "Bitch, you gonna give me all that motherfucking money that that nigga gave you."

I said, "Baby, I told you the man didn't give me shit." I wasn't parting with that $20. 'Cause fuck that, the man had licked the dick, and I needed my money for him licking it.

So I was trying to pull my panties up ,and we were about to drive past a police car. He couldn't ride by with a damn ski mask on so he yelled, "Bitch, don't look at me!" and he pulled his mask off. I was so surprised that the first thing I did was I looked dead in his eyes!

He drove like he knew where he was going. We got to this abandoned-looking area. He pulled over, jumped out of the car, and came around on my side.

He said to me, "Get out," and I did. He said, "Pull those fucking panties off—pull all of that shit off." He had me stark naked. It was almost dawn. He took me to the bushes and he said, "You're gonna give me everything you got." I said, "Baby, I don't have anything."

"All of that ass and them titties?" he said. "You got everything I want right now right there."

I thought, "Oh, okay, so it's turned into *this* now."

So I just dropped down, and I started sucking him, "Mmmm mmm mmm mmm mmmm," on my knees in the bushes, his gun still right there upside my head.

"I wanna fuck you," he said. And he put a condom on.

"Oh, my God," I said. I mean, what is the procedure for that when you have a gun to your head? Then he just spit on his dick, and he rammed it in.

I was nervous, bitch! And, you know, spit and ramming and nervousness are the ingredients for a milkshake! So when he pulled his dick out, it was covered. It was covered! Like a Milky Way bar. I said, "Oh, my God." I thought, "Please don't let this man kill me because I shitted all over his dick!" But he looked at all that dookie and his eyes lit up. It was a turn-on for him. I said, "Thank you, Jesus," for that.

But then he told me, "Turn around and face the tree." And I thought, "What? This is it? Is he gonna kill me in the middle of nowhere, naked?" He said, "Count backward from one hundred."

I said, "Ninety-nine, ninety-eight, ninety-seven, ninety-six, ninety-five, ninety-four…" By ninety, he threw me the car keys to the car and said, "Do you know how to drive a stick?"

"Hell no, I don't know how to drive no fucking stick-shift car!"

He said, "Don't look! I told you not to!"

I said, "I can't help but look, baby. I'm looking!" He got into a car that had pulled up nearby, a gold Nissan Maxima, and pointed the gun at a woman in the driver's seat. They sped away, leaving me right there, naked with the Toyota.

As I'm walking out of the bushes, police cars pull up. One of the girls who was working the streets with me that night jumps out of one of these police cars, and the guy who was robbed was in the back. But she had led them to where I was. I'm thinking, "How in the hell did she know where I was? Was this a setup?"

One of the officers comes up to me and says, "Uh, sir," like he can't tell I'm trans, you know, because this was Miami. They respected nothing. He said, "Tell us what happened."

I said, "Well, first of all, I'm not a sir."

He said, "Excuse me, you're naked. You're a sir."

So I thought, "Okay, whatever. I'm the motherfucking victim here, okay? So don't come over here with this bullshit." I started to tell them what happened, the usual prostitute-on-the-street story. "I was talking to a friend, and he was getting ready to give me a ride."

The cop said, "Cut the shenanigans. We were already informed about what was going on." The owner of the Toyota shrugged. "Baby, go ahead and tell them."

I said, "Fine. Well this guy pulled up and he offered me $20 to suck my dick, and I told him not to pull over there to this fucking abandoned bushy place. But he did, and some crazy-assed, maniac, trans-loving, ski-mask-wearing fool crawled through the bushes and pointed a double-barrel, sawed-off shotgun in the car, and he stole the car—and that Toyota idiot ran—and the ski-mask guy kidnapped and raped me. That's what happened."

"Do you wanna go to the rape center?" the officer asked. I declined. Like they're gonna care that a Black "man" was raped by another Black man. The dick was good, I'm not gonna lie. I would'a did all that stuff, honey—he didn't have to bring the gun!

Now, a big old commotion started to come through the cop's radio. Then the officer said to me, "Let's go, we've apprehended a suspect!"

Well, let me tell you what this fool with the shotgun did. He had to have been stalking me walking the streets all night. He had parked his car on the other side of the street, where the bushes were. When the other queens, the other girls working the corner, found that out about all this, they busted out all the windows of his car and flattened his tires. So, I guess the accomplice, that woman in the Maxima, was trying to take him back to get his car, but when he got to it, he couldn't move, 'cause the queens tore that motherfucker to the ground, baby. And he was caught just a few feet from the scene of the crime.

The police rolled right up on him. They said, "You're under arrest for kidnapping and rape of a man."

He couldn't handle that. "Man, I didn't rape no motherfucking *man*," he said. "I ain't do shit!"

They asked if I could identify him. Well, of course I could. I looked, bitch!

I got into the backseat, beside the girl who had been

working the corner with me that evening and my client. As soon as they brought the shotgun guy over, she starts screaming, "That's him! That's that nigga right there! Take that bitch to jail!"

And then that fool broke out of the cops' grasp and tried to run! It was crazy.

After a few weeks went by, I was asked to come downtown and speak with the investigator.

I said, "Well, how long do you guys have him for?"

"Oh, he's released," this investigator told me. "He got out. His bond was $50,000. He's been out of jail for the last week."

I was shocked. I said, "Do you honestly think that I'm gonna sit up here and press charges on this man, when he could kill me on the street? Y'all don't have any protection for me? I'm a queen. A man will kill me for twenty bucks. This man kidnapped me, stole a car, stole jewelry, and raped me. Why does this man get a bond? Because I'm a queen."

So I didn't press charges—what was the use?

But that was my last night working the street. After that night, I vowed to myself not to fall for the temptation. "Madison, bitch," I said to myself, "you have so many things to look forward to in life. This could have been a moment it all changed, and all people would have said is, 'Well, she deserved it, because she was a whore.'" I knew queens who had been murdered on the streets of Miami, and the police didn't give a fuck. Like you're one less piece of trash on the sidewalk.

During that time when I was working the street, it was very difficult for girls I knew to transition and work at the same time. I don't think anybody walks that street for nothing less than money. A lot of us can't get regular jobs because the first thing that people are worried about is which damn bathroom we're gonna use. I've worked so many jobs, and every time, they didn't wanna say the obvious reason that they were terminating my position: I'm transgender.

That drove me to the street. I had gotten raped and robbed, and I let it go because my lesson was a good one: I survived this stuff so that I could tell this story to new girls thinking about the business. It's not all you think it's cracked up to be. Anything can happen to you on the street. You may not be as lucky as me—you might not get away with your life.

And if you're thinking of robbing some boy pussy, you just might get shitted on.

TAKING THE RISK!

A Q&A WITH TS MADISON

One of the things people find so surprising about this story is your sense of humor about it all.

I think of myself as an especially strong soul, because most people don't like to talk about the traumatic things that have happened in their lives. I always hope that my survival can be like a road map for someone else. Having a sense of humor about it is part of taking the power back from the situation and laughing in its face.

Have you been told that some of your stories show how trans sex workers face a degree of discrimination most people would never even think of?

Yes. I am honored to be able to be both entertaining and educational about something so sensitive and predominant in our community.

MARCY LANGLOIS

SURRENDER

I grew up in a trailer, and at times we had no running water. We didn't have money for anything more than the bare necessities, and sometimes not even enough for those. My mom was only nineteen when I was born. My father was a twenty-five-year-old with a bad drinking problem.

I was born into this tough situation with a cleft lip and palate, and all the medical complications that can come with those. My mom fed me with an eye dropper every twenty to thirty minutes, because I didn't have the ability to suck.

I ended up having about nine major surgeries, with many more procedures throughout. They took a bone out of my hip and put it in my jaw. They pulled all four wisdom teeth. They put plates and screws in my upper jaw, trying to expand it and prepare it to be broken. And that was just one surgery.

When I wasn't at the doctor's office or the orthodontist, I was at the speech pathology center, and if I wasn't there, then I was at the ear, nose, and throat specialist. I had an eleven-millimeter underbite, three front teeth, and braces that stayed on my teeth from kindergarten until my senior year in high school.

Going to school and being around children who were

picking on me, I always felt inferior. The only way I knew how to compensate for that was by outdoing everybody at everything. I tried to run the fastest, be the best basketball player, the smartest, funniest student, anything to distract from the way that I looked. I needed to be perfect.

Then, as a young girl in Catholic school, I started to realize that, rather than being attracted to boys, I was attracted to girls. "Oh, great," I thought. In addition to my cleft palate, my alcoholic father, and our poor upbringing, I now had another challenge to overcome.

To make matters worse, something happened one night in first grade that disturbed me. My parents had gone out and were trying a new babysitter, a man. At some point during the night, I remember waking up, with my yellow-footed pajamas unzipped. I was on my back, and my panties were pulled to the side. The light was on in my bedroom, but the babysitter was in the bathroom on the other side of the wall. I heard water running, and then I heard the light click off in the bathroom. I closed my eyes, and I laid there. I pretended I was asleep, because I didn't know what else to do. The man fondled me, then zipped up my pajamas and walked out of my bedroom. He turned the light off as he left. I never told anyone about that.

In middle school, I started fooling around with drinking and smoking. I was looking for any way to get rid of the self-hatred that I so intensely felt, any way to escape my body. Alcohol became a crutch for me. I drank to forget my circumstances, telling myself I didn't deserve anything good. "Who would ever love you?" I thought. "Who would ever want you?"

Drinking and drugs were destructive, but they were also helping me make friends. In my junior and senior year, I felt like I was really starting to turn the corner, beginning to leave all of the pain from my childhood behind me.

At seventeen, I had my final surgery, and I felt like I was entering a new life.

It was January 31, 1994, and it was a really cold day in Vermont. I was preparing to go to work at my after-school job, and my mom suggested that I take my parents' car instead of mine, since their car had heat. "Sure," I said, and I drove downtown.

A song came on my mother's tape deck that I wanted to listen to. I danced to it in my seat as I drove through town, speeding a bit as I began to enter the busy part of town, where my grandparents' diner sits beside the fire station. I could see some of my grandparents' regulars were outside on the street. I start downshifting, and I notice as I'm looking ahead that there is a car pulled out from the sidewalk in front of my grandparents' diner, trying to come across my lane of traffic. I keep downshifting, going through my gears, and I start to recognize that the driver does not see me. He's not stopping, he's not swerving. He just keeps coming.

I jerked my head around, looking to see how I could possibly avert a crash. The driver kept moving toward the brick fire station on my right, and I was sandwiched between the station and the oncoming traffic.

I hit his car broadside, and my car spun several times. As I was walking over to the other car, screaming, my whole body felt like an electrical wire was on. I felt like this might be a dream, might not actually be real. There was smoke coming

out of the hood, smashed glass everywhere, blood everywhere. I could smell the rubber skid marks smoking on the
road. The whole time, I was screaming.

I looked into the car. The driver was an old man, who
seemed to be in shock, and had some cuts and bruises. But
the woman sitting in the front seat of his car had her neck
bent over to the side, her head collapsed on her shoulder. I
had no idea if she was OK.

I looked in the back seat, and saw two women. One was
resting her head on the shoulder of the other, her eyes
open, staring back at me, as if to ask, "What have you done
to us?" That image has haunted me almost every single day
since.

My aunt and uncle came out from the restaurant, trying to
get me to go inside. I could not for the life of me calm myself down. I felt like I could no longer grasp reality. I just
wanted to know if those people were OK, but no one could
tell me. So they dragged me through the restaurant at dinner-
time, screaming at the top of my lungs.

They wanted me to go to the hospital in an ambulance, and
I refused. "Not until all the other people in the other car go,
am I going," I said. I eventually got in the ambulance, though,
asking the whole time, "Are they OK? Are they OK? Are they
OK?"

As we're getting ready to leave the hospital, the nurse
comes in to go over all the paperwork with me. "When
there's an accident like this," she says, "it's normal to, you
know, be upset, and maybe have trouble sleeping, and have
some anxiety...But it is even worse when there are people
who die."

I said, "What do you mean, 'When people die?'" I looked at my mom, who looked devastated. She said to the nurse, "We weren't gonna tell her until we got her home."

There are no words to describe the feeling of being responsible for taking someone's life. I found out that it was not just one life—both women in the back seat had passed away. The shame and the guilt were so immense. Instead of sleeping that night, I made my plans for tomorrow. My mom was going to pick me up from school, and we were gonna go to the hospital and visit the woman that was hanging on. For some reason, I felt that if this woman lived, I would have some sort of relief.

As I came out of my school the next day, my mom held open the door. The first thing I said to my mom was, "How is she? Do you have an update?"

She just looked at me, and I knew. "I'm so sorry. I'm so sorry, Marcy." That felt like the end of me. I was so angry at myself, at this God that they had taught me to believe in, at the guy that had pulled out in front of me. I said to myself, "I killed them." And my life would never look the same.

I found out where one of the women was buried, and I would sit at this woman's headstone and scream at the top of my lungs. I asked her to forgive me, to give me a sign that I was forgiven, even that I deserved to be alive. I would tell her how sorry I was, and how sorry I was for her family that no longer had their mom or their grandmother. I went there almost every day.

When it was time to go to college, I didn't want to go, because all I wanted to do was die. I started to drink and use drugs every day to escape the guilt. I was trying to kill myself without pulling the trigger. For the first six weeks of college, I never attended a single class, and at the end of it, I called my mom and said, "Mom, if you don't come and get me, I'm gonna kill myself."

My mom said she would come and get me only if I would leave Vermont. I had to do something different with my life, she said, because if I stayed there, I would never make it. She was right. In the town where we lived, I had to drive by the scene of the accident every time I left the house.

So, I agreed. I worked a couple of jobs to save money, and then left, following that road of addiction all around the country, trying to outrun myself, hoping that I'd be a different person when I moved to a different place. I went to Florida. Eventually, I decided I would move to Alaska, and on my way there, I stopped in Colorado.

In Colorado, I met up with a friend named Tracey, who had a little girl named Brianna. Tracey and I had always had a special connection, and when I visited this time, it really came to life. We soon moved in together. Since she had a daughter, I was forced for the first time to make difficult choices. I couldn't drink all day, but I also didn't know how not to. I'd go to work, then leave work to go do shots at the bar, then go back to work. I would tell myself in the morning, "I'm not gonna drink today, no matter what happens," and I'd be drunk by noon.

I had picked Brianna up from school one day, and she was talking about her day. I had been drinking already, of course, since it was already three o'clock in the afternoon, and I was driving back to the bar with her, when I realized, "Marcy, you are not listening to her at all. You don't even care what she's saying." That's when I realized that I was treating her exactly how my dad had treated me.

I'd sworn I'd never make that mistake, that if I ever had kids I would participate in their lives. That night, I decided to attend my first twelve-step meeting, and, thank God, I haven't had a drink since.

For the next five years, I focused on just staying sober and went to a lot of meetings. Then my body physically started manifesting all of the psychological roadblocks I'd never worked through. I got a sinus infection that wouldn't resolve for years. I started having heart palpitations and psoriasis all over my legs and arms. I had seven or eight anxiety attacks a day. The doctors couldn't figure out what the source of my troubles was, so I finally went to a naturopathic doctor, and she told me, "You have to address the trauma that you've gone through in your life, and unless you do that, these physical issues are just gonna get worse."

I started seeing a therapist two to three times a week, while Tracey was helping me to stay sober. I worked, as I focused on my recovery, to help keep the driver of the other car from going to jail. He was seventy-eight years old, and he shouldn't have been driving that day, but I know that he had suffered, just as I had. I had contacted the state's attorney in our area and requested that, rather than taking any legal action against him, they revoke his license permanently.

One day, about two years into my therapy, and about seven years into my sobriety, and about fifteen years after the accident itself, I had a major breakthrough. My therapist had me repeat after her, narrating what had happened on the road that day. "I was driving down the road, and I hit this car, and it was an accident." We said that over and over. Then, on my own, I said, "I didn't kill them. I didn't kill them. I did not kill them." Soon, all of these emotions and memories flooded me. She told me that we were going to hand this experience of the car accident over, give it to the power that was greater than me, because it was too big for me to carry anymore, and I didn't have to do it.

I felt like the spirit of the universe touched me in that moment, and I cried like I had never cried before. I don't know if I've ever been as vulnerable with someone as I was in that moment, and it was so unbelievably powerful, so freeing. It opened my heart. And who it opened my heart to was me.

I had been caught up for so long in the shame and the guilt that I had felt, but I had never taken stock of what I had lost. When I was able to finally look at my own pain, to have compassion for myself in it, that's when I turned the corner.

I am healing. It is a continuous process. I think the day that I arrive will be the day that I will die. Until then, I have this journey of healing that I continue on.

The only way we can learn is through experience, and I believe the most important lesson for all human beings to learn is to love ourselves unconditionally. When you're a lesbian in a Catholic family going to Catholic school, and the world tells you that you're a piece of garbage because you don't look like everybody else, and when you believe you killed three people, to love others and to love yourself unconditionally seems like a pretty tall order. But that's what I choose now.

TAKING THE RISK!

A Q&A WITH MARCY LANGLOIS

Do you recall why you decided that *RISK!* was a place you could share your incredibly personal story?

After completing my work with the Story Project, a small, local storytelling nonprofit, I shared this story on Facebook. An acquaintance from my hometown sent me a message, telling me that she felt like I should submit it to *RISK!* I began researching the show online and sent in my pitch.

After being on the podcast, I had thousands of people visit my website and Facebook page. To open my heart and my soul and share it with the world has enriched my life with a deeper level of compassion and empathy. When I opened up, it felt like I gave others permission to open up as well, which generated a reciprocity of connection within our struggles, conflicts, and trials. We could walk through our experiences together. This isn't about me anymore. My hope is to encourage others to heal their own wounds so that the world can be a better place. We all have a continuous responsibility to do our own work. If we want the world to change, it starts with us and our own stories.

Because this story was so emotional, you took care not to rush it, and developed it in rough drafts over time. Was that process in itself at all therapeutic for you?

Our stories are always developing and evolving. The process of unraveling all of this story to be able to put words to things that I felt at such a deep level was, indeed, therapeutic. Walking back through my experiences in a way that would allow me to articulate to the listener exactly what I was experiencing was grueling at some points and rewarding at others. Based on the feedback that I received from listeners, I knew that my story had a significant impact on their lives. It had created inspiration for some, and a dose of truth for others. Some said they experienced a renewed sense of commitment to tackle the challenges they were dealing with that needed to be faced. I believe it's very therapeutic to isolate what we suffer from and show each other how we share these burdens.

KYLE GEST

DYLAN

I'd been a fat boy for most of my life. I was occasionally bullied and increasingly shy, trying desperately to pretend that I wasn't. Then, halfway through sixth grade, this other slightly standoffish, somewhat heavyset kid showed up, and my teacher Mr. Wheatley said, "Hey, Kyle. Why don't you show Dylan around?"

Dylan had this kind of unusual look to him. He had dark, narrow eyes, but an otherwise fair complexion. I gave him the grand tour of the school—the library, the gym, and the computer lab, where I swore to him that the teacher was really named Mrs. Macintosh. He thought that was pretty funny.

"Oh yeah," he said. "I think the principal told me about her. But I hear she's kind of a bitch."

"Yeah, you're probably right," I said.

I wasn't wildly popular in elementary school, but I had a few friends, and I thought that Dylan could be another one of those friends. That week, though, when I had my back turned, I discovered that Dylan wrote "Jew" on the back of my Nike T-shirt in big pink highlighter.

I said, "What the fuck, man? That shirt was expensive—why did you do that?"

He just laughed. He took another swipe, and made a vertical line down the front of my shirt. I wasn't even Jewish, but I was pretty pissed off.

"Fine," I said, grabbing another highlighter. I took a swipe across his shirt. He shoved me against my desk and said, "Don't write on my fucking shirt."

I was as big as he was, so I shoved him back, took a swipe at his shirt, and said, "Fine. Then you don't write on *my* fucking shirt, OK? We're even, right?"

I put down my highlighter to demonstrate a truce. But he took his and swiped it across my face, opening an inch-long gash along my right cheek.

He said, "Yeah. *Now* we're even."

So it was much safer to stay on Dylan's good side, even if he was being a prick. As far as he was concerned, I was actually his friend somehow. But for me, it was just this bewildering, whiplash back-and-forth of thinking "He's a nice guy," "No, he's a bad guy," "No, he's a nice guy."

For example, the first day I gave him my lunch money, it wasn't the classic bully scenario. He didn't beat me up or give me a swirly. He just asked me, "Kyle, can I borrow a dollar?" As long as he paid me back, I obliged. And he did pay me back, almost always. In fact, if he was late, he would actually double it, paying me back twice what I lent him.

But after about a month of this give-and-take, this back-and-forth, he decided he wanted more money when he already owed me some from the day before. "Sure, man," I told him. "No problem. But, you gotta pay me back what you already owe first."

He weighed those words and he said, "Why can't I have

a dollar now?" I said, "Well, you still owe me a dollar. It wouldn't make any sense if I lent—"

And he sacked me with his fist, right in the balls. I crumpled. He stood over me, and said, "You don't trust me? I'm supposed to be your friend. Now lend me a fucking dollar or you get nothing."

I lent him his dollar, and he paid me back.

Dylan kept a hunting knife in his pocket, which he brought to school for "utility," he said. It wasn't so much the violence that scared me about Dylan; it was not knowing when it was coming. Out of the blue, I'd be smiling through gritted teeth and pretending that, yeah, a meter stick across my knuckles was pretty funny.

In an effort to start anew, and to get away from Dylan, I picked the least popular high school to go to. I kept the fact that I would go there a secret.

As I was turning in my application, Dylan asked me, "Where you going next year?"

I said something about how I didn't actually know. I'd chosen one at random and didn't even remember.

He went off to the stack of forms and went through it, and before I could do or say anything, he saw that I'd be going to Garibaldi. Now, he would be, too.

On the first day of high school, I met Dylan in the hallway. He ducked low, like he was gonna deck me the way he often did, but then he stopped short and put this thin-lipped smirk on his face and opened his palm. He wanted to shake hands.

"I think we should have a truce between us," he said, as if I was ever the instigator.

"Yeah, sure," I said. "Why not?" I shook his hand, the bell

rang, and we went our separate ways. And then, I realized what I had just done. I had just cemented the friendship with Dylan that I never wanted to begin with.

To his credit, he didn't hit me as much. He did get bigger and he hit harder now. I wouldn't give him the satisfaction of reacting as if it hurt.

The other kids noticed that, and when they would ask me, "Doesn't that hurt?" I would tell them, "No, actually, I have this really high pain tolerance, and I don't actually feel anything."

Then they would want to test that theory, and they would start to hit me, too. Even though I was black and blue and green underneath my shirt, and every time they hit my shoulder it was excruciating, I kept a poker face. I wouldn't let them call my bluff.

Instead, I started avoiding the hallways at lunchtime. My buddy Sean and I spent our lunches lifting weights at the school gym. We got stronger—real strong, actually—but it didn't matter, because Dylan decided to follow suit, and before long, we found we were in a competition over who could get stronger.

I started skipping class to avoid him, a whole month straight at one point. Everyone thought I'd dropped out of school. When I came back, the only lie that I could think of that would justify that long a departure was that my grandmother had died. They wouldn't let me make up my assignments, and I was gonna fail five of my eight classes, so I begged my mom, on my hands and knees, to write me a note about my grandmother.

The problem was that I had earned an association with

Dylan. We were two peas in a pod, as far as my teachers were concerned, because we were always together. Despite the fact that I was an A student, in their eyes, I was a delinquent just as bad as the little shit in class carving swastikas into the desks.

In the end, I failed five classes. I'd be repeating the ninth grade.

On the upside, it had become summertime, which for me meant no Dylan, and a pile of video games. I did my best to avoid him.

About midsummer, I got a call from my friend Sean. "Kyle, are you sitting down?" he said.

"You bet. I'm playing *Metal Gear Solid 2*. I'm absolutely sitting down."

"Dylan stole my brother's car," he said.

"He *what*? What are you talking about?"

"Dylan came over. We hung out late. He was crashing on my couch downstairs, and when everyone went to sleep, he stole my brother's car."

"How do you know it was him?"

"My brother Colin heard his engine start up. He looked out the window, and there was Dylan, booking it off in his car."

The car had turned up on the side of the road with a couple of valuables missing, but Dylan was nowhere to be found.

The question for me wasn't why Dylan had stolen the car, because Dylan did a lot of things for no fathomable reason, but how he thought he would get away with it. Was he planning to drive cross-country with it and make a break for it? Did he want to go to jail? Was he gonna come back to school and say, "Hey man, sorry I stole your brother's car." You never knew.

The new school year rolled around, and I didn't know if he was dead or if he'd dropped out, but Dylan was not there. I was waiting for the wave of relief to wash over me, but it didn't come. I only felt empty because most of my classes that year were with kids a year behind me. I was no longer the fat kid in the school—now I was also the stupid kid. All I wanted to do was miss more school.

The principal warned me that if I missed more than a day a month, he would come to my house and personally drag me back to school. What he didn't know was that I couldn't sleep. I couldn't function. I was full of anxiety. And by the second week, I was already skipping class.

One day, I woke up to the sound of my doorbell at eleven a.m. Mom and Dad were at work. My sister was at school. I couldn't see the front door from my bedroom, but I had a feeling that I was in trouble. I moved slowly, thinking that if it was my principal, I wouldn't want him to know that I was home. The doorbell rang again, and I peered around the corner just enough to see through the frosted glass. It was Dylan.

He knocked this time, putting his hands against the glass, trying to peer in, and I ducked behind the corner. My heart was in my throat because I couldn't think of a good reason he'd be there. He'd stolen my friend's car. He'd been missing for months. And as far as he knew, I should be at school.

When I looked back, though, he was gone.

Then I heard the sound of furniture being dragged in my backyard, and I realized that the door to our deck was open for the cats. I was frozen. I was unarmed, unsure what I could possibly do, and before I could do anything, he had climbed up the balcony into my kitchen, and we were standing face-to-face.

We were like two deer in headlights. There was not a word exchanged. My dog, a golden retriever, gave him a sniff and wagged her tail excitedly.

His hand was in his pocket. I knew that he kept a hunting knife on him, and I knew that he was unpredictable, but I didn't know if he would hurt me. I opted to put up the only defense I'd ever known to work against Dylan. I treated him like my friend.

I said, "Dylan. Wow, it's been a while. I haven't seen you in *forever*! Uh, are you going to a different school now? What's up?"

"Yeah," he said. "I'm going to MRSS."

"Oh yeah, with uh, with Ross and Chris and those guys, right?"

He said, "Yeah. Listen, um. I gotta meet somebody. I'm sorry. I gotta go."

He took off through the front door, and I panicked.

I told my parents that we needed to get a security system because I felt like he was gonna come back. They tried to assuage me and told me to go to school. "He's not gonna come back. You already caught him once—he'd have to be an idiot."

But I knew that Dylan did things for no fathomable reason.

The next week, I called my mom as I did every time I got home from school. I was walking around the living room, when I tripped over something. "Hey, Mom," I said, "the cats knocked the DVD player off the stand." An overwhelming sense of anxiety hit me.

I looked down the hallway, and my bedroom door, which I always kept shut, was sprung wide open, and I sprinted down the hallway. My mom was asking me what was wrong, and I told her everything from my video games to my systems to my movies—my entire collection of electronics—was gone.

I called the police and I gave them a description of Dylan. We did a search of the house, and it looked like he had broken in through a window, but there was no way that he himself would've fit through it. The officer suggested that maybe it wasn't him, but I knew that wasn't true. I knew that even though Dylan couldn't fit, he had accomplices and friends who certainly could.

Sure enough, the officer, a mere day later, drove by Dylan toting around my PlayStation 1. It was the single item he couldn't sell because it had stickers all over the lid. When he returned it to me, the officer said, "If it's any consolation, Dylan says that he's sorry."

I might have felt bad for him, but the next day, he was already out and having coffee with his friend across from my mom's store. Because he was only fifteen, it turned out he couldn't be tried in adult court, which meant that, between the car, and the thousands of dollars in electronics he'd been stealing, and whatever else he'd been doing in his absence from school, he must have gotten to feeling invincible.

I became increasingly paranoid, terrified that he would come back to my house a third time. I was afraid to sleep in my own house, in case next time I wouldn't wake up in time for him.

But I was afraid to go out, too. I dropped out of high school. I couldn't go anymore. I was done.

About a month went by. I was noticing knocks on my door when nobody was there, hearing people that didn't exist whispering in my basement. If I slept too long, I told myself, he would come back.

It was five in the morning one day, when a thump hit my door. I leapt out of bed, sprinted down the hallway, and turned on all the outside lights. It was the newspaper delivery.

I figured that I might as well be up for the day, so I read the paper. The front page said something about Ross, one of the dorkier kids from my elementary school. I hadn't seen him in a while. I remembered his mom, Colleen, driving a carpool of kids to school.

The day before, Colleen had come home to a stranger in her house. Actually, it wasn't exactly a stranger. She knew this person, this heavyset kid, but he was not supposed to be there.

When the kid realized he'd been caught, he hit her. She tried to fight him off, but while he was only fifteen, he was very strong. He improvised, and bound her arms with a roll of duct tape he found. Then he pulled down her pants, and he raped her. When he was finished, she told him to take what he wanted and go. He said he was sorry, but it was too late for that. He taped her eyes shut. He taped her mouth shut. And he slit her throat with a hunting knife.

But somehow, that didn't kill her. So the kid searched the

garage and took a gallon of gasoline. He doused her and the rest of the house and he set it all ablaze.

"The suspect can't be named because he's underage," the article said, "but he was found in the family's car, smoking their cigars with his friends and the wedding ring he'd taken from Colleen's finger."

I put the newspaper down, and my mom, who had gotten up to get ready for work, asked me why I was crying.

The news went national. Because the crime was so violent, they said, the boy would be tried as an adult, which meant that both his image and his name could be released. And there he was on the front page of the *Vancouver Province*: Dylan.

The defense argued that Dylan had fetal alcohol syndrome, which meant that he tragically lacked a conscience. A psychiatrist in the case said that he shows no remorse for his actions and called him "untreatable." The judge was at a loss, and he said Dylan was "unspeakably evil."

Dylan, the boy who I'd once considered my friend, got life in prison with a chance of parole after seven years.

I should have felt safe. But I didn't. The fact was, Dylan didn't work alone, and while he was locked up, more people came to torment Colleen's family. They cut the tails off their horses and rattled their chains in the night. I felt like my family was next on their chopping block.

My anxiety was higher than it had ever been, because all this had taken years, and not a day went by where I didn't flinch at every creak, crack, and moan in my house. Somebody was on the roof, I thought, or in the bathroom or in the basement. Every year that went by, I dreaded the family friends who'd innocently ask, "Kyle, what have you been up to?" The answer was zip, nothing. I'd been in hiding.

I had dropped out of high school and I hadn't done a god-damn thing. I wish I could tell you that I had a revelation where everything turned around and I forgave and I forgot and I felt safe in my own house. But I had a serious case of PTSD. The only cure for that was time. To this day, I still don't have my high school diploma.

But I do have my bachelor's degree. It turns out, the secret benefit to having a sad story is that universities everywhere accept you. College reshaped me into the person I have always wanted to be, and it gave me a profound love for story-telling. It also gave me back the sense of trust that I'd been missing for so long, and I am infinitely grateful for that.

It's been thirteen years since I last saw Dylan, and I don't expect to see him anytime soon. The more I talk about the re-lationship I had with him though, the more I wonder if maybe I haven't seen the last of Dylan. Every once in a while, I see a kid with that black mop and those beady little eyes and an ex-pression way too stoic for his age, and I swear it could be him.

TAKING THE RISK!

A Q&A WITH KYLE GEST

How does this story compare to what you do on your own storytelling podcast?

With *The Lapse*, I'm typically the one listening to the story. But I use the same principles when interviewing someone as I do when crafting my own story: Don't write everything down, especially not in the early stages. I build and practice my stories from memory. There's honesty in the sound of someone thinking.

How do you feel about how this story ends on such an unsettling note?

It's part of the reason people still approach me about Dylan today. Some of them have questions, others, condolences. Nowadays, I have to gently turn down the condolences. I'm OK, even if Colleen and some others aren't, and I mourn them. This story is a snapshot of how I felt at the time, a snapshot of my PTSD. That folks are still talking about it, to me, suggests it's more relatable than you might first guess.

A BRIDGE TOO FAR

CHRISTOPHER RYAN

OUTSIDE THE
COMFORT ZONE

I was on track to do a PhD in literature at Oxford and then be a tenured professor somewhere by the time I was thirty. Then I found a loophole in the student handbook that allowed me to skip most of my junior year of college and still graduate on time, so I decided to go to Alaska.

I hitchhiked there from New York, and during that experience, I met so many amazing people who had no clue who Nietzsche was, or Joseph Conrad, or Emerson, or Thoreau— all these people that I was studying, these ideas that were so important to me. But from the passenger seat of the car or truck of any number of these people who drove me through the wilderness, I started to look back at my friends, who were all certified geniuses, and realized they were also sort of assholes. I no longer wanted to be like them. They were good to me, kind—it wasn't that. But they wouldn't have been so kind and generous to any of these new people I was meeting had they stumbled into *their* high-IQ world.

But here I was stumbling into this other world, and people were taking me home and feeding me, and letting me sleep on their sofa. I was welcomed into their lives.

That's how I was thrown into my midlife crisis at twenty.

I'd realized I was going in the wrong direction. And so what I decided was, until I'm thirty, I'm not going to commit to anything. I'm just going to travel the world, have adventures, and let life do what it will to me. Then, at that point, I'll be better able to decide what to do with my life.

Just the other day, I was talking to a friend about travel. He'd made a bunch of money over the decades, and he felt like, "Now, what do I do? I thought this would make me happy, but instead, I'm just lost." I was telling him that the thing about money is that it buys you comfort, but comfort is numbness. The meaning of life and the interesting things that happen in life—the surprises—are things that happen when you can't afford comfort. When you're backpacking, as opposed to flying on your private jet to a five-star hotel. I told him how I'd found that you meet the interesting people when you're hitchhiking. Of course, you've got to stand by the side of the road and deal with Jesus freaks and maybe even murderers or rapists, but if you're as careful as a hitchhiker can be, and you're lucky, you're going to meet someone fascinating. Most of us pay to avoid this hassle if we can. We opt for comfort. But that's the fatal mistake, because what protects you from inconvenience also removes you from life.

After Alaska, my life remained full of change because of my travels. Soon, I was marking the date by full moons. I can remember in Kashmir, at Dal Lake in India, seeing a full moon, and thinking I wanted to be at the Taj Mahal for the next full moon before working out how soon I'd need to depart to allow for the usual setbacks and still make the deadline. A month later, I'm at the Taj Mahal for the next full moon, and I look back and say, "That was a month? That feels like years." It was just so much packed into that one month, and that's what gave me the sense that the length of your life isn't measured in years, but in experiences and friendships and surprises and discomforts. That's what measures time, because time is a measure of change.

Now, the most discomfort I ever felt came when I was twenty-seven. I was in Tikal, Guatemala, and it was the full moon of April in 1989. My girlfriend, Ana, met me in Guadalajara, and we traveled together from there. Just a couple months before, we'd been at Monte Albán, near Oaxaca, an amazing complex of ruins. We'd been there for a full moon, and since I had some LSD with me, and we'd met some people in Oaxaca, we invited them to join us. Five or six of us went up and spent the night there tripping in a pretty bizarre experience. So Ana and I had decided to repeat the experience at Tikal.

One of the things that I very much respect about psychedelics is their ability to remove cognitive filters. I imagine that's why they're such important teaching tools in many traditional societies, and perhaps why they're so forbidden in ours: because they tend to reveal truths that we spend all our energy and time trying to deny and avoid. They bring those things right up to your face. That can be terrifying for people who are very invested in their denial, or it can be extremely liberating if you're trying to overcome it, if you're someone who just needs a nudge to get through the fire, to get out on the other side.

My relationship with psychedelics was that I would often take them in sacred places in order to absorb more of the experience of being in that place. That's why we used them in

Tikal, this magical Mayan ruin of a massive city that has been overtaken by jungle for the last 1,500 years.

Fabrizio and Solange, the two friends who joined us on this hike, didn't know that Ana and I were going to take acid. We never mentioned it to them. So unbeknownst to them, we took the acid about an hour before we would be at the top of the temple, so that we'd be tripping by the time we got up there, but we'd still be more or less reliable for climbing over the boulders and the roots that lead to the temple, and the pipe ladders drilled into its sides that lead you to the top.

We finally got up to the platform where people linger. It's above the tree line and you can see a stunning stretch of lush, jungle canopy below you. You hear the howler monkeys. It had been a little before dusk when we had set off. By the time we got up there, the moon was starting to rise and the sun to set. Above the sunset, I saw this huge bank of clouds, thick storm clouds. I could see rain in the distance, with a rainbow farther off.

Ana and I were tripping pretty strong at this point. Fabrizio and Solange said they were going to go back to the campsite, since it'd be dark up there soon. The clouds were starting to block the full moon. Ana and I weren't feeling like doing any walking at this point, so we said, "Sure, we're just going to hang out here. You guys go ahead." I went over to the ledge of the temple to hold a flashlight for them. They needed the light descending this ladder that was probably thirty feet straight down the side of the temple.

They got to the bottom of the ladder, and said, "Okay, we'll see you back at the campsite."

I turned to go back to Ana, and I felt this sting, this bite on my foot. I shone the light down and saw a scorpion scampering away from my foot and up the wall.

I looked on the wall, and there were others—four or five. I suddenly realized that this whole temple was covered with scorpions.

Like an idiot, I was wearing sandals in the jungle. I went back to Ana, and I said, "Hey, uh, I just got stung by a scorpion, you know, so be careful. They're all over the place here."

"Is that dangerous?" she asked.

"I don't know."

By this point, there was no sign of people in the ruins in any direction we looked, and it was pitch-black. Except for these two guys sitting over on the ledge. We walked over to them and it turned out they were Italian, didn't speak any English. But since Ana spoke Spanish—she's Puerto Rican— she could communicate with them in stops and starts. She asked if they knew anything about scorpions, saying her boyfriend just got bit.

"Wow," they said. "No, we don't know about scorpions." While we're talking with them, a Guatemalan guy came up the ladder. He was a night guard with an old bolt-action rifle.

Ana said to him in Spanish, "Do you know anything about the scorpions—are they dangerous?"

"They're lethal," he said.

Ana immediately started crying. The Italian guys were upset, too. We were all going through our individual grief. And the LSD was hitting me at full volume now. I needed to get down from the temple, because there was no way anyone could carry me down. We'd come up this series of ladders, and all sorts of arduous jungle terrain where you couldn't land a helicopter or even drive a car. We were days from the nearest hospital. So initially, I just sort of felt I needed to focus on getting myself down before it became impossible for me to move.

Ana was very upset—from my perspective, inconveniently so. I was so shocked, I felt I couldn't afford to really be compassionate with her. I just needed to do what I could to increase my chances of survival. One of the Italian guys said, "Look, I'll stay with Ana, you guys go ahead."

I started going down the ladder with this other Italian guy. Working our way down toward the jungle floor probably took us twenty minutes or so. I remember someone had told me there were some American archeologists who were working somewhere in the vicinity, investigating the temples and ruins. I thought, if anyone's going to have an antivenom—and I didn't even know if there *was* an antivenom—it would be them. I needed to find them.

At this point, I could feel the poison running up my leg. It was like a burning, chili-pepper sensation running up along the bone. When it got to the top of a muscle, it would freeze the muscle. My leg was pretty much stiff all the way to above the knee, so I was dragging my leg as we were plunging ahead through this jungle. Because of the acid, I remember being especially floored by all these amazing, glowing insects and centipedes. Enormous bugs that would just zoooooom by me and bathe me in irridescence.

Inevitably, we got lost. There were no signs anywhere. There were just pathways going from temple to temple. That's when I had time to think about what I was going through. I was walking with this kind, Italian stranger, saying what I believed were my last words to someone who didn't understand English.

I remember he would put his arm around me sometimes and touch my back. I was crying part of the time, and other times I was laughing. I'd never really even seen the face of my companion because when we went over to talk to them, it was already pitch-black. I guess he'd never seen mine, either. And yet, we were walking through this darkness together, sharing this incredibly intimate moment.

The next thing I felt was the anguish my parents were going to face. They had been so generous, so selfless in the way they accepted all the crazy shit I was doing, the risks I was taking with my life. To give them a dead body in return didn't seem right.

Once the poison got up to my hip, my whole right leg was just frozen, and my tongue started to swell. My throat started swelling, and I couldn't swallow. I realized I was salivating a lot. I was spitting and my lips were tingly. I was observing the sensations and thinking, "This is when the poison's going to get to my heart and lungs, and that'll be when it's over."

That is when I arrived at this moment of peace—the most unexpected thing of all. I was looking at my life and thinking, "Okay, I'm twenty-seven years old. That's pretty young to be dying. But man, what a way to die! This is a cool fucking way to die. My friends are going to hear about this, and they're going to raise a glass. There's going to be a lot of sadness, but there will also be big smiles, and they're going to think, 'Wow, that guy, he had his fucking adventure. That's what he wanted. He had it, and he died doing what he loved.'"

They'd be right. I had done a lot of amazing things. I'd been around the world, loved beautiful, wonderful women, and they'd loved me. I'd been paid lots of money to do silly jobs, and I'd mustered the courage to quit those jobs and go off and do what I wanted again. From that moment that I stopped being afraid to die, I felt peace. I felt happiness. I even felt pride.

But we were still stumbling around, trying to find these archeologists, and we came to a little parking lot. There was a Guatemalan kid there, maybe fourteen, fifteen years old. The Italian guy explained the situation to him, and the kid looked at me with huge eyes, and he said, "Come, come!" He took us to this little hut and banged on the door. Bang, bang, bang, bang! Finally, a light came on, and this guy opens the door. He was obviously shit-faced, drool hanging from his mouth.

The kid said this was the doctor, and who was I to argue? The man sat me down on a chair and he looked at my foot where the scorpion had stung me. He asked me to describe the scorpion to him. I told him everything I remembered—two and a half, three inches, sort of green, gray color."

And he said, "Oh, no, no, no, no, no. This is alacrán, not scorpion!" And that is when I learned that there are two different, but similar-looking creatures that we would call, in English, scorpions. But in Guatemala, *el escorpión* is a very small, red thing that will kill you. But the sting of the alacrán, which is a bigger, gray-green thing, is sort of like a rattlesnake bite or something. It can fuck you up, but it won't necessarily kill you if you don't have heart problems, or you're not old, or a child.

"Look," he said, "you're still alive now, and this thing bit you two and a half hours ago. You've already passed the most dangerous point. You'll be okay."

He gave me a pill, which must've been an aspirin or a Tylenol or something, and he scooped some water out of this bucket he had sitting there and gave it to me. I had been traveling for a long time, and of course I knew that you never drink water out of a bucket in the tropics. But this guy had just told me I wasn't going to die, so I would've done anything he said.

I took the pill. We thanked him and then went back to the campsite. Ana was at the campsite with Fabrizio and Solange, and they had some beer. We told them the story. By now the moon had come back out, and we could see it peeking through the canopy of the trees.

My tongue and lips continued to tingle for days after that. They were still tingling when we went to this place an hour south of Tikal to stay at a ranch that had been bought by an American couple who'd adopted a few Guatemalan kids and created a guesthouse traveler stop. The husband who helped run it, Michael, was a really sweet, wonderful man, and one morning, maybe a week after we'd arrived, I woke up with a really bad headache behind my eyes. I went down for breakfast, and I explained to Michael what I was feeling, and he looked at me. "Man," he said, "I think you have hepatitis."

It turned out I did. I'm sure I caught it from that jungle doctor's bucket of water.

I had to stay there at Michael's place for about a month. I remember lying there, and there was a bottle of water next to the bed. I wanted some of the water, and it took me ten minutes to gather the strength to reach out and grab the bottle of water, and then another ten minutes to bring it back to my chest, and another ten to bring it up to my mouth. I didn't mind. I was alive.

That night in the ruins gave me the chance to go through the process of dying without actually dying. I was given an amazing gift. It was almost like a vaccination, where they give you a weakened strain of the virus so you can survive the real shit down the road.

If a month with hepatitis is what I had to pay for that gift, so what? Whatever I have to pay, I'll pay it.

TAKING THE RISK!

A Q&A WITH CHRISTOPHER RYAN

How do you embrace new life experiences now that you are older?

I don't wander around unfamiliar jungles in sandals as much as I used to, but I still try to remain open to new experiences and risk failure as much as I can. I think one of the things that makes us old is accepting the notion that we can't afford to take risks like we did when we were young. In fact, we can afford it more. After all, the older we are, the less unlived life we're risking. Nobody can steal money that I've already spent.

What are your aims in sharing this story with the world?

I hope the story helps people overcome some of the stigma attached to psychedelics and to our mortality. We're all dying every day. The day of our last breath is not the day we die, it's the day we stop dying.

THE STRANGER

I fucked a couple of girls in high school, which remains a shocking thought for me to process on all sorts of levels. One of them, the girl to whom I lost my virginity, was my older brother Billy's girlfriend. Because, if you're fucking girls just to convince your Irish Catholic family you're straight, you might as well fuck a girl that it will get back to your Irish family about. Now, when I fucked girls, I would pretend it was a guy, saying to myself, "It's Keanu Reeves, it's Keanu Reeves, it's Keanu Reeves, with his head screwed on backwards and his shoulder blades dislocated!" Actually, if I'm being completely honest about the celebrity I was thinking about, it really dates me. So the truth is, it was, "It's Leif Garrett! Leif Garrett!"

But this story isn't about the girls I fucked. It's about a boy I fucked. When I say "boy," I mean he was eighteen. But I'm still a bit uncomfortable telling the story because I was about nine years older than he was at the time, but now I'm a parent, the father of a teenage boy. So my position *now* is that no one of any age should fuck someone so young but still totally legal! But that was not my position when I was twenty-seven.

I had just moved to Seattle, and there were two things I did not know how to do when I arrived. One of them was drag and the other was how to type, which was really weird because I was moving to Seattle to work at a newspaper, where I very much had to type. Back when I started my column, "Savage Love," I was living in Madison, Wisconsin, while writing this column that only ran in Seattle, so it didn't occur to me to take a pseudonym. Then I moved to Seattle, which I hadn't been expecting to do, and my column was this huge hit in town. But nobody knew what Dan Savage looked like. Somebody in Pike Place Market was even selling T-shirts that said, "I am Dan Savage."

After I got here, people started asking me to do public events, speak at political fund-raisers, host gay bingo. I wanted to go out and do these things, but I didn't want anyone to know what I looked like, because if someone would write into my column, saying something dumb, I would brutally mock them. I didn't want that person to know what I looked like if I didn't know what they looked like.

So when I started doing public appearances, I did them in drag. I didn't know how to do drag, but I had a friend named Zora who would dress me up, paint my face, put a wig on my head, and shove me onstage. Soon enough, my apartment was full of wigs and gowns and makeup.

Next, I had to learn how to type. So I became the guy at the paper who entered in all the personals. I forced myself to do this all night long. But that also meant I got to read every personal before it went into the paper.

One of them came in from a UW student who said he was into uniforms and domination. I thought that sounded kind of sexy, and he sounded sexy in his description of himself.

So I jumped on him first, because I had his phone number—everyone running a personal would need to give us their phone number so that we could confirm their ad. I called him up and said, "I'm entering your ad right now, but I'd rather be entering you." Not really. I said, "I was entering your ad and…I'm interested!" So we made a date.

Now this is pre-internet. No pics, no texts—I'd never invited someone I'd never laid eyes on to my apartment before. But soon, there he was, and he came in carrying a big, green duffel bag. He was stunningly gorgeous. Half Asian, half Italian, a shock of black hair, slight and pretty, the way I like my men. He excused himself to go into the bathroom. Ten minutes went by. I was thinking, "What the fuck is taking so long?" Then he comes out of the bathroom in full Erik Estrada CHiPs regalia. Boots up to his knees, California Highway Patrol tan pants with the stripe, the shirt, handcuffs, and helmet. One of the things he said he wanted me to do was to handcuff him.

"Alright," I said. I took his handcuffs from him and got his wrists in them, and we started making out roughly. I pushed him against the wall, and I started opening his shirt. He had a bra on.

"Hmm," I thought. "What do I do with this?"

Now, I have a degree in theater. As you may know, the first rule in improv is that you never say no. You say, "Oh, a bra. Sure! Of course. Don't we all have bras on?!"

So I took the helmet off his head, because the visor was bruising me on the bridge of my nose and my chin as we were making out. I just wasn't sure what I'd do with the bra yet.

He said, "Call me a bitch."

"You're a bitch!" I said, "With a bra on, and that's awesome. You're just really, really fucking pretty." We're making out, and I feel him growing hard. But as we're rolling around, he sees all the drag on the shelves on the other side of the room. And this is where it starts to get really fucked up.

He asks me to put one of the wigs on him. "Yes, of course!" I pop the wig on his head, and he climbs completely out of the California Highway Patrol uniform and into my drag. He puts this giant, beautiful Zoro wig on, and in that and his bra and panties and a camisole top of mine, and these big, high-heeled, patent leather boots (that I still wear on Christmas morning every year) I realized something: This person who was the picture of masculinity when he stepped out of my bathroom was now a girl.

And because he's a stunning, half-Asian, half-Italian man who is slight and pretty, he is the hottest girl I've ever made out with. Pretty much the only hot girl I ever made out with.

All of this happened in my basement apartment, an apartment that had a bonus room, a tiny, cave-shaped space under the stairs, which was a perfect little fuck room. The renter before me had covered the walls of this little cave with mirrors and there was a hook in the ceiling—it was the early nineties in Seattle, and everybody was into S&M then—and I of course had the mirrors and hook up because, why not? So I pulled this pretty boy into this room, and suddenly I was staring at myself from every angle while I made out with a beautiful girl.

I had some rope, and he wants to be tied up. So I oblige. Because I am accommodating that way. I tied his wrists over his head, to the hook in the ceiling. At one point, I go to the bathroom and there's his duffel bag. I think, "I'm just gonna look in his wallet and find out what his real name is."

That's when I see from his ID that he's eighteen. I'm twenty-seven at the time, so I'm within a decade, but still, I'd never been with someone quite that young before. I think to myself, "OK, take care with this kid."

I came back, and he's staring at himself in the mirror, transfixed by this image of himself as this truly stunningly gorgeous, trussed-up girl.

I fucked him in his ass, which was fine. It was what he wanted, condom on, of course. The whole time, he stared at himself in the mirror, as I lifted his pretty little skirt over his insanely pretty butt, and pulled down his panties. He kept saying, "Call me a bitch, call me a whore!" so I did.

His legs were together. He asked me to tuck his penis back so that it would look like he had a vagina.

But as I fucked him in the ass, holding firmly to his tits (which were actually my tits that I would wear when I was in drag), I found myself thinking, "I can't believe my dick is hard!" I was so turned on! When I had fucked actual girls when I was younger, I had to clamp my eyes shut, concentrate as hard as I could, and force myself to think, "It's Leif Garrett! It's Leif Garrett!" When I fucked girls, I had to picture a guy, but now I was fucking a guy who was the picture of a girl! And it was so hot! And to my surprise, I felt straight for like five whole minutes! I had never felt straight when I was fucking actual girls. In fact, I felt even *gayer* fucking actual girls—fucking girls confirmed that I was gay. I'd have my penis in her vagina, thinking, "I am the gayest girl-fucker ever." But with this boy dressed as a girl, however, there were no thoughts of anyone else, no distractions. I was just thinking, "This is the hottest straight sex I've ever had."

The inevitable end came. He shot geysers. I hadn't seen anyone shoot that far, ever. And anybody who has had sex with someone just beginning to explore their kinks, knows what happened next. I could see him instantly shutting down, the shame washing over him as he realized I now knew him in a way that perhaps no one else in his life did. There wasn't a horny, hard dick overriding those shame feelings anymore. He was exposed.

So I tried to help him feel comfortable. I helped him get out of the drag. But he just packed up his shit and bolted before I could really even say goodbye.

But...he accidentally left behind an expensive watch and his panties. I waited a couple of days, and called his number. The phone number was for some sort of group—his apartment or his frat—and someone else answered, but when I asked I was able to get to him.

"I'm calling because you left your—"

"Please," he said before I could say *very expensive watch* or *cheap panties*. "Please don't call me again. I never want to do that again."

I felt terrible. I felt like I was the instrument of his shame. I wondered if I'd let things go too fast and too far. I knew that everything had been requested or OK'ed and he had consented to everything we did, but he was obviously still reeling from being known the way I now knew him, and that made me feel the ache he must have felt. I was familiar with that ache myself.

I never got to to tell him that I had this expensive watch and these very cheap panties, which I still have to this day because I'm a pack rat.

I think about that kid to this day. That was twenty-two years ago, so he is forty or so now. I would love nothing more than to meet him again. Not to have heterosexual intercourse with him again, but just to see how he's doing. In our sexual and social development, most of us have certain experiences where something explosive or transcendent went down, some moment where we were utterly uninhibited, and then we went careening back to "normal life," but nothing was ever truly "normal" for us ever again. It's so rare to circle back, and to be able to meet up with those people again years later. If I could do that with this guy, I would ask, "What was going through your head? And if something was wrong, I apologize. But I would really love to know who you were at that moment and who you are now, because I think I could have played some important part in your sexual self-discovery, and I hope it was a positive thing, ultimately, even if it didn't seem to be two days later when I tried to return your panties and your Rolex." And so, if you read this, and you're now a healthy, self-loving, non-shame-warped kinkster, I'd love to know. Give me a buzz, send me an email, let's have a conversation.

TAKING THE RISK!

A Q&A WITH DAN SAVAGE

What do you like or dislike about telling stories on-stage, as opposed to on the page?

You interact with the audience when you're on stage, and feed off their energy, and very often that energy winds up shaping and directing your piece. It's not about playing to the crowd, it's about playing with the crowd. Really playing *with* them, in the "hey, let's all jump on the swing set together!" sense, not the "toying with" sense. I love that.

You've made a career of encouraging people to come out about issues in their private lives. In the long run, do you feel like it's helping?

I think more and more people are out now about more and more things—and that's wonderful. I really feel that the LGBT community modeled something important for the straight community. Telling your truth, even a difficult one, even one that you can only tell at great personal risk, is liberating. It's freeing—and who doesn't want to be free?

This is a story about trying something for the first time. Why do you think so many stories go there?

Those experiences are electrifying—your first bungee jump is always way more exciting than your thirtieth bungee jump. You're a lot likelier to crap your pants that first time!

JJ

JUDGMENT DAY

I was born and raised on the borderline between Bushwick and the East New York section of Brooklyn, in a family of Jamaican immigrants. It was the 1980s, and crack was abundant in the neighborhood. I grew up around drugs—my father hustled, and I had other relatives who played that game.

My mom would tell me real simply, "Life is about choices. The time you spend going to a party is the time you could have been studying." So when something bad happened, she would always reflect back on the choices that were made leading up to it. "When you're young," she said, "there are some bad choices you can rebound from, but some you can't rebound from at all."

As I went through school, my mother, being the proud Jamaican woman that she is, pushed me to go to college. I felt torn at first, because that wasn't the norm in my neighborhood, even though she had gone to college. It was a neighborhood in which you would see, even as a kid, a lot of things you shouldn't. Not just drugs, but murders—some people I knew killed a few people. There was a guy in my neighborhood named Shoe Shine who was notorious for being a gangsta. He was a robber, a drug dealer, and even rumored to have killed a few people. He went to jail several times for different reasons.

Growing up in my neighborhood, it seemed easy to fall
in with people like Shoe Shine. For one, your tolerance for
risk is higher when you're younger—you don't have children,
you don't have major responsibilities. Two, in a neighborhood like that, your life expectancy is low. You know you
may not live past twenty-five, you don't see a lot of wealth in
your household, and most times, you don't feel like you have
much to look forward to. As a result, your risk/reward calcu-
lation is not like everyone else's.

The people that I hung around did not go to college. They
were lucky if they made it out of high school. Since my
mother and family were such an influence in my life, I had
done very well in school, earning the highest SAT score in the
school's history. Based on this, my teachers pushed me onto
a different path. They invested more time in me than in the
usual high school kid.

College was a rude awakening for me, because in high school
I had relied on my above-average memory and natural intelli-
gence; in college, there was too much information to remember.
I had to learn how to study. On top of that, I felt isolated—for
the first time in my life, I was surrounded by people who didn't
look like me, at a small college in Connecticut that was almost
completely White. Even the few Black people I met there had
grown up in suburban circumstances I hardly recognized. Shit,
to me they were just White people in Black skin.

I busted my ass to get out of college. I still don't know
how I pulled down good grades. When I got out of college,
I had to figure out what it was I wanted to do with my life,
and I decided to go work on Wall Street. I could have gotten
an apartment with some friends of mine in the city, but since

my mother lived in a brownstone in Brooklyn, and her tenants were moving, I decided I should move into the empty apartment in her brownstone. Stupid mistake. I called this me trying to give back to the community, but in hindsight, it was stupid. I had always heard about something called "Black flight," which is when a Black person gets educated and starts to make a decent living, then never returns to their community, their roots. I didn't want to be that guy. I wanted to always empathize with what was still going on in these urban environments. To this day, I still do.

One thing I noticed when I moved back was that some people in the neighborhood can get jealous; they don't appreciate what you've accomplished. Your newfound knowledge is not appreciated or celebrated. In fact, in some cases, it's ridiculed.

One day, I was coming home from work early—that was rare in my sixty-hour weeks—and as I was walking down the street, I saw some guys I'd known pretty much all my life. I'd played a lot of basketball in the park with them on Sundays. They were OGs to me. They were huddled around a car, talking. "Hey, what's up, banker?" they shouted, jokingly. One of the guys had been shooting the shit about something, but now he wasn't the center of attention, so he flashed me this nasty look. This was Shoe Shine. At the time, I was coming into my own. I was dating a lot of women, and generally was well-liked and active in the neighborhood. He'd seen me around a lot. I never really talked to him, and maybe he felt a way about it. I don't know. I began talking to one of the guys in the group, and he immediately said, "What are you doing over here? You don't belong over here."

I looked at him with a crazy, confused face, and said, "What? You ain't my father. I'm a grown-ass man. You can't tell me where I can and can't be. You a grown-ass man. I ain't talking to you. Mind your business."

His friends started laughing at him. He was offended. He was yelling, "Yo, you know who I am and what I do. You know how I could hurt you?!"

I looked right at him. I wasn't hearing none of that shit today. "So come and do it, then," I said back.

He lunged at me, and I moved. He swung at me and missed. He reached around his waist, like he had a weapon. I used my laptop bag as a shield to protect me from his blows, and then I threw the bag down. I said, "Okay, what you got, a knife or something?" He didn't. He was just trying to scare me.

He swung at me again. Now my hands were free, and my boxing instincts kicked in. My immediate instinct was to fight back, so I threw a few punches at him, and two or three connected. He was shocked. I was getting the best of him. "Open the trunk! Open the trunk!" he said, to one of his friends. When someone says *open the trunk*, you know he is going to get his gun. That's when I realized, OK, this was not a game anymore. I hadn't been around that level of intensity in a long time, and it just set me off. But I needed time out. So I ran. I ran from the street that I was on all the way to my house.

Growing up, I always kept a gun in my house, a nine millimeter. I have had it since I was sixteen. Illegally. Thankfully, I never had to use it. I've shot it a few times, but never at anybody. I had it, because in my neighborhood, you always hear stories of folks' houses getting broken into, or people needing a gun and not having one. But when I saw that gun that day, I was so angry that I pretty much forgot about everything that I had going for me. I began thinking, "OK, how am I going to get away with this murder I'm about to commit?"

I got the gun, I put on black gloves, and I ran outside. It was about six o'clock in the evening in late August. I was running toward the car where Shoe Shine was at. From down the block, he saw me coming. He knew I would come back. 'Cause that's what people from my neighborhood do. They come back to finish things. That's what we know.

But my friend's brother, Peyton, saw me coming, too. He knew what was going on. He was one of the guys I was talking to at the car. He knew this was about to be a bad situation real, real quick. Peyton also was G'ed up. He had been in and out of jail and put in work on the streets. When Peyton saw me coming with the gun, he ran toward me. "Don't do it, don't do it!" he shouted. He was blocking me. "Don't do it. You gonna lose too much. It ain't worth it."

I was shaking, but I would not drop the gun from my hand. I said, "Peyton, move out the fucking way." But he wouldn't.

He said, "You gonna shoot him, or he gonna shoot you. You don't want to do this." He moved out of the way, but he said, "You're not going to do it!"

I started to point the gun. He said, "Naw, no, no!" He grabbed my hand, and I pushed him away, and he grabbed my hand again. I was going to do it.

And now there were all these people looking at me and Peyton in the street. He said, "If you do this, you gotta recognize, there's no coming back from this. You don't want to be like this, this is not you!" And he pushed my hand down.

And I didn't do it.

I was furious. I wanted to do it.

Peyton walked me back to my house. He said, "Yo. Put the gun away. Go in the house." I went in the house and up to my roof. I was looking around, thinking, "Where can I hide the gun, just in case someone calls the cops?" So I hid the gun and came back downstairs. I stayed in my house that night. For about three hours, I was more furious than I'd ever been that Peyton didn't let me do it.

Then after that phase of rage, I was in a state of shock. I thought, "Wow. I almost shot somebody. I could be in jail right now." So I prayed to God. I said, "God, I gotta make some choices. Because if this sort of thing is going to keep happening to me now that I'm back in this community, then I might need to leave again for a while." Lo and behold, a month later, I went to a seminar about business school grad programs. I applied to Harvard Business School, and I got in. How ironic.

We live in a society where for a lot of men, all they have is pride. And pride can be a dangerous thing, especially around young men with nothing to lose. It's important to have pride—in your work, in how you carry yourself. You have to have enough pride not to let yourself be bullied. But if you let too much pride get in the way of what's best for you, it can get you in trouble. There are a lot of people in jail right now because of pride.

So I still think back sometimes on what my mom told me about choices, and how there are some you can't come back from. I know, from that day, I could lose everything I've worked for in a split second.

TAKING THE RISK!

A Q&A WITH JJ

It was back in 2013 when you shared this story on *RISK!* Do you have any other thoughts, looking back on the story now?

My story is not unique. As a Black man in America who grew up in poverty, my story is typical. What is not typical is that I did not resort to violence and end up in jail or dead. But I have more stories. Stories about police brutality, stories about racism. If I had the time, I could write three novels about each stage of my life so far. I'm just happy that someone might learn from this little piece of it that I shared.

HAM AND SAMURAI

Psychologists say that you should try to think back on what your first memory is and see if it might say something about you. I know mine does. I was about three years old, crawling around on the red shag carpet in our dining room and watching the dust motes float in through the sunshine, when I had the first conscious thought I can recall ever having. "Wow," I thought, "I *really* like boys' butts!" I know that memory says something about me, because that little thought is also more or less every other thought that I've had since that Saturday afternoon.

But for a long time, I kept that thought to myself. I grew up in Cincinnati, the most conservative city north of the Mason-Dixon. In my hometown, it didn't just seem like homosexuality didn't exist. It didn't seem like *any* sexuality existed. Frankly, I wasn't sure how the city kept on, you know, populating.

So by the time I was eighteen, I'd had very little sex and I was *very* horny. I convinced my parents to let me go to New York, somewhat for the film school at NYU, but frankly, also for gay sex. The thing was, I wasn't used to socializing in romantic or sexual ways. The straight kids I'd gone to high school with learned how to flirt at the dances and on dates. But by the time I got to New York, I was in the habit of being terrified to talk to anyone I might find attractive. I had no idea how to "cruise" at the gay bars.

Then one day, I was in a bar in the East Village called the Boiler Room, where the gay guys from NYU would hang out. I was talking to a platonic friend of mine from school there, and I said, "You know, I really wanna get laid tonight. But I don't want to have to start a *conversation* with someone first!"

He laughed. "Well, actually, you're in luck!" he said. "There's this secret new place across the street you'll want to see!" He said that down an alleyway across the avenue was what appeared to be an abandoned building. "You'll know you're there because someone spray-painted the number 82 on the door," he told me. "If you push open that door, you might be afraid the building will come crashing down around your feet, but it won't. Then you walk down one flight of stairs, then another, then another, and at the bottom, you'll find a little man. You give him $10, and he'll open a door for you, and it's a sex club in there! It used to be where the Rolling Stones would shoot heroin together," he said. "But now, it's just guys having sex with other guys!"

Now *that* sounded like the New York I'd spent most of my life fantasizing about. "Wow," I said. "Compared to standing around in this bar trying to start conversations, that sounds so much more efficient!"

"Yeah, and the best part," he said, "is that it's all guys from NYU, since they normally find out about that place from others in this bar, so you don't have to worry so much about running into guys who look like Santa Claus in ass-less chaps," which just happens to be the way I look now, in my late forties.

I ran over and found the building exactly as he'd described it. I pushed the creaking door open, wondering if the building would collapse. I went down one flight of stairs, and another, and another. And there was the little man! I paid him $10, and when he opened the door, I was instantly enveloped in smoke. I found myself walking through a labyrinth of hallways pockmarked with little doorways into, ironically enough, closet-sized rooms. When the doors weren't closed, guys were hanging out in the doorways, giving nods to whomever they might be interested in who was passing by. It hadn't occurred to me that my social anxiety might tag along with me to this place from across the street. Even nodding at guys in doorways felt like too much. I quickly learned that someone with my lack of confidence could get a lot of exercise at three in the morning, walking around and around that maze.

Now, remember, I was studying film at NYU, and the week before all this, one of my professors had shown our class a movie that changed my life. It was *Seven Samurai* by Akira Kurosawa. The teacher had said, "This is one of the ten greatest movies ever made. There is so much to get out of it!" Well, what I got out of it was that, in the last two hours of the movie, the main samurai, played by Toshiro Mifune, was only wearing what looked like a diaper, and he looked great! Watching him run around bare-assed in the rain was a eureka moment for me. I thought, "I like guys that look like samurai!"

So, as I wandered the hallways of this sex club, I found one doorway that intrigued me. It seemed empty at first, blanketed in shadows. But looking closer, I saw that there was someone waiting in the back of the tiny room. I saw that he had these beautifully fierce Asian eyes. Then I looked even closer and saw that he had a ponytail on the top of his head—like a samurai! I thought, "Well, if this guy doesn't run a sword through me, I might've just hit the jackpot!" He gave me a nod, and I gave him a nod, and then I jumped on in.

Then, self-doubt set in. I had never done this before! I'd never learned about typical safety measures to take or even the etiquette for sex clubs. I thought, "What is the best way I can start this interaction?"

"Let's go back to my place!" I found myself blurting out. So we went up one flight of stairs, and another, and another, and out in the lamplight, I finally saw that this guy did not look like a samurai. He had a big, beaky nose and a skeletal frame. He was endlessly twitching and sniffling, and I thought, "Oh no, he's *on* something."

I wanted to get out of this now, but the thing is, I'm from Ohio, so I don't know how to be rude. I thought, "I could say I have an appointment! But with who? The nighttime dentist?" So I found myself saying, "What's your name?"

"Ham," he said.

I said, "Ham?" He said, "No, Ham." I said, "Ham." He said, "NO! Ham!!!" He was not a chipper dude. I said to myself, "Kevin. The last thing you should be doing is bringing this guy back to your place!"

So we went back to my place. As he closed the door behind us, Ham went into command mode. I was thinking I ought to put on some Miles Davis and light some candles, but Ham pointed at the opposite side of the room and shouted, "Stand over there!"

I thought, "Oh wow!" Was he doing this thing I'd heard of called "dominance and submission"? I'd taken enough acting classes to know I should probably be "yes and-ing" this moment, playing into the submissive role. But also, I was from Ohio, and I didn't know how to say no.

When I got to the opposite side of the room, Ham yelled at me, "Take off your clothes!"

"Ham, do you think we could tone down the volume a little bit?" I asked. The walls were paper thin.

"Take off your clothes!"

I did. I thought, "Kevin, tonight might be the night you have another transcendent eureka moment! Maybe you'll see the light, and understand the joy of dominance and submission!" It seemed like a perfect rationalization for not knowing how to say no.

Ham studied me for a bit, still standing by the door twelve feet away, and that's when he really laid it on me. "Put the shoes on your balls!" he said.

I paused.

I said, "P-pardon…me?"

"Tie them to your balls!" he barked. He looked at me as if he were thinking, "How'd this guy get this far in life without learning to tie his shoes to his balls?" Ham had to show me what he meant. He wanted me to take the laces of my Converse sneakers and tie them together, like you might if you were going to throw them over a telephone wire, then wrap this contraption like a propeller around my balls so that the shoes would end up dangling at my shins. And frankly, at this point, I was just so curious as to where the hell this might go next, that I did what he said!

Now, I wear size eleven, so that's a lotta shoe. But also, I had the heaviest arch supports that money could buy in those suckers, because Converses are not very good for your feet. I was in the process of learning that they're also rather rough on your balls. So I was standing there, very bowlegged and feeling very pinched. "Okay, Ham," I said, "let's get to the next part as quickly as possible!"

Without budging from his spot by the door, Ham pulled down his pants and started whacking off like a madman. He got all red in the face and sweaty and out of breath. I thought, "Well, this should be over soon, because he must be the world's fastest masturbator!" But then I remembered he must have been on something, and those kinds of drugs can make a man have to go on and on and on. So the minutes were ticking by, he was jerking off to me from the other side of the room, I was feeling *reallly* pinched and I had nothing to do!

"Uh, Ham," I said. "Could we maybe take it to the bedroom and switch it up?"

He looked stunned. He was so offended. "What's your problem? YA LOOK GREAT!"

I thought, "Well, I must be *some* kind of fashion statement, at least."

I let him go on for a while, but then I tried to move toward him. "WHOA, WHOA, WHOA!" he yelled. "WHAT THE HELL IS YOUR PROBLEM?! YA LOOK GREAT!"

It was the strangest debate I have ever had. We went back and forth arguing for a good ten minutes, but no matter what

I proposed, he insisted that my wanting to move on to other activities was proof there was a flaw in my character, because wearing nothing but shoes on my balls was such a good look on me.

Finally, I had had enough. I could see that it was time for this kid from Ohio to show some dominance. So I grabbed his jacket, opened the door, and threw it out into the hallway. That broke the spell. Ham turned to me, looking utterly defeated, all the wind out of his sails. I felt a little sorry for him, knowing I had ruined all his shoes-on-balls plans for the evening. He picked up his jacket, and started putting on his clothes. But, like a politician on election day, he had to get that point in one last time. "Man," he said, "you don't think you have a problem? You look great!"

"Thanks, Ham," I said, "but it just kind of wasn't working for me." I let him out the door.

I turned around and remembered something—I had brought a full-length mirror up from a pile of things left out on Ludlow Street earlier that day. So now, I found myself looking at my whole self, completely nude…except for my shoes. I thought, "You know, Ham might have been crazy. But he was right about one thing. I looked great!"

These days, decades after that night with Ham, I host the *RISK!* podcast and live show, where people tell true stories that, as we put it, "they never thought they'd dare to share." A couple of years ago, a friend of mine told a story at the show about attending an erotic biting workshop. Afterward, I asked him, "Where *does* one attend an erotic biting workshop?"

He said, "Oh! I'm going to this kink camp in a few weeks. You should come along!"

"I don't know," I told him. "I may have told stories about sex on the show before, but I still don't know anything about bondage or dominance and submission."

He rested a hand on my shoulder. "Kevin," he said, "take a risk!" It felt like my show was speaking to me.

The weekend I went to the kink camp, I finally had my *real* eureka moment about the joys of dominance and submission. Late in the weekend, I ended up in a circumstance where I was blindfolded and tied to what they called a Saint Andrew's Cross, while a man who looked a lot like Santa Claus in assless chaps was doing horrible things to me, and I loved it. At one point, I started to feel a pinchy sensation downstairs, and the man leaned into my ear and whispered, "You know what I just did, boy?" "No, sir!" I said. He said, "I just tied my Doc Martens to your balls." My first thought was that my balls must have some sort of magnetism for various kinds of footwear. My second thought was, "Doc Martens? I have come a long way!" So let's just hope that the next time, it's not snow skis.

NIMISHA LADVA

AN AMERICAN FAMILY

I belong to an Indian immigrant family. We didn't come straight from India to America. Over the generations, my family moved from India to East Africa, where I was born. Then to England, where I got my accent. And then finally to America, where I live now. I grew up with a version of Indian culture that my grandparents carried with them when they left India, a version that is nearly a hundred years old. One of the things I often heard growing up was that I had a responsibility to protect and uphold my family's *izzat*, my family's honor.

When we came to this country, my parents saw that many of the Indian Americans here were professionals—but neither of my parents had been to college. To fit in, and to maintain the family honor, it became very important that my brother and I "study well and marry well." Translation: Become a doctor, or marry a doctor. There was one problem: I faint at the sight of blood. Plan B became Plan A. I was supposed to find a nice Indian doctor to marry. You can imagine my parents' disappointment, then, when I told them I wanted to marry David, a nice Jewish boy from Chicago. He was not a medical doctor.

My father took it well for the most part—better than I

expected even—except for one time. We were driving on a mountain road at night. Suddenly, from the passenger side, he grabbed the wheel.

I screamed, "Oh my God! Dad! What are you doing?"

He screamed back, "Just leave me on the side of the road. To die."

For the record, I did not leave him on the road.

Then, there was my mother's reaction. It came in daily doses on my voice mail and went something like this:

Me: "Hi, this is Nimisha. Leave me a message. Bye!"

My mother: "Ni-mi-[sob]-sha-[sob, sob, sob, sob, sob]. Ni-mi-SHAAAAA!!"

Except for my name, no additional words were necessary.

At one point, David hears such a message. I tell him how I feel.

"She leaves these for me *every single day*. David, I am killing my mother. I am killing her, with this, with us."

As soon as I say this, I see him do something that surprises me. He smiles.

Then he says, "You are not making her react this way. She is choosing to react this way."

"Are you kidding me?" I say. "What kind of stupid, post-therapy, White man thing is that to say?"

To me, at the time, his comment might have been the dumbest thing I had heard from him. It said to me that he had no ability to understand how difficult being with him was for me and my family. The dutiful immigrant daughter who lashed out at him knew that when your parents are upset because of something you do, it is your fault, and your responsibility to make it better. The rest of the conversation didn't go well. He reminded me that he was Jewish, that things had happened to him, that he wasn't all White privilege or just a walking pile of micro-aggression. It hadn't yet crossed my mind that I had my own racism to deal with.

Things weren't going well with the other people around me, either. Family members would ask, "Nimisha, are you sure about this? You know when you marry out of our community, there is no coming back."

Or they would ask, "Nimisha, are you sure you've given other options a fair try?"

Or they would just shake their heads in disappointment.

I was having doubts. He certainly didn't look like anyone I thought I would marry. When I met him, he was wearing gold-rimmed glasses—which were ugly, and not in a cool way. He was from the Midwest, a place I knew nothing about. He was wearing a red, cotton jacket, and I assumed this was a way to avoid being hit by farm machines, a leftover habit from his childhood among cornfields, because, what did I know?

As we get to know each other, however, signals along the way tell me that even though he doesn't look like the man my family and I thought I would marry, he is the right choice for me. One day, he says he has a surprise for me. We get to his place, and there, laid out for me, is a proper English tea. There are scones in three flavors, cucumber sandwiches with the crusts cut off, real Devonshire cream, jams and jellies, and imported butter. He's been special-ordering from Whole Foods and a local bakery. Then I see the tea.

"You have Harrods' #5 Breakfast Blend? It is my absolute favorite!" I tell him. "I had no idea they carried it at Whole Foods."

"I know it's your favorite. I had my friend ship it here for you."

"From England?" I ask.

"From England," he says.

I hadn't told him it was my favorite. He had simply paid enough attention to know. I never imagined it was possible for someone to be so careful and observant about what I liked, about what would make me happy. I wasn't imagining. David was real.

To my parents' credit, they started to change their position on David as well. To my surprise, we got to the point where we were actually planning a wedding. My father asked David if he wanted a rabbi at the wedding. David was so pleased to get a yes from everyone that he was happy with an Indian wedding.

Indian weddings can be fancy. In India, a groom might arrive on an elephant. In America, I have been to weddings where the groom arrives on a white horse. Because the ceremony would be conducted in bare feet, David said he was happy to arrive on his white feet. Indian weddings can also last for days. Ours would be on the shorter side, two days.

Typically, the groom's family and the bride's family separately celebrate the days before the actual wedding ceremony. On the first day of my family's celebrations, my parents thought that, rules notwithstanding, David should come over and enjoy a little bit of five thousand years of Indian culture.

He comes by himself and meets my extended family. In the middle of all the cooking and chanting, my mother announces she is making something for David, by herself, for him especially. We both have to stay away because she wants to surprise him. I am delighted she is doing this for him. She isn't into crafts; the closest we got to doing crafts as children was sewing buttons back onto my father's shirts. I think to myself, "Here is my Hindu, voice-mail weeping mother, offering to make something special for my Jewish husband-to-be." She has come a long way, and I feel proud and happy.

She tells everyone that what she is making is a *luun*, which, frankly, is a massage tool. Let me explain. It is a small brass vessel filled with mung beans and covered with decorated cloth. It's used during the wedding ceremony to help the groom tolerate the demands of sitting on a low platform, legs crossed, reciting Sanskrit *shlokas* as he awaits the arrival of his bride. A young relative—in my case, one of my cousins—is tasked with sitting behind the groom with the *luun*, shaking it (it makes a pleasing jingle), and running it down the groom's back.

My mother asks my cousins to bring her various items. "*Kanku app jaldi!*" Bring me some red powder! And then, "*Liloo capru!*" The green cloth, too! Finally, she says she is done. The room falls silent as David and I sit next to each other, waiting for her to present him with his gift. As she walks toward us, I am bursting with joy. I never knew I could have such feelings for a mere craft object.

She leans in, puts her hand tenderly over David's head, and gives him his gift. That is when I see it for the first time.

My mother has painted a swastika on it.

My vision tunnels. I am transformed into fear and sweat and little else. There is silence from everyone, but especially from David. It is as if someone has died. Then, finally, my mother speaks.

"David, you don't like it?"

She sounds genuinely hurt. My father, reading the situation, offers some cross-cultural context.

"You know, David. The swastika has been in Indian culture for centuries. It means home, it means family. It is common in Hindu weddings."

Still no response from David.

My mother speaks again. "Those Nazis stole the swastika from India. They are very bad people!"

I feel some relief that we can all agree about the Nazis. It's enough to pull me back into the room, into what is going on. I'm suddenly aware that I should have seen the swastikas coming. I had grown up around them my whole life. But I didn't. I had been so consumed with my own family agreeing to the wedding, that I hadn't thought enough about David's family, my future family. Other relatives chime in about the prevalence of swastikas in other cultures, but the din of their explanations makes David's silence all the more unbearable. I can think of no way to get out of this mess by myself.

Then, I finally hear David.

"Mom," he says to my mother. The room is silent again. This is the first time he has used this form of address with my mother. We all hear the newness of it. "Mom," he repeats, "we can't have swastikas at our wedding." In that one word, we hear forgiveness, we hear love. It changes everything. We snap back to our senses and into action: We must protect the *izzat* of David's family. We check the decorations and my wedding sari and the *mehndi* designs on my hands—no swastikas! I realize then, we aren't just an immigrant family, or a Hindu family, or a Jewish family. We are an American family.

TAKING THE RISK!

A Q&A WITH NIMISHA LADVA

This story is even more poignant now than when you first told it, as there is currently such a cultural backlash against immigrants and against Jews from some factions in America. How does it feel to look back at it?

I feel even more grateful that *RISK!* gave me the opportunity to bring this story to a larger audience. Telling this story helped me articulate my identity as an "American" to myself. It reminds me that being American is a process—for everyone—not just a fixed identity.

Have any of the people mentioned in the story heard it and reacted?

David, my husband, has heard it and loves it. My parents heard a shorter version and wanted to know why I have to keep telling people "all my personal business." They asked, "Is it necessary?" In their own process of becoming American, they are both supportive and ambivalent about this storytelling business. Whenever I need documentation for one of my stories—say, a photograph, or an object—they always find it for me. They know "sharing my business" is necessary for me.

Were you inspired to share more stories after telling this one?

Yes! At the time I told it, it was the longest story I had told on stage—and you know what? I didn't pass out on-stage, as I had feared. And people liked it! So now, in fact, I have written and performed a solo performance play, *Uninvited Girl: An Immigrant Story.*

MOLLENA WILLIAMS-HAAS

SLAVE

I was a science fiction geek as a kid. When I was four or five, I started watching *Star Trek*, the original series. I had the hugest crush on Captain Kirk—I thought he was the hottest man who had ever walked the planet. There was one episode in which a green Orion slave girl dances for Captain Kirk, as someone discusses with him how the Orion slave girls are the most desirable women in the galaxy. I saw that and thought, "I want to be an Orion slave girl!"

But the big turning point for me came in the episode with Khan. Khan is a bad guy, but a woman on the crew falls madly in love with him, and he asks her to betray the *Enterprise* for him. "No," she says, "I can't do that," and then he knocks her to the ground. He says, "You may stay or you may leave, but do it because it is what you wish to do!" And she comes crawling across the floor back to him, begging him to accept her. And five-year-old me thought, "Yeah!"

I had started developing fantasies about submission. I thought it would feel liberating to have someone treasure me so much that they owned me, that I belonged to them. That idea was so hot to me.

A couple of years later, we hit 1977, and *Roots* comes on

television. And now I'm watching people who looked like me being treated rather poorly by White people. Seeing other Black people enslaved and beaten and humiliated, their families torn apart, so graphically for the first time made me feel horrible for having found submission so exciting in other contexts. Being the bright, precocious kid that I was, I thought, "Okay, I gotta figure this out." If slavery was White people doing bad things to Black people, and since all White people couldn't be evil, then I reasoned that perhaps there was someone who owned slaves who was actually nice and treated them well. Maybe it wouldn't be so bad to be a slave, if your master was nice to you. What if your master was Captain Kirk? He would never whip his slaves, I decided.

I remember asking, "Mommy, would being a slave be okay if your master was nice to you?" You can imagine the look on her face. "Lord Jesus," she must have thought. "Help me with this child!" She prayed a lot.

"No," she told me. "There is nothing ever okay about slavery. Slavery is the worst thing that people can do to other people. It can be worse than death." My conclusion, then, was that my fantasies about submission were really about something worse than death, and there was no way I could ever tell anyone about the fact that it was kind of sexy to me.

Fast-forward to my twenties. I was in Los Angeles at Barney's Beanery with three of my girlfriends, swilling beer in a booth right by the pool table, and this guy was on the other side of the table, playing pool in a very dapper suit with his friends. He was tall, and pale, with green eyes, dark hair, and a British accent.

I'd never had anyone give me a look that so clearly said, *I could have you if I wanted*. I looked back at this man, thinking, "You don't get to look at me like that!"

At one point, he came around to the side of the pool table that was closest to us in order to aim for a difficult shot, and bent over so his ass was within a foot of my face. I tapped him on the butt and said, "Um, excuse me, could you please try not to intrude on our booth?"

He turned around. "Oh, sorry, love!" he said. "Cheers. Didn't mean to put me bum in your face!" And with that accent, I could have melted into a puddle right then.

To apologize, he offered to buy me a beer, which I, of course, accepted. Then he invited himself to join us in the booth. He told us that he'd just flown in. He was on tour with a band. He had me wedged in against the wall so that the normal gestures of conversation meant brushing knees.

I couldn't make eye contact with him, and then when I did, I couldn't look away. He was magnetic, and he knew it. His arrogance was maddening to me, but also lured me in. I would giggle and blush when I tried to address him, and my friends looked at me, baffled, never having seen me react this way to any situation.

I agreed to go out with him the next night. We had dinner. At one point in the evening, I had gotten up to go to the bathroom, and when I came out, I felt a hand around my neck. The man had grabbed me by the throat. He pulled me into the bedroom of his hotel suite, threw me up against a wall, and leaned against me.

"You've been a very bad girl," he said. "You've been teasing me all night."

I was flustered, stammering "I...Um, I'm sorry?"

"Do you know what happens to bad girls?" I told him I didn't.

He started pulling off his belt. To this day, hearing that slow slide of a leather belt through the loops of a pair of pants makes me dizzy. He took off his belt and wrapped it around my neck, pulling it really tight. I was having a hard time breathing. He yanked me toward him, and picked me up off of the floor and threw me down on the bed. He was pulling my underpants down, throwing up my skirt, and beating the crap out of my ass with his hand, as he continued choking me with the belt, saying terrible things to me about what a bitch I am, and what a slut I am, and what kind of whore do I think I am, the way I tease him.

I thought to myself, "This is a lot like what a sexual assault would feel like." And yet, I was more turned on than I'd ever been in my entire life. I was wet and shaking, and begging him to have mercy. I didn't beg him to stop—at no point, in fact, did I say no. Rather, I just asked him to please have mercy. But when it came time for fucking, he said, "You are going to have to beg for it."

"How dare he?" I thought. But I said, "Please, oh my God, please fuck me!"

He proceeded to have the most violent, aggressive, greedy, selfish, piggish sex with me, and I think I probably had an orgasm for the entire hour of it.

Afterward, I lay there, spent, and he jumped up and grabbed a cigarette, suddenly chatty. "Okay," I thought. "At some point, I'm gonna freak out, and tell him this is not okay." But I didn't. And we fucked again the next morning, and then the next evening, and had this two-week-long affair the whole time he was in LA. Then he flew me up to be with him in San Francisco, and he flew back home to England.

He and I had had such an amazing bond, and I was convinced that, despite the fact that we could not be together, living in different countries, we were somehow destined for each other. No one else, it seemed, would ever understand what I needed in a sexual or emotional relationship.

After he returned to London, we kept in touch. We would have lots of phone sex. One day when we were on the phone, masturbating, he said, "Do you know what would be really hot? You know what would turn me on? If you were my slave, and I owned you."

My whole body froze. "You imperialist fuck," I thought, "you son of a bitch."

I said, "I would not be—Who do you think you are?"

"Oh, you're right," he said. "You'd make a terrible slave. If you were a slave, you would be knocking over pitchers of milk in the kitchen just so you could get punished."

And we laughed. I confessed that I was turned on by the idea. "Well, you should write about it," he said. "Write me a story."

I started writing this story about the poor innocent slave girl, who was being terribly abused by the evil British sea captain who had visited her plantation, and it was just completely politically incorrect. It was like, the worst bodice-ripping romance novel ever. But as I was writing, I was thinking, "Oh my God, the ghost of Martin Luther King is going to rise from the grave and say, 'Girl we did not march on Washington so you could masturbate to fantasies of being ravaged by some White man!'" And I'd say, "But Dr. King, it feels so good!" I would email him these stories, and my Brit would tell me how incredibly hot they were.

I finally shared this with a friend of mine, another Black woman, who I expected to tell me I was sick bitch. Instead, she said, "No, it is hot. But it's hot *because* it's fucked up. It's transgressive." I thought, "Yes, we have fought so long and so hard to own our own bodies. And to have a sexual desire to lose that control? I'm a feminist. I'm an independent Black woman. What the hell am I thinking?" I had amazing amounts of guilt about it.

Interestingly, I was having this conversation with my friend, the evil British sea captain of my fantasies, and he said, you know, "Why would you deprive yourself of something you want, because of your politics?" He said, "Your pussy doesn't care whether or not your fantasy is politically correct. It knows what it wants." And I thought, "Well my pussy is a terrible, terrible creature then. And deserves lots of spankings."

I started exploring online. I started going to kink events. I finally asked some other Black women in the scene, "Have you ever had fantasies about submitting to someone, and having the fact that you're Black be a part of the scene?" "Sure," they said. But just fantasies. You just couldn't *do* that. There weren't very many other people of color involved in the leather and kink community in the early nineties, and of the few of us who were present, most did not want the topic of racially charged slave fantasies brought up. Their fear was that, if we acknowledged those kinds of fantasies, every racist mofo in the five-hundred-mile radius might suddenly rise up and decide it was okay to call Black people niggers and bring back slavery.

The first dominant I experimented with in the kink scene would not do anything remotely resembling slavery. "I can't," he'd said. "If you choose to do that at some point in your life, that's fine—just leave me out of it."

Then, finally, after many months, I met another dominant in the kink community, this very funny Jewish guy who was happy to do it. We were able to joke around a lot about racial and cultural tensions as we negotiated how our play would go. We would do a scene in which I was coming in for a job interview and he was reviewing my résumé skeptically.

"Wow, it's really funny," he would say. "You're awfully articulate for a colored girl. I mean, Black girl. What are we supposed to call you people now?"

Eventually, the scene degenerated into "Well, if you want this job, you're gonna have to suck my big White dick."

It was so wrong. But the rush was incredible. At the end of that scene, I said to him, "I hated you. I hated you purely for a good couple of hours. But, God, that felt good." To have the permission to feel those conflicting, uncomfortable feelings was incredible. I came to understand that I really could explore this stuff, as long as it was with someone I trusted. Someone who knew me well. I knew I was getting into deep water, but I thought I knew how deep the water could go.

Eventually, I decided I wanted to do a somewhat more elaborate scene, but I knew it would require a thorough negotiation beforehand. My friend G was experienced in kink, and we had lots of mutual friends. We decided it would happen at a kink play party, but we didn't specify a date. In the middle of some upcoming party, my partner would initiate this scene. We would have the element of surprise. He would grab me and throw me into the dungeon, calling me all sorts of terrible names, most of them racially charged. That was our negotiation. G was also from the South. He no longer had the accent, but he could play the redneck well. In normal circumstances, he's gentle and sweet. But in the kink scene, he's a skilled sadist.

Over the next couple months, I saw him at a couple parties, and I was on edge, never knowing when he might break out into this act. So the anticipation kept building, which was really hot.

Then, one night, I was at a kink play party and I was chatting with a friend by the snacks. "Oh, did you hear that there was a fire yesterday in so-and-so's barn?" my friend asked. I looked at her, baffled. "What are you talking about?" I said. "I don't know anyone with a barn!" Then, suddenly, I found myself with a bag over my head, being pushed down and dragged into the dungeon.

I was thrilled. I thought, "This must be it!" I started getting into the headspace for submission.

G took the bag off my head, yanked me up by the hair, and threw me up against a wall. "Hey y'all, look what we got here!"

I heard the accent and I thought, "Oh my gosh, this is going to be hilarious," in that way that some of the race play I'd done before had had a ridiculousness to it. But then he called me a "nigger bitch," and asked me who the fuck I thought I was. I could I feel myself surging with anger—I don't like that word. I started trying to kick him in the balls, but he restrained me and pushed me back, getting some help from folks around us at the party. Soon, there were three or four people holding me down and tying me in rope.

"Well, I know y'all saw what happened last night at the barn," he said, grinning at me. "And are you gonna be a good nigger and tell me what you saw, or am I gonna have to beat it out of you?"

I thought, "Oh, I see. This will be one of those scenarios in which he'll be the evil redneck who was going to find some excuse to beat the crap out of me." That's what he did. At first, he was just slapping my face, then using a whip. But he just kept repeating this question, "Tell me who burned down the barn?"

Nowhere in our prior negotiation had there been any mention of a barn. So, clearly, I didn't have the information he wanted. He was just going to beat me until he got tired of it, I thought. We had discussed that my safe word was "red," so he knew that would be like a stoplight if I should choose to yell it out. But as his spankings and whippings continued, they were beginning to overwhelm me. I began to feel confused and afraid.

The first inkling I had that something wasn't quite right was that at one point, I had gotten loose from the rope, and started running toward the door, and was caught and dragged back by a bunch of people. Now, mind you, these are all friends of mine who were recruited to help in just that situation. But somehow, I couldn't see them that way in that moment. I thought, "Why aren't you helping me escape from this evil man?"

I was becoming disoriented. At one point, I remember I was on the table, and then I blinked, and the next thing I remember, the table was falling away from me. One part of my brain knew I was losing my grasp on what was actually happening. I was beginning to experience momentary blackouts. But the scene would not let up. After one of the terrifying blackouts, I found myself hanging, by my hands, from a hook in the middle of the dungeon. He was striking my back with his whip. I was terrified every time I heard it snap, and felt an overload of the fight-or-flight impulse.

"Tell me who burned down the barn," he screamed, "you fucking stupid nigger!" I moved on from my initial rage to flat, empty terror. When I looked at his face, I didn't recognize him at all. I could not see my friend. I saw a White man who had zero regard for my humanity.

I blacked out again. Then, he took out a knife and pressed it against the lower part of my stomach. He grabbed my head and turned it around so I could see the people standing and watching us, twenty or thirty White people staring at me. I found out later that our scene had gone on for so long, and had been so epic, that everyone else at the party had stopped their own scenes to watch.

But in the mental space I was in, I could not see a bunch of kinky folks standing around watching a scene. No, they looked like a bunch of White people who were helping this person torture me.

As he held my head to face them, he leaned in and whispered in my ear, "I could cut you open right here in front of all these people, and no one would do anything, because no one gives a fuck about another dead nigger."

At that moment, I felt him push the knife against my stomach. And I thought, "He's right. No one cares."

"I'm gonna give you one more chance to answer my question," he said, "and tell me who you saw burn down that barn. Otherwise, I'm gonna slice you open slow, from your guts to your neck."

I wish I could say that I fought back, that I was overcome with a sudden burst of strength, and broke free from my shackles, and grabbed him by the neck. But in fact, I only prayed that he would slit my throat instead, so that I would die more quickly.

I have never felt so bereft and alone in any situation before. It was genuinely terrifying.

Soon, the host of the dungeon party came up behind G and told him, "We're almost at closing. You have to end this scene."

G had lost track of time, too. He said, "Oh, okay, well, I guess we'll end the scene here." So he put his knife away, untied me, and pulled me down on the ground. Then he went to find me water and a blanket, to fulfill the proper post-scene care duties.

But as he approached me with a blanket, I started crawling backward on the floor, screaming and crying. "Get away from me," I said. "Don't fucking touch me! Don't touch me!" And then, everyone in the room finally realized there was a problem. I was slowly snapping out of it. I was becoming aware that the man before me was someone I knew who had been performing a scene with me, that we had been doing some kink. But I felt he had gone too far. I was furious and terrified.

My other friend, the Jewish guy who had done the racist job interview scene with me, was there. He began taking care of me. He said to G, "She's not really gonna want to deal with you right now. You just need to go to your separate corners."

My friends took me home, and I was not even fully present. As the hours passed and I tried to force food and water down, I was trying to figure out what had happened. I went to sleep and woke up the next day, still angry and afraid. At this point, kinksters had started talking about the scene online. People were bewildered and fascinated by the scene and its aftermath, and everyone had an opinion.

Many were convinced that I was at fault, saying I should have safe-worded if I was having a problem. Others said that G obviously went too far, and wondered why he didn't take time-outs to check in with me at times.

When I finally spoke to G about it, I said, "There was obviously something wrong. Why didn't you stop the scene?"

He felt terrible. "But, we both knew you had a safe word" was his response. It turned out he'd directed the woman at the snack table to tell me who burned down this fictional barn: that confusing interaction was the basis for the information he wanted me to confess to him in the scene. But while she'd been rambling about a barn, I was focused on the snacks! I hadn't followed what she was saying at all.

The truth was, I couldn't safe-word. In a way that had never happened before, I'd become truly lost in the reality. I had no idea that my brain had the capacity to believe my life was in danger when it was not. The idea that I could have stopped it all by saying, "red," simply did not occur to me. I felt the depth of the power of this taboo I'd been toying with for years on a whole new level.

I wish I had been able to reconnect with G more quickly.

For the first couple of weeks after the scene happened, I was going through an emotional process that neither one of us understood.

To this day, I'm still unpacking the lessons I learned from it. I had a taste of what it is like to have your life in the hands of someone who genuinely disregards your humanity. I find an immense freedom in the fact that I was able to survive. I know, in a way that few do, the strength of taboos, of racism, of hatred, of fear.

People come up to me now and then and tell me about the fantasies they want to enact, but explain why they're afraid of playing them out. "Excellent," I tell them. "You absolutely should be afraid." It doesn't have to stop you, but that fear should give you pause. If you can work through that fear and excitement, I tell them, finding a way to explore your psyche and take responsibility for what happens on the other side, then take the journey—because holy crap, even though it could be dangerous, it could also be amazing...and hot!

TAKING THE RISK!

A Q&A WITH MOLLENA WILLIAMS-HAAS

This story digs into our nation's racial tensions in surprisingly revealing ways. Do you ever get pushback from sharing this story? Did you worry some might take the wrong message from it?

If by "pushback" you mean folks who despise the idea of using BDSM to address racial issues, then yes. I am not sure what the "right" message is, so I cannot say that there is a "wrong" message. It is not a fiction, a morality tale, or a piece of entertainment. It is my life. As such, there is no right or wrong message to be gathered. Folks will come to their own conclusion, and relate (or not) to suit their individual experience. My hope in sharing it is that it helps someone, somewhere, to gain some insight, some empathy, some bit of information that might shed some light into what is usually an obscure, dark aspect of the human experience.

Have you engaged in race play much in recent years, or has that particular kink become less interesting to you over time?

I don't feel that anything that changes us becomes less "interesting." What has been true for me is that some experiences bear repetition and some, not so much. The experiences I have had were invaluable to me and, should the spirit move me toward further exploration, I would certainly consider it.

You seem to do more improvising than the average storyteller. Do you ever write things out or create outlines?

I don't use outlines and notes for standard storytelling. Much of my belief around the tradition of storytelling is about a direct spiritual and emotional connection with the listener. Having a script, for me, places the story into the realm of "performance." As a performer, I love that! I perform my solo show, *HYENA*, with a script, as I am working with an orchestra, and the performative nature of it works well in that approach. But when I am telling a story, I need to be *with* the audience in a way that removes the safety net of scripts and outlines, which renders each person in the house a friend, rather than an audience member.

Any other thoughts or feelings you'd like to express about the story, the experience of having it on the podcast, or the thought of having it in this book?

To be honest, I haven't listened to the whole story. I don't enjoy listening to myself on recordings, and I don't necessarily enjoy reliving this particular experience. Over the years, I have had quite a few people contact me to share that this story was important for them, because they didn't see themselves, their curiosities, their desires, and their fears reflected in the BDSM and Leather experience. That other people felt validated by my own experience makes the more difficult aspects of the experience more bearable. Perhaps having this story in this book will help it find its way to the eyes of someone else who is hungry for it, too.

MICHAEL IAN BLACK

THE RING OF FIRE

I'm a person who has always, even before having children, been fairly conservative in my proclivities. Before children were even a thought in my head, before I was even married, I never drank, never smoked cigarettes, and had never done drugs.

But then I got married. For our honeymoon, my wife and I decided to go to Amsterdam. We went for the whores, and for the Anne Frank house.

The trip started off beautifully. While we were checking in at JFK Airport, the woman punching in our info looked up and said, "Are you on your honeymoon?"

"Does it say that on the computer?" I asked. "How did you know?"

She pointed to our rings. "They're all sparkly and bright! They look brand-new."

We admitted that she was very observant. We had just gotten married and were indeed on our honeymoon.

"The Anne Frank house?" she asked.

I'm kidding—she didn't say that. But she did congratulate us. She handed us our tickets and we said, "Thank you," and then we looked down and realized she had upgraded us to first class. "Wow, thank you so much!" I said.

"Have a good marria—" she said, and by that point the person in line behind us had interrupted her.

I've always wondered what's in the upper passenger level on the the 747 planes, and that day, I found out that what's up there is magic.

It's essentially a salon up there. You get your own big chair and it goes back, and as soon as you get in, the flight attendants give you a bag filled with gifts—little slippers that you can put on, and an eye cover, and collectible earthenware filled with liqueur, which surprised the hell out of me.

"Thank you very much!" I say.

"Enjoy your earthenware." The flight could've gone on forever, I am so contented.

I am almost disappointed when it lands and I have to leave and go to Europe. "Europe can't compare to this," I think. And the truth is, it doesn't.

That's not to say that we don't have fun. We do, and it is lovely. We are swapping apartments with a couple, which is how we could afford the trip, and the Dutch couple had this nice apartment overlooking a canal. The first thing I do when I get to the apartment is think to myself, "I'll bet this Dutch couple that we're renting from has topless pictures of the hostess." They were Dutch, so it seemed a sure bet.

I go to the photo albums, and there are. I study those for a little while, thinking this is a really good honeymoon. We're there for a couple days, going to little shops and eating little Dutch sandwiches.

Eventually, something starts gnawing at me. We walk through the Red Light District to see what it's all about. There's nothing erotic about the neighborhood. But I can't shake the thought that since I'm here, I should get high. So I say to my wife on our last night there, "You know what we should do? We should get high."

She's fine with it. We just had this big, Italian dinner, and at the end, I said, "Take me to the place where you get high."

I'm assuming my wife knows where to go because she's gotten high before, so she's an expert in my eyes. She finds us one of the coffee shops, which are back in the Red Light District. The cafés where you smoke pot in Amsterdam are these shitty little rooms with red walls and Bob Marley posters, and terrible music, and one asshole American, passed out in the corner because he could not handle his pot.

We get what they call a space cake. Since I've never inhaled anything, I'm afraid of doing so. Instead, I had these brownies that are half chocolate and half lawn clippings, just choking them down.

I'm waiting for it to kick in, and twenty minutes go by, then a half an hour go by. Nothing is happening. I say to my wife, "Do you feel anything?"

"I don't know," she says. "Be patient."

"I'm *being* patient. Nothing's happening." Another ten minutes go by, and I tell her I don't think it's working.

"I feel OK," she says.

"Well, it's not working for me," I say.

What I fear is happening is that we just had this big dinner, so the active ingredient in the pot got absorbed into my food, and it's not going to work. "Go get a joint," I say, happy to make her do everything, which should have been the first signal that perhaps I was high.

"Are you sure? We just had this space cake, and I think it's going to work if you just give it—"

"Just get the fucking thing," I say, because apparently that's how I now talk to my wife. She gets up slowly, and she buys a joint.

"You have to teach me how to inhale," I say, "because I've never smoked anything in my life." She demonstrates and gives it to me to try.

I puff the joint as best I can. "It's not working," I say.

"Just try it again."

I do, but I don't feel any effect. "It's not working."

"Well, I'm high."

"Well, I'm not. Pot doesn't work on me."

The joint gets smaller in my fingers as I continue to drag from it.

Then, all of the sudden I hear somebody screaming bloody murder. "He's dead!" a woman yells. "Oh my God, he's dead, he's dead!"

"What the fuck is going on?" I think, and then I realize I'm unconscious, and the person who is screaming is my wife. I have become that asshole American passed out in the coffee shop because he could not handle his pot. "He's dying," she says, "he's dying." I feel the little, thin arms of the Dutch boy who works there pick me up off the floor and put me back onto my stool. My eyes kind of open a little bit, and my wife goes, "Is he going to die?"

"Nobody ever died from pot," the boy says, and then he disappears in a puff of smoke.

"What happened?" I ask my wife.

"You were yelling that it wasn't working, and then your head hit the table and you fell onto the floor."

"That doesn't sound good."

"It wasn't," she said. So we agreed to leave, and we get up and walk out, back to the apartment where we're staying, except that now, we are both walking like panda bears. We've become panda bears, which is a surprise to both of us. Even though it sounds cute, it's not, when you realize that it's late at night and even during regular business hours, it's tough to find bamboo in Amsterdam when you're a panda with the munchies.

We make it back to our apartment, and I climb the stairs as a panda bear would, and get into bed as a panda bear would, and my wife tucks me in. I wake up like eight hours later, and I am still a panda bear. "How long is this going to last?" I ask her.

"It'll stop soon," she tells me, but it doesn't. It goes on for almost the whole day, and we have to go to the airport, because it's time to return to America. We're now changed people. We're haggard, and I remain semi-panda. We walk up to the airline desk and I say, "Show them your ring. Just hold up your hand and show them your ring."

As we approach the clerk, I ask my wife to kiss me. "I don't want to," she whispers, and I say, "I don't want to kiss you either, but do it! Pretend that we're still in love." The clerk looks up and she asks, "Going back to New York?"

"Yeah," I say, as she looks back down. "We were just on our honeymoon."

"Uh-huh."

"It was great…We saw the Anne Frank house."

She types some letters into her computer. "Congratulations," she says, looking up and handing us our tickets, which are coach.

We get onto the airplane, and the seats in coach are now much smaller than they would have been had we never been in first class. They are infinitely smaller, the seats in front infinitely close. We are infinitely tired and infinitely no longer in love because of this long evening that we just had. My wife says, "I don't think I can do this." I don't know in that moment if she means sit in coach for eight hours, or the marriage.

Then, I swear to you, a Russian women's basketball team proceeds to board the plane and sit all around us. They're the biggest people, male or female, I have ever seen.

There's a stereotype about Russians that all they do is drink. I am here to report to you that that stereotype is absolutely true. It was the most awful eight hours of my life, and I thought to myself, "If we can survive this infinite evening of just tripping out of our minds on pot, and being exhausted, and coming back to our shitty New York apartment, we can survive anything."

We land at JFK and I'm feeling pretty good. In fact, we're starting to laugh about it, saying we'll survive anything. Then, a couple years later, we end up having children.

TAKING THE RISK!

A Q&A WITH MICHAEL IAN BLACK

Do you find it freeing that you don't have to be funny the whole way through when telling a story?

Yeah, I don't particularly worry about funny in a story-telling format. I'm just focused on telling a good, concise story that moves.

Can you remember hearing others tell true stories and it making an impression on you?

I've always loved good storytelling—I remember actor and comedian Toby Huss telling a moving story in the early nineties about an RV or something. It was the first time I understood that comedy and pure storytelling could be integrated.

IN PLAIN SIGHT

JONAH RAY

HIGH FIDELITY

My alarm goes off. I had just moved to California, and I was keeping my alarm on the other side of the room from where I would sleep because I'd become good at hitting the snooze button without looking or even waking the fuck up.

It is tuned to the most obnoxious radio station I could think of when I set it. "Butterfly" by Crazy Town starts to play, a song that I'm happy to hear because I hate it. "Come my lady, come, come my lady. You're my butterfly, sugar—"

"—Baby."

I get up so fucking fast I get a head rush. I run across the room. But before I can turn it off, the song fades out and the DJ comes on. "All right," he says. "Just to reiterate. Two planes have flown into the World Trade Center buildings in New York City."

I wasn't sure what to think. Two planes had crashed into New York City and this guy still felt the need to play "Butterfly" by Crazy Town? "The Madonna concert tonight is canceled," he said. "And Disneyland is closed."

These are the things that people are gonna be upset about? None of us know what to do that day. I hear the news, and then I boot up my dial-up internet, and wait an hour for the photo to load. The whole scene looks pretty fucked up.

I have to go to work, though, so, I just do what we all do—those of us lucky enough not to be at the site of the attacks—and I go into a haze to work at the record store I just got a job at in Venice Beach, California.

The year 2001 was not a good time to work at a record store, what with the entire recording industry failing. The married couple that ran the store, Bob and Nancy, are typically stressed about making rent each month, and the state of their relationship is largely a function of how well the record store is doing at any given moment. With Napster in its heyday, their marriage isn't at its best.

Bob is a portly fellow, loud and boisterous like Jack Black's character in *High Fidelity*. He's the kind of shop owner who tells you to your face that what you're buying sucks. Once the movie *High Fidelity* comes out and takes off, people come into the record store and say, "You ever see *High Fidelity*?" And he says, "Get the fuck outta here, Jake." He calls people Jake like it's a placeholder name.

On 9/11, I try to proceed with all my normal duties, putting out the new releases, hanging up new posters. Customers take the same approach to the day, coming into the store and browsing what records they would go home and then download for free.

"Ugh…Crazy, huh?" someone says, flipping through CDs on a rack. "What's going on out there? Boy oh boy…How is that new Slayer album? Weird that it's called *God Hates Us All*, huh?"

That was nonstop. In between, I'm being yelled at for not

sweeping because my bosses' marriage and livelihood are falling apart.

Bob and Nancy get into a big argument over the fact that they shouldn't be selling bongs. "We don't need to sell bongs, we're a record store!" Bob says.

"We're a record store in *Venice Beach*," Nancy says. "We gotta give the people what they need."

She walks out in a huff, and Bob and I continue silently doing what we always do. It's just an odd day in part because of how normally it proceeds.

We're making virtually no sales. Then later into the evening, a cute little punk rock couple comes in—two little young, high school crushes, sharing earbuds, listening to the Smiths. They're adorable. They start grabbing stuff and stacking it on the counter, which is really good to see—these two kids aren't letting the world events ruin their day of getting new records, being in love, and listening to depressing Morrissey songs.

They are having a blast, talking to us about music.

"Oh, you like that?" I say. "You should get this."

Soon they are done, getting everything they want, which will cost a lot of money. They give us a credit card, which my boss runs. I put their stuff in a bag and hand it to them.

"See you around!" I say.

The whole interaction was proof that love does exist, even in the darkest times.

After a couple minutes go by, my boss goes, "You know what? I feel like I shoulda checked the ID on that credit card."

"There's better things to concern yourself with now," I say. "Being as the world is ending and all."

"Nah, it's gonna bug me," he says. "I hope that doesn't bite me in the ass."

About an hour later, the young punk rock lovers come right back in, cute as ever. They start getting tons more shit, grabbing entire racks of records and just putting them on the counter. "What's that thing?" they're asking each other. "Is it expensive? Put it in the pile!"

My boss flashes me a look that says, *Oh, fuck*. He goes to the girl, who's close to us in the front of the store, and he says, "Hey, uh, God, I'm so sorry about this, but I would really like to see that ID that you used with the credit card."

"Oh, yeah," she says. "Totally. Don't worry about it."

She walks over quietly to her boyfriend on the other side of the record store and leans into his ear. My boss just turns to me. He says, "Lock the doors."

I start locking the double doors. I get one done, and my boss starts coming over to help me with the other, and then he turns, and we see the boy sprinting.

He tries to squeeze through the door, but my boss grabs his hair, throws him on the ground, locks the door, jumps on top of him, and starts screaming.

"Why the fuck would you do this?" he says. "Why would you do this?"

"Aahhh, I'm sorry, I'm sorry!" the kid says.

"Why the fuck would you steal from me? From my family?" Bob is broken. Like a damn had burst.

"I don't know! I'm sorry!"

Bob starts to cry. "Why would you wanna make it so I can't feed my kid?" he says, but now he can only get the words out piecemeal between sobs. "These...these Strokes records aren't gonna send her to college!" The boy, who's wearing a Dead Boys T-shirt, starts to cry, too.

Then the kid is hugging my boss, both of them crying now in the middle of the store. The girlfriend is sobbing, too, and the tears start streaming down my cheeks, because I'm nineteen. I don't know how to handle real shit yet, either.

We all begin to commiserate about what a shitty day it is. Eventually, my boss pushes the boy away and says, "Alright, though, listen, I want my shit back. You bring my shit back!"

"We will. We'll go get it," the boy says, and they both start to leave.

"No," Bob says. "You stay. The girl goes and gets it." So this was like a hostage situation.

We let the girl out and then start waiting there. My boss has a cordless phone for the business in his hand, and he's pacing back and forth. He's pounding the receiver on his head, like it's a gun. "She's not coming," he says. "She's not coming."

He starts to dial 911, but the kid pleads with him. "No, no, no, no, no, no, no! She's coming, man. She's coming back! We love each other. She's coming back." Bob would hang up the phone, then he'd do it again, and the cycle would repeat.

She finally comes back, and puts all the stuff on the counter. My boss goes through the receipt. Puts everything back in. Everything is accounted for. He slams the register shut. It makes a *ding* sound.

He looks up at them, smiles, and goes, "Thanks a lot, guys. Come again!"

And then he turns to me. He goes, "You can take off an hour early if you really want to." And I did. Then I just cried the rest of the night.

TAKING THE RISK!

A Q&A WITH JONAH RAY

Have you told this story other places?

I've only told parts of the story to friends here and there. There's so much sadness in it that I hate to burden people with it at a comedy show, for instance, when we're having fun.

I am so much of a passenger in this story. I was involved in a way, but more so, I was just a side character to the central drama. So it does feel a bit weird to present it to people. The story still feels like the demo version of the story I'll put into my autobiography when I'm seventy-five...it'll be called *What If I Tried? The Story of an Unknown Comic*.

DAVID CRABB

EVERY DAY IS HALLOWEEN

One night when I was five years old, a babysitter allowed me to watch David Lynch's *The Elephant Man*. It was the most terrifying thing I'd ever seen. But for two hours, I couldn't look away. That night, I could hear the Elephant Man wheezing beneath my bed, waiting to reach out with his melted claw and pull me under, where he would drool all over my face while falsetto-screaming. I barged into my mother's room to tell her I couldn't sleep.

Three sleepless nights later, my exhausted mother flipped through the *TV Guide*. "Look, honey!" she said, "*The Elephant Man* is on tonight. Let's watch it together."

Panic struck me. I thought, "Is the punishment for watching *The Elephant Man*—watching *The Elephant Man* again?"

My mother wasn't one to let a teachable moment go. So that evening we watched the film together. Each time I would begin to cover my face in a blanket, my mom would interject with commentary like, "The nurse earlier cried because she was scared, but Anne Bancroft is crying because she's touched by his poetry," or, "Yes, they call him the Elephant Man, but his name is John Merrick. And even though he looks like a monster, he loves opera and building models."

By the time the most violent scene arrived, in which a vagabond group of drunks break into Merrick's room to terrorize him, I was standing on the couch in my footie-pajamas, screaming at the television.

"Leave Mr. Merrick alone!" I yelled. "The Elephant Man didn't hurt you!"

Three hours earlier, I'd made a cape out of newspaper and tried to fly off the dining room table like Superman. But now my hero was a long-dead, horrifically deformed, British sideshow freak with a penchant for tea and theater.

That night, I must have looked under my bed a dozen times, hoping to find Mr. Merrick, with his huge, malformed skull and jigsaw-puzzle face, screeching with delight to see me and drooling all over my face as we hugged.

The Elephant Man was probably the beginning of my love of dark things, but there was also the influence of my mother, Geri, a tiny, fire-headed Newfoundlander with a house full of knickknacks: Royal Doulton china sets, tiny ceramic sculptures, and weepy-eyed Precious Moments dolls. On her bookshelf you'd find engraved Bibles, old copies of *Good Housekeeping* magazine, and every copy of *Jonathan Livingston Seagull* ever printed. But looking closer, you'd become confused, noticing a Zodiac manual and a compendium of the Salem witch trials. Looking higher on the shelf you'd find copies of *Charles Manson: In His Own Words*, *The Stranger Beside Me: The Shocking Inside Story of Serial Killer Ted Bundy*, and *Killer Clown: The John Wayne Gacy Murders*.

At a certain point, you no longer noticed my mother's collection of tiny wicker angels and positive-affirmation books for the trail of prostitute murders and crime procedurals splayed out before you. Hers was an odd collision of interests, no less for a thirty-five-year-old single mom managing a maternity store. I was convinced that she'd much rather be dusting for fingerprints over the corpse of a partially cannibalized stripper than selling nursing bras at the mall.

By the time I was thirteen, I'd probably seen every horror film ever made, with my mother serving as a guide throughout the gruesome journey.

"See, honey," she'd say, as we watched *Friday the 13th*, "he's not trying to hide his identity with that hockey mask. He's just vulnerable. If you saw your mother beheaded by an angry teenager, you'd be upset too."

Halfway through *Halloween*, she rolled her eyes and said, "Michael Meyers doesn't have a case of sibling rivalry. He has a Peter Pan complex. I've dated men like that."

As *A Nightmare on Elm Street* ended, she was incensed. "Those parents acted with vigilante mentality when they burnt that man up in his work shed. Now, he'll kill their children in their dreams for years to come." She sighed. "Who's *really* the monster?"

I identified with these blade-wielding maniacs as outsiders because, as a preadolescent who threw like a girl and listened to a lot of Taylor Dayne, I was one, too. Being a gay person was a prospect that terrified me more than the Elephant Man ever did. I thought I would lose my father, then my mother, then the rest of my family, and then the few friends I had, and then I would get sick and die alone of AIDS: the omnipresent boogeyman of early-nineties MTV youth culture.

Next, Madonna's new public service announcement about AIDS!

Next, someone in MTV's Real World *house struggles with AIDS!*

Next, TLC will be here in jumpsuits made of condoms to rap about AIDS!

Michael Meyers had nothing on the "gay cancer."

My anxiety about who I was becoming made me want to disappear. I'd tried throughout sixth and seventh grade to "blend in," and it hadn't worked for me. I'd attempted dating girls and joining school clubs. I'd tried to play a sport that involved a ball that I wouldn't instinctively run away from. Every attempt at mainstreaming just made me stick out even more. So instead, I decided to become a wall-flower. In most middle school portraits, I can be seen wearing a variation of the same costume: pleated khakis, brown loafers, and a button-down, collared denim shirt. I basically looked like a tiny, chubby lesbian employee of Blockbuster Video.

Two months into eighth grade, I was invited to the Hal-loween party of a popular boy. My mom, excited about this opportunity for me to socialize with my peers, gave me carte blanche to purchase any costume I wanted. I found a red-and-green-striped sweater, a small-brimmed hat, and an eighty-dollar, latex Freddy Krueger mask that wrapped fully around my head.

The night of the party, I nervously put on my costume and spirit-gummed myself into the mask. Waiting for my mother to get off work and pick me up, I checked and double-checked myself in the master bathroom mirror. Something wasn't right. I wanted to be excited about my costume, but I was let down, bored by achieving the very thing I'd set out to do—looking exactly like Freddy Krueger.

So, I took some liberties.

Beneath my mother's vanity was her makeup kit. I proceeded to cover the mask in a full face of hot-pink blush, green eyeliner, and blood-red lipstick. I put on my mom's floral-print dress over two brassieres stuffed with toilet paper, and topped it all off with a giant, yellow hat, which I decorated with plastic flowers from the dining room table centerpiece.

My mother honked the car and I ran out, terrifying her as I pounded the glass and screamed, "It's me! Fredericka Krueger!" On our drive to the party, she was in full hysterics, begging me to stop, as I revealed a basket full of ketchup-soaked breadsticks and exclaimed, "Lady fingers! Hahaha!"

Five minutes later, I clicked up the sidewalk in three-inch heels and burst through the front door in-character, falsetto-screeching at anyone in sight through my burn-victim mask.

I was a monster. *And I loved it.*

I peered through the tiny eyeholes of the rubber headpiece at the most popular kids in eighth grade, all of whom howled with laughter as I pegged them in the face with bloody Twinkies and ran my flicking tongue against the pink-painted rubber blade of my glove.

"Fresh meat. How sweet!" I cackled at three giggling cheerleaders who'd never given me the time of day. In the living room, I spun in circles while throwing Slim Jims from my apron, screaming "Teen jerky!" like a terrifying, transvestite sprinkler system, as a crowd of teenagers howled. The mask was like a rubber oven around my head, but I kept it on and stayed in character, meeting more people in two hours as Fredericka Krueger than I'd met the last three years as David Crabb. I was, for the first time in my thirteen years, the life of the party.

Two hours later, I screeched, "Goodbye, kiddos. See you in hell!" to a room of forty peers, who all screamed back "Goodbye, Fredericka!"

I walked outside into the eighty-degree San Antonio night and ripped off my mask for some much-needed fresh air. I tossed it in my basket and looked up to the stars, feeling hopeful, giddy, and, for the first time, popular.

As I waited for my mom in the yard, the school's star athlete, John Drummer, pulled up with three friends, each of them dressed like a member of the band Color Me Badd. I beamed at them and said hello, ready to make more new friends. But my smile was met with sneers from the group, who looked me up and down in my dress, apron, and heels. As they passed me and broke into laughter, it occurred to me that, without my mask, I was just that weird nobody from school, dressed as a lady.

"Hey! It's a costume!" I yelled, but they were already walking into the house. I reached into my basket and held up the latex mask as proof. "See? I'm actually Fredericka Krue—"

The door slammed shut.

I laid in bed that night realizing that Fredericka was the life of the party, not me. Although Fredericka and I both stuck out, she did so in a way that people liked, and weren't suspicious of. Somehow, she made me feel "normal."

I couldn't be Mrs. Krueger all the time, but maybe I could

become someone else, someone people liked, who had friends—someone who was eccentric but safe. How could I become the most socially successful version of myself by morphing into someone else, and still be me?

I would answer that question two years later, not with the guidance of my mother, but with the help of my new assortment of freaky friends: black-lipped girls named Raven and Salem; boys with painted fingernails who wore dog collars; people who made face jewelry from office supplies and wore capes in earnest; freaks and delinquents my father would look at and say, "D.J., your friends look like superheroes going to a funeral."

I became a goth kid. For the next three years, my new friends would never tell me what to wear, they would never reject the part of me I'd thought was unlovable, and, most importantly, they reminded me that, if I wanted it, every day could be like Halloween.

TAKING THE RISK!

A Q&A WITH DAVID CRABB

How have you changed as a storyteller since you first told this story?

I'm a little more interested in pathos now, although I still love the sound of a room full of laughter. I suppose that many of my stories since this one are about that union—the place where emotions go high and light, then low and dark within a short time. I love stories that are sweet and salty. One of my co-creators and directors, Josh Matthews, calls this "Hug 'em and hit 'em," which sums it up perfectly. In a lot of ways, this story was one of the first I've crafted in which I realized how I might be able to process heavy reflections (being young and suicidal) in a way that was funny. It's a model I've tried to keep and applied heavily to my memoir, *Bad Kid*, which features many anecdotes from this story.

Are there any little ways you bent accuracy to get at the emotional truth of the experience?

My answer to this is always yes, because it's impossible not to. Most of those ways I probably don't even realize.

A friend of mine from way back just recently reminded me that I wrote a sketch for a middle school play about "Freddy Kruger Press-on Nails." A few old friends also remember this sketch, which I have zero memory of. So, hilariously, the idea of a drag-Freddy existed in my mind on some level months before this party would happen, in spite of it seeming like a fresh idea that Halloween night. I also changed the name of the bully, because I think everyone should be protected from the choices and mistakes they made as kids.

Did telling this story help you to better understand that part of your life?
Yes, actually. This story didn't end up in my book, but it served as a kind of origin experience which has informed a lot of my other work. I think the idea of "origin stories" are great, but ultimately unrealistic, as we are influenced by way too many factors to pinpoint the bulk of our identities on one night or one party or one car crash, etc. This night obviously isn't the *only* reason I'd become goth or come out of the closet. But when I teach storytelling, I like telling my students to consider each story they tell as a mini-origin story, in terms of how it changed one relatively small thing about themselves in a big way. I think this story is a part of the inspiration for that mind-set.

JC CASSIS

THE DOWNWARD SPIRAL

A couple days after Halloween a few years ago, my mom called me to say that she'd received a call from someone with an Irish accent so thick, she could hardly understand him. What she gathered was that the caller was my uncle Fred's boss, Michael, and he was trying to track down one of Fred's relatives. My mom is Fred's sister. Michael had told my mom that Fred was in the hospital in intensive care and had never given Michael an emergency contact.

Fred hated Michael, it turned out, and had never told him anything about his life, but at some point, he had mentioned he had a sister in New York. Since Fred was unconscious, Michael had the police help him break into Fred's house, looked into Fred's call records, and called the only New York number in there, which turned out to be my mom's.

Michael told my mom that Fred had been walking barefoot around his neighborhood in Miami, Florida, with bloody gashes, scrapes, and bruises all over his head and arms. The cops had taken him to the hospital, where he proceeded to have a stroke, and was diagnosed with advanced lung cancer that had spread into his bones. He was about five-foot-nine, but he only weighed ninety-three pounds.

"I can't believe it," my mom said to me, shaking her head. "But I always said I knew one day I'd get a call like this. Fred was always so secretive about his life. When we talked on the phone, I'd say, 'Fred, we've *got* to keep in better touch. You're my only brother, and I'm your only sister. What if something happened to you?'"

No one knew why Fred was so beaten up—maybe he'd been attacked by criminals in the street, as a cop who had told us how Fred was found had guessed. To not even know what had happened to Fred deeply disturbed my mother. Up until then, her biggest frustration with Fred was that he wasn't friendlier or more open, but now we didn't even know how long he'd be alive. So, four days later, we went down to Florida to visit Fred in the hospice that he'd been moved to. Michael picked us up at the airport to drive us there, and on the way, he unloaded about everything that was going on.

"I went to Fred's house after he was found," he said, "and I took some video because you won't believe me until you see it for yourself. The smell of mold when you walk in the door would knock you over." He explained that he could barely even breathe in that house. There were buckets of water spread everywhere around the floor to catch the rain falling in. Vines from the outside had grown in through the ceiling, and the pool was covered in algae and moss. It looked like the house was about to collapse.

He handed me his iPhone and I watched the horrifying video.

We arrived at the hospice and opened the door, and immediately the smell hit us: old people, disinfectants used to clean up bodily fluids, illness, depression, hopelessness, nurses who hate their jobs, and patients who hate their nurses because they're the only ones around to take out frustrations on. The tears welled up in my eyes, and as I asked one of the receptionists where room 10 was, I realized how much my throat ached.

When we looked into room 10, my mom and I were really confused. There was just one skinny old man with this sunken face, lying asleep on the hospital bed, with his head tilted up and back, and his mouth hanging open, with only three teeth in it. But he had an aquiline nose that I recognized from my childhood, the last time I'd seen him, and the short, straight, brown hair I remembered, and hands that were the male version of my mother's. There were scrapes and bruises on his forehead, and big scabs on his head and arm.

This man, who looked like he had just died at the age of ninety-seven, was my uncle, who was still alive, and only sixty-eight. I was terrified by the look of him. My mom's jaw fell as she studied him. "He looks like he's already dead," she whispered to me.

For all the wisdom that my mom has, I often can't believe how she lets herself say the utterly wrong thing within earshot of others. "Mom," I whispered, "not in here. Let's step outside and talk to the nurse." I couldn't hold my tears back anymore, but I didn't want Fred to hear me cry. I also didn't want to cry in front of this nurse I'd never met, so I turned my back to the nurse and my mom as they spoke about Fred.

The nurse assured us he was comfortable, despite how rough he looked. "We're giving him lots of pain medication," she said.

"Can he talk?" my mom asked.

The nurse hesitated. "He has trouble because of the stroke. But he makes some noises when we go in to check on him."

"Should we wake him up? We'd like him to know we're here."

"You can try talking to him and he'll hear you, but he might not respond."

My mom and I walked back into the room. "Fred, JC and I are here. We came down to see you." I couldn't talk. My throat was so tight that the only sound that would come out was a sob if I tried. "Fred, we love you," my mom said, "and we'll be back later, okay?" Fred didn't wake up, and we had to go see his house, so we turned and left.

Michael drove us a few minutes down the road to the house that my uncle had lived in for the last forty years. There was yellow police tape cordoning it off. Michael had gone with the police to break in and have the locks changed after Fred was hospitalized, and now he opened the side door and led us through the garage. Inside, I looked up at the huge hole that had opened up in the garage's ceiling and the chunk of plaster that had smashed onto the floor below in a scattered pile.

"You see how this door handle's broken off?" Michael asked. He was leading us from the garage into the house. "I think Fred cut himself on the handle when it broke, because it's all sharp and jagged. I think that's where he got those gashes on his arm." He paused, then added, "That's why there's blood all over the house." Hearing that filled me with dread.

Michael gestured toward a bloody hand swipe mark on the door. When he opened it, I was shocked and terrified to see similar swipe marks and handprints all over the dryer right next to the door. I could only guess that Fred had fallen, cut himself on his way down, and then tried multiple times to pull himself up. The dryer had been slippery, and he was covered in blood, and it looked like it had taken him many tries to get all the way up.

As we walked carefully into the house I gripped my arms tightly around my chest and tried to stay as compact as possible. I didn't want anything in that house brushing against me and startling me. I looked up at the ceiling, where little rays of Florida sunshine were poking through huge holes. The floor underneath us was squishy with mold because of the rot of so many years without a working roof.

The electricity to the house had been cut off, so the only light that was coming in came through this small window over the kitchen sink that had a diamond-pattern gate over it, as if it were a window into a jail cell. Among the ruin of this kitchen and this house, the dishes were clean and put neatly into a drying rack next to the sink. It was a bizarre bit of normalcy and order in this otherwise disastrous house.

Then we looked into the living room, and we couldn't believe our eyes. The entire floor was covered with rubble from the ceiling that had caved in everywhere. There were leaves and twigs that had blown in from outside, and vines growing down the walls and hanging down from the ceiling. Cobwebs lined every stuffed chair, each of which had exploded and collapsed, with stuffing bursting ousaying not of every rip in the fabric.

There was a calendar from 1996 on the wall, and a stack

of bank statements over a foot high, dating back to the early nineties, on a table. The papers on the bottom of the pile had become bonded to the table by black mold that had started growing beneath them.

I looked at one of the buckets collecting water on the floor and saw that there was a beautiful black lizard floating in it. I've always loved lizards, and my brother and I used to chase them and catch them every time we would come down to Florida as kids. Part of me hoped that maybe this lizard was still clinging to life, and we could fish him out of the bucket, and at least prevent any more tragedy from happening in this house, but as we approached, it became clear that the lizard was already dead. I couldn't help thinking about how this innocent little animal had come into this horrible place, and then slipped into the bucket of water and died of exhaustion, forever struggling to get a grip on a slippery plastic rim. No one had been there to help him.

We moved into the bathroom, and there they were: more bloody handprints on the door, and a semicircle of dried blood around the foot of the toilet. The evidence had become undeniable that something had gone wrong mentally with my uncle. I imagined him picking himself up in that entrance-way where he had fallen, bloody and cut up, and wandering over to the bathroom to pee for a minute, while his blood just flowed freely from his arm to the floor.

"Oh, look," Michael said. "A swarm of mosquitoes have started living in the toilet." Thankfully, before I could look, he had flushed them away. The clear shower curtain was yellowed and cloudy, but the shower itself seemed utterly clean. The house was full of such contradictions.

As I was looking into one of the closets in the bedroom, something poked me from behind. I jumped and screamed.

"Boo!" It was Michael, and he was laughing at my reaction.

"Oh…that's funny," I said, inwardly marveling at his cluelessness and trying to be friendly in spite of my outrage, "but now's not really the time."

I couldn't believe that this man who had only just met us was trying to have fun while we were experiencing one of the most frightening and heartbreaking moments of our lives. I could definitely see why my uncle would've hated this guy.

A few minutes after we had entered the house, the heat, humidity, and horror had started to weigh on us. "I think I've got to get out of here," my mom said. We walked out into the driveway as the sun began to set, bathing us in strong, yellow light.

"Excuse me, are you Fred's family?" A pretty, middle-aged brunette woman was coming toward us from across the street. "I'm Arlene, Fred's neighbor. We lived across the street for thirteen years." We introduced ourselves and shook hands.

"I'm so sorry about what happened," Arlene said. "You know, my husband is friends with the police officer who picked him up, and he said they took him to the hospital. Is he alright?"

"No," my mom said. "He's been moved to the hospice because he has advanced lung cancer."

"Oh, gosh. I'm so sorry. You know, we would always see him in the neighborhood, walking, or riding his bike. He would wave at us, if we said hello. He was always polite, but he really kept to himself, never really talked to anyone, in

fact. My kids would sometimes play ball out here, and one time, I remember the ball went over into his yard, and I just remember him saying, 'I don't mind them playing out here, but if you could please keep them away from my house, I'd appreciate it.'"

"When I called him," my mom said, "if I could ever get him to pick up the phone, he would never tell me anything about how he was doing. We had no idea how bad it was."

The next day, we went back to the hospice to see Fred. This time, he was awake. "Fred, it's me and JC," my mom said. "We came down from New York to see you."

He looked up at us and tried to speak, but could only groan.

Though my mom has trouble understanding unclear speech, I've lived my whole life in New York City, interacting with people with thick, foreign accents, so there's little spoken English that I can't understand. For the whole time that we visited with my uncle, I served as a translator for my mom since his speech was so unclear. "You've come a long way," he told us. "You didn't have to do that. I don't want all this fuss."

"Well, we heard you had an accident. We wanted to see if you're alright."

"I'm fine," he mumbled, "but I hate it here. I hate these people."

"The nurses?"

"Yes, I hate them all. I want to leave."

"You've had a stroke," we told him, "and you need to recover before you can go home."

"I didn't have a stroke." He was in denial.

The nurse came in with a tray with milk and a meal with

meat in it. My uncle had been a vegan for over twenty years, and not a noncommittal, eternally lapsing, aspiring vegan like me, but a hardcore one who had never slipped up.

"Do you have any vegan food for him?" I asked the nurse.

"We have vegetarian options," she volunteered.

"Okay," I said, "but he's vegan, so he can't eat milk, or eggs, or butter, or cream, or any animal products at all. And most things have animal stuff in them. Is there a way he can have something that doesn't have any animal stuff at all?"

"I'll see what we can do," she said. "We didn't know he was vegan—no one said anything." It was just another in a long list of heartaches.

After the nurse left, my mom said, "Fred, we would have visited you years ago if you had invited us, and I invited you to visit us every time we spoke on the phone. Why didn't you come see us?"

"I didn't think you wanted me there. I remember when I visited, you were pushing me like this," he said, as he jerked his palm forward and back.

"When was I pushing you?" my mom asked. "I don't remember that."

"I was asleep, and you woke me up," he said, "and you were pushing me and pushing me. And when we went out to eat, you got so upset that I was asking what was in the food, but I'm vegan and I can't eat a lot of the things. It just seemed like you didn't like having me there, and I didn't want to bother you anymore."

"Oh, Fred," my mom said, "I didn't mind that you were asking about the food. I might have nudged you to wake you up, but I didn't mean to push you like that. I was happy that you came to visit, because we don't see each other that often. I always told you on the phone that you were welcome to come back, and we would've loved to see you."

"I just didn't think you wanted me around."

I remember the last time we had seen my uncle, when he had come up to visit us in New York all those years ago. We had been shocked by how different he looked. The previous time we had seen him, he was still married to his ex-wife, Alana, and they were a happy couple living in that house in Florida when it was still in good condition. They used to visit with my mom and dad and brother and me, and we enjoyed hanging out with them.

But then they got divorced, around the same time my parents did, in the midnineties, and Alana took all their pets and moved up to New England to start over. They had no kids, and my uncle was left alone in the house. It was around that time that he quit smoking, went vegan, and stopped telling my mom much of anything about his life. He never said why Alana had left him, but he was clearly very upset by it.

He stopped keeping in touch with people, and he would just bike alone for miles and miles every day. At the hospice, he told us that just before he had been admitted to the hospital, he was cycling ninety miles every weekend, which was hard to believe about a man with advanced lung cancer that had spread to his bones. When I looked at his bare leg that was sticking out from under his sheet, however, his long, thin thigh was all lean, toned muscle, tanned up to the knee and then glistening white to the hip.

When he had come up to visit us ten years ago, he was markedly different from the man we remembered. We went to a pool, and he took off his shirt and took a nap on a lounge chair, curling into a fetal position on his side. From the biking and veganism, he had become almost frighteningly slim, and his vertebrae poked pointedly out of his skin.

We noticed on that visit that he was missing about five of his back teeth. My mom asked him why they were gone and whether he was taking care of his dental health, but he just got annoyed and said, "I'm fine. Leave me alone."

Back in the hospice, I couldn't help but feel guilty for not having reached out to Fred much myself. I'd been an adult for years and I never really tried to see how he was. "Fred." I said, "I'm really sorry that I didn't make more of an effort to talk to you and see you. I would've liked to see more of you, and I could've tried harder to make that happen."

It was one of the few times in my life where I've gotten to face having done something in a way that I regret, and apologize directly to the person who deserved the apology. Looking back now, I know that nothing I could have done would've been likely to have made a real difference in what was happening in his life. I couldn't have stopped his downward spiral. But at least he would've known that I cared about him.

Every night that we were there in Florida, we would go back to our hotel and my mom would be a wreck. I hadn't seen her so stressed since her own divorce and battle with cancer about fifteen years prior. "I just don't understand how he could live like that," she said. "It's heartbreaking. How can he live in that house?"

Each time she'd say something like that, I'd try to explain it as best as I could. It seemed that he'd gotten to the point where it didn't really register with him. When you watch something deteriorate slowly over the course of fifteen years, you just don't see it with the same eyes that someone takes to it when they see it for the first time. That's what I believed had happened with Fred. He let his house go to waste bit by bit. He didn't fix a crack in the ceiling, and it just got bigger and bigger until a huge chunk collapsed, and then the roof was coming down around him.

By that point, maybe it was too overwhelming and he just continued to let it go, and it continued to get more over-whelming until it passed the point of no return, and he just accepted his fate. Here he was in this clean, comfortable hospice bed, in a clean, bright, well-kept room, and all he wanted was to go back to his dark, moldy, dirty, falling-down house.

Our visits to Fred in the hospice each day got a bit awk-ward after the first few minutes, because he was not a super-social person and he wasn't really interested in small talk. He was interested in trying to get out. After about five rounds of him just begging us to help him get out, and us telling him that the nurses had said that they couldn't even safely move him into a wheelchair in his condition, he started to get sneaky.

Instead of saying he wanted me to pull him out of bed, for instance, he just said, "Pull on my arm."

"Are you sure I won't hurt you?" I said.

"No, you won't hurt me. Just pull on my arm. I want to sit up." I pulled on his hand, and he pulled as hard as he could to lift his torso into a sitting position, but he didn't seem to be making it all the way up. So, I reached behind him to support his back, and his hospital gown was open in the back, so that my bare hand landed on his bare back.

I could feel that he was just skin and bones, and yet he felt so heavy. I couldn't get him all the way up, and so finally he gave up and sank back into the mattress still holding my hand. "I want to get out of here," he said, looking into my eyes pleadingly. "Can you please pull me out of the bed, so I can get out of here?"

"I'm sorry, Fred, but the nurses said if you get out of bed, you'll get hurt because you can't hold up your left side."

I'll never forget the way, as soon as I said that, his face went cold, and he snatched his hand away from mine.

Each time the nurses would come in to help him adjust his position or check in on him, I noticed that they would put on latex gloves, even if they were only touching his back or shoulder. It almost seemed insulting, like they couldn't even touch his shoulder, as if he were dirty. I knew it was probably just policy, but it still made me sad.

I thought about how Fred had probably barely been touched by anyone in twenty years. Now, in his final days, I just wanted him to feel a warm, loving touch from someone who cared about him. I tried to give him what physical affection I could—holding his hand as we talked, stroking his hand with my thumb, and smoothing his hair as he drifted off to sleep. It wasn't going to save him, but I had read somewhere that human touch is absolutely necessary for our well-being, and I believe that on a deep, psychic level, it meant something to him.

After that visit, we had to go back to his awful house to gather as much documentation of everything as possible.

Everyone we had spoken to about what was going on had said that we had to get his ID, wallet, bank statements, deed to the house and cars, mortgage statements, and anything else that would prove who he was and what he had. That would help us to settle his estate when he passed.

We gathered everything we could find, and it amounted to about four huge garbage bags full of papers and files. Everything was moldy and dusty, and we didn't want to get all the mold into our hotel room, so when we got back to the hotel, we sat on the outdoor walkway outside our room and sorted through my uncle's whole private life. As we worked, all these bewildered vacationers padded by to get ice and bring it back to their rooms, stepping around our stacks of moldy financial records, and politely acting like they didn't think we were insane.

When we were finally done with all the sorting, we threw three huge bags of documents into the Dumpsters behind our hotel, and we brought the important papers, as well as a box of photographs from throughout my uncle's life, into our room. This flimsy cardboard box of photos had been on a high shelf in one of his bedroom closets, right by a water-damaged wall and under a hole in the roof, but somehow, miraculously, it had survived all the Florida storms completely untouched.

As I flipped through the pictures, I saw my uncle laughing with his friends on a boat they were sailing. There he was getting married to Alana, looking happy and healthy, surrounded by friends and family. There he was in his twenties, standing next to my mom in the Caribbean. There he was at a house in the country with Alana and their friends, talking and laughing in the summer. There he was with my brother and me when we were little kids, all of us smiling, hanging out in his house.

In all of them, he was someone who had ceased to exist a long time ago. I wondered if divorce and depression were really all that it took to wreak havoc on a life. Over and over again, this whole experience was showing me why you can't give up on your happiness when bad things happen. You can't push everyone away and expect to survive.

The next day, it occurred to me to try to find something that we could bring to Fred in the hospice that he could actually eat. Luckily, there was a raw, vegan juice store in the strip mall by our hotel. I picked out a green gazpacho, a carrot-orange turmeric juice, and some other flavors.

We got to the hospice and told Fred we had picked up some raw vegan juices for him. "Let me see it," he said. In true vegan fashion, right up to the end, he scrutinized the ingredient list, assuming there'd be something problematic in there. Thankfully, he was willing to try it.

Since the left side of his face was droopy from the stroke, and he had only three teeth, it was hard for him to drink without liquid dribbling down his chin. So as he sipped the gazpacho, I held a towel around his chest, and each time he dribbled, I gently wiped his face. "It's good," he said after the first sip, and for the first time in a week, I felt some relief.

Finally, he was making an effort, and his spirits were improving. I knew he'd never get completely better, but I hoped that at least he might get to the point where perhaps he could get out of bed and walk a few steps. To think of him never being able to get out of bed again for the rest of his life was more than I could bear.

Since we hadn't known what the situation would be before we went to Florida, we had booked our flights to get there on Thursday and return on Saturday, and it was already Saturday afternoon. We realized that we had to leave to catch our flight, so we started saying our goodbyes, not knowing if we'd ever get to see him alive again.

My mom leaned over the bed and gripped his hand in hers. "We have to go, Fred, but I love you. You're my only little brother and I love you, and we'll come back soon, okay?"

"I love you, too," Fred said. His eyes were wet with tears. It was his most sincere statement since we'd been there. It seemed that in that moment, they were patching up whatever misunderstanding they'd had years ago, and finally he was letting his guard down, and letting us in.

As we turned to walk away, I saw him smoosh his fingers into his sunken cheek and look desperately sadly out the window, as if he knew that the only people who were there for him were leaving, and there was no path for him out of that room. I felt so horrible leaving him stranded there. But I was glad that at least now we knew what the situation was. We knew that he hadn't been attacked. We had gotten some quality time in, even if it was too late. Now that he was eating something, perhaps there was even some glimmer of hope.

Two days later, I called the hospice from New York to check in on him, and the nurse said that his ability to swallow had completely broken down. The juices that I had brought were too thin for him to ingest safely. His only option was to drink this stuff called thickened water, which has the consistency of honey. We decided we should go back down that night, and we ended up staying for five days that time.

It was five days of hospice visits, Fred begging us to get him out of there, and nurses saying no to every single request he had. There was nothing he could do, they said, besides have a little thickened water and rest. With everything that was going on, I knew that my mom and I had to make sure we took care of ourselves, too, by taking a moment every day to just relax and enjoy the Florida weather, the sunshine, and the hotel pool.

One afternoon, I'd gotten into the pool and was dog-paddling around the edge, when I saw this little black shape floating in the water. I swam closer and I noticed it was a baby lizard, exactly the same kind I had seen dead in the bucket at my uncle's house: black, with a raised ridge along its spine and a pointy little face.

It was clearly panicked—it had been struggling to get to the edge of the pool for a few minutes. But the pool was lined with these slippery tiles, and it couldn't get a grip. I grabbed it and fished it out of the water and climbed out of the pool, and I could feel its tiny little heart pounding on my index finger, and see its eyes half closed in woozy exhaustion.

I always feel bad for animals when I'm holding them, because I realize that, to them, I'm this huge monster that could kill them at any moment, and they're these tiny beings completely at my mercy. There's no way for them to know that I would never hurt them, that I love them, and that I just want them to be happy. "It's okay," I said to the lizard. "You can relax. I just wanted to save you from the water. I just want to hold you for a second, and then I'm gonna let you go."

I thought about how the lizard's skin was covered in pool chemicals that were probably really bad for it. I took my water bottle, which was full of really cold water, and I unscrewed the cap and poured a little water over its body to rinse it off. As soon as the water hit the lizard, it immediately sprang to attention, and flew off my hand and onto the ground. As it wriggled along, I herded it into the grass so that it wouldn't get stepped on.

I don't know why my uncle had to go through all this shit, and why my mom and I were the only people who could be there for him. But I was so glad that at least this experience had allowed me to be in the right place at the right time to save this lizard. It was the only time that I felt good during that whole trip.

As the days went on, Fred's condition got worse. He slept more and more, and spoke less and less. Each time I would put water in his mouth, just a drop at a time with the tip of my finger, he would try to grab the mug from me and tip it into his mouth and drink normally, and each time he did I had to remind him that he couldn't do that, or he would choke. I shuddered to think how parched and desperate he must have felt, and how it must've seemed to him that everyone was trying to take even the simplest pleasures away, when really, we were only doing what we were told.

I had already started telling my mom not to bring water for us to drink in his room, since he couldn't do it himself. She didn't realize that even gum would get her in trouble, when she took out a piece and started to chew it. "Can I have a piece of your gum?" Fred asked. I popped out of the room to ask the nurse if gum was okay. "I'm sorry, but no. That's not safe. If he chokes on it, he'll die."

"Fred, they said we can't give it to you because you might choke."

"I don't care," he said. "I want some gum. Give me a piece of your gum, please."

"I'm sorry, Fred, I can't."

"I don't fucking care what those fucking nurses say. Can I have it, please?"

It was awful. There wasn't anything we could do around him that wouldn't remind him of something he couldn't do or couldn't have. When he finally started to nod off, we said, "Okay, Fred, we'll let you get back to sleep, but we'll come back tomorrow, okay?"

He turned toward us and cracked open his eyes a bit. "Don't come back," he said.

"You…" My mother and I looked at each other, confused about how to proceed. "Well, we'd be happy to come back," she said, "if you want us to."

"No, don't come back. I don't want you to come back. I don't like all this fuss."

That would be the last thing he would ever say to us.

People often imagine that dying alone is the worst way to pass on. I don't know if it's how I'd prefer to die, at least if I have the option of having friends and family around, but when I spoke to other people who had also recently lost loved ones, many of them said that their relatives had also wanted to be alone when they knew that they were going to die. So we did as Fred wished, and we flew back to New York that night.

When I got back to New York, I called the hospice every day to see what was going on. Each day, the nurse would tell me that Fred still hadn't had any water and couldn't swallow—he just slept a lot and was being kept comfortable.

As the days went on, I felt worse and worse, thinking about how he must have been feeling. Seven days with no water, no food, no movement. Eight days, nine days. I imagined that his life must be so bad at this point, that I was hoping, for his sake, that it wouldn't go on much longer.

Then, five days after we had last seen him, I got a call from a Florida number on my cell phone. I already knew what it was. When I picked up, I heard the nurse finishing a conversation with a colleague, before putting the receiver up to her mouth.

"Ha, ha, I know!" she said. Then she turned to the phone.

If my life were a movie, the dark comedy of the nurse's callous timing would have made me laugh. But in real life, in that moment, it was just sad. I heard the nurse abruptly change her tone when she addressed me. "Miss Cassis?" she said, tentative.

"Yes, it's me," I said, waiting for her to say it.

"I'm calling to let you know that, unfortunately, Fred has expired, as of about noon today."

"Okay, thanks for letting me know, and thanks for all you guys did for him. We really appreciate it."

"Of course," she said. "I'm so sorry for your loss."

Finally, the worst of this bizarre horror story was over.

There are a lot of things that could've made this whole experience easier to deal with. If my uncle had taken better care of himself, for example, or if he hadn't been mentally ill. Or if he'd been nicer and more likable. It was really weird to try to make conversation and spend quality time with someone who sometimes didn't seem to want us there, or who only wanted us there to take him home.

It had been awkward, too, as a pretty progressive person, to sit there with Fred in the hospice while he watched Fox News and started talking about how much he hated Israel. The last thing you want is to have an awkward political discussion with someone you haven't seen in a decade who is about to die.

There was also this feeling lingering in the air the whole time that we were only there because we were related, and we were the only ones who were going to help him. It's so bizarre to feel like you're supposed to love someone simply because they're family, and also be fully aware that if it weren't for the family bond, you'd have no bond with them at all.

I felt like I had been giving a lot of myself, trying to be super-nice and think of his every need and accommodate it, and not getting much thanks. Then, when I thought about the frame of mind Fred must have been in, I realized I couldn't possibly hold any of his crankiness against him. I hoped I would be kinder and more grateful if I was ever in his situation, but there was no way of knowing what I would do.

A week before he died, I remember Fred saying, "When I die, I want to be, uh, incinerated. Is that the word? What's the word?"

"Cremated?" I said.

"Yeah, cremated. Whatever's the cheapest, with the least amount of fuss. I don't want anything special."

So that was exactly what we did. We had him cremated, and his ashes were spread at sea, because he was always happiest when he was sailing. I can only hope that leaving his body freed his spirit to be in a happier place.

A couple months later, my mom and I got the opportunity to have lunch with Fred's ex-wife's sister, Janette, whom we hadn't seen in nearly two decades. We went out to lunch with her, and we talked for hours about my uncle's life before everything went downhill. It was an incredibly meaningful conversation to me, because after all the horrible things that we'd been through, and all the sad things that my mom had told me about my uncle's life, Janette was finally showing us his happy times, saying things like, "We used to have a wonderful time with Fred. We used to go sailing and we would have great conversations, and everyone would be laughing. Fred was so funny and so sweet."

Then, Janette looked at me sincerely and said, "And I just want you to know that your uncle was a really great guy before all this happened."

Hearing that made me cry. It was such a comfort to know that there had been a time in his life when things went right. As tragic as it was that he wasn't able to sustain that joy through the end of his life, the fact that he had been able to experience it for at least a few decades out of his sixty-eight years was a huge comfort to me. I was incredibly grateful for that lunch, for meeting Janette, for her telling me those things. I can only hope that, wherever Fred is now, he's at peace.

TAKING THE RISK!

A Q&A WITH JC CASSIS

Why did you want to share this story?

I've been working behind the scenes on *RISK!* as the producer and business manager since 2011, and when I hear everyone else's amazing stories on the podcast, I always think, "Wow, I wonder if I'll ever go through something that intense and be able to tell a moving story about it." Then my mom and I went through this crazy experience with Fred. It was so emotional, and after having worked on the show for so long, I couldn't help but think, even as I was standing in Fred's house, "Well, I guess now I have an intense story to tell…" My brain seems to block out a lot of details and aspects of emotionally intense experiences that I go through if I don't write them down immediately, so I knew I had to tell the story very soon after going through it. Telling it for the podcast helped me to process the sadness and move forward, as well.

Did any of your relatives hear the story and share their feelings about it?

Yeah, my mom, dad, and stepmom listened to it, and my mom sent it to pretty much everyone she knows. My mom said that listening to the story really helped her start to heal from that experience as well. My dad said he didn't understand why I was so emotionally affected by the experience, since my uncle and I had barely spoken for the previous fifteen years, but I am always deeply saddened by deaths, and by the thought of anyone living in deep, terrible, and prolonged misery, especially when it's partially preventable. The thought of my uncle letting his life go down the drain for fifteen years instead of finding ways to heal from his divorce and build a new and happy life for himself, when he had the means, is incredibly upsetting. It was a very strong lesson and reminder that no matter what life throws at you, you have to pick yourself up and take care of yourself and keep moving forward. That's what I choose to do.

AMES BECKERMAN

LIKE MOTHER, LIKE ME

I was thirty years old. This was three years ago. I've always had a really complicated and uncomfortable relationship with my body. Another thing is, I'm a nervous person. I'm self-conscious, often manic, and paranoid. My mom, Randi, is my best friend. She's also a nervous, paranoid, manic person. All those things.

Basically, we're the same person. I just spent thirty years doing a comedic impression of my mother at all times. I gave in to her shopping addiction, her love of a good Coach bag. We would hide shopping bags in the car while my dad was home. And then, when he would go to work, we would bring them into the house so he wouldn't find them. We did everything together. We were like Russian dolls. Except I felt like a drag queen, and she had no idea.

So here's the thing. It's really complicated, because I loved doing feminine things. I loved going to get a pedicure and sitting in the next chair and chatting with her about everything. And the thought of watching the game with my father and his friends sounded like the worst idea for a Sunday.

But I just wasn't in love with being a woman. So I went ahead and did all the girly things. I would get my acrylic nails filled every week. I would shop at Lane Bryant. I did everything you can think of that's feminine. Then, in one attempt to feel comfortable with my body, I got into this habit of excusing myself after every meal and sticking my fingers down my throat. In another attempt, I had weight loss surgery. I lost one hundred pounds. Still, I just wasn't happy as a woman. I tried it all. I just was not comfortable.

And then, I had this great idea. I decided, "OK, I'm a lesbian!" So I just spent all my nights listening to CDs of Melissa Etheridge and Tracy Chapman while eating fistfuls of pussy.

I even married a woman. I got to go to David's Bridal with my family and try on all the dresses. And at the end, when I found my perfect dress, I rang a bell and felt like, "Yes! I'm a woman and I did it all!"

Till I just couldn't do it anymore. A day finally came when I said out loud, "I am done. I can't do this. I need to transition. I'm a man." But I just didn't know what to do about my mom. I thought, "I know she's not gonna disown me, but what is she gonna do with a son? Never mind just a son, a trans son."

So, my mom was living in Florida and taking care of my grandmother, who was dying of cancer. And here I am in New York City, growing out my leg hair and my armpit hair, worshiping the six chin hairs I have, and hoping I wake up the next morning with six more. And I'm binding my chest. If you don't know what that is, it's when you wear this compression garment that's itchy, sweaty, and really tight around your tits, to create the illusion that your chest is flat.

And here my mom is in Florida; she has no idea what's going on and there's no good time to tell her. I couldn't do it much longer. On February 16, 2015, she calls me. "Amy, I think Grandma's dead. She's not moving."

I thought, "Oh, boy. Yeah, she's probably dead."

And my mom says, "OK, Cookiecrumb, I gotta go. I'll call you back." She used to call me that. She called me back ten minutes later, in manic mode. "Amy, uh, these people in here, Central Holding, they're-they're taking her body out. And they're being such dicks! Like, you would think they would be nice to me, because my mother's dead! I'll see you in Boston. Bye, Cookiecrumb."

So, as soon as I get this news, I jump on the Megabus to Boston, and I meet my mother at the Holiday Inn in Dedham, Massachusetts, where I was gonna stay with her for a few days for the funeral. The trip was rough, because I didn't feel like it was the right time to come out to her. But if I took the binder off my chest and wore a dress, I was gonna feel shitty about myself. So there were just a lot of emotions that were happening to me all at once.

I get there, and I meet my mother, and she's grief-stricken, and just, like, crazy. I mean, she's yelling about bagels. "We're gonna have the shiva, but I don't think we have enough bagels! Amy, call the deli! Order a dozen more!" Then, she throws herself on the bed, and she's crying.

The next morning was the funeral. Now, what we would normally do before a family event, is that the two of us would be together in the bathroom, getting ready and chatting. This time was different. She was putting on her makeup in the bathroom, and I was standing outside the bathroom, ironing a crappy dress shirt that I bought at Buffalo Exchange. And she just kept looking at me suspiciously, and going back to her makeup. And finally she looks at me and she says, "Why are you so masculine?"

I lost it. I don't even know what got into me. It's like I suddenly had verbal diarrhea. Like, my mouth just, like, spilled the beans everywhere. I said, "Mom, when I go back to New York City, I'm changing my name from Amy to Ames. I'm going on testosterone, and I'm gonna have top surgery to remove my breasts." She didn't believe me. She said, "Can't you just be a tomboy? Look at me. I have short hair. You can just be a tomboy." And then she went right back to doing her makeup. Then she came out of the bathroom again, and looked into my eyes till she finally said, "You're gonna be so hairy! You're gonna have so much chest hair. You're gonna be like a gorilla, like your father."

And I said, "I hope so! That's all I want."

So we went to the funeral. The whole ride was quiet. I sat behind her, and she sobbed the entire time. I knew that she was mourning two losses: the loss of her mother, and the loss of her daughter.

After the funeral, she came to New York City with me for a few days, just to get away. We just hung out, doing the things we normally did. I forced her to watch the first season of *Transparent* with me. I introduced her to some of my trans friends. We got takeout. She had a lot of questions that I wasn't able to answer. She wasn't sure if it was her fault, or if she did something. Or if there was something she could've done to prevent this. And I told her there wasn't. And then she said, "Were you lying? Did you not like getting your nails done with me? Did you not like doing all the thing we did together?" And I said, "Mom, of course I enjoyed that.

And I'm gonna continue to enjoy that. What do you think? I'm a flamboyant gay man!"

So I chose to involve my mother in my transition. I included her in every aspect. I informed her about all of the medical changes that would happen on testosterone. And when I had top surgery, I went to Florida, and she took care of me.

I took it slow with her about using new pronouns. I knew that, over time, she would understand that it's *he*, *his*, and *him*. Even though she would forget once in a while to call me Ames, and blurt out, "Amy," I was really relaxed with her, because I wanted her to be comfortable with the process.

After a few days of recovering from top surgery in Florida, the two of us went to the mall. And, instead of going into the women's shopping section, she went with me into the men's section, and she helped me pick out some shirts for my newly flat chest. We did all the same stuff. I was just her gay son now. It was a transition for both of us.

TAKING THE RISK!

A Q&A WITH AMES BECKERMAN

Has your mom heard this story?

As soon as I got booked on the *In It Together* show that the *RISK!* team produced, I called my mom and told her that I was going to perform the story about her on stage! She was trying to fly in from Florida for the show, but she wasn't able to make it. I really want her to hear the story because there's a lot of emotion in it about our relationship, and she would really love it.

At that show, you had a ten-minute time limit. Did that affect how you told the story?

There are a few details of other family members' reactions that I really wanted to include, but couldn't. My stepfather was present for most of the interactions, but because he is deaf, he didn't fully understand what was happening some of the time. Also, at this time, my brother was battling an addiction to opiates (that nobody knew about), and when I told him, he looked at me and said, "So you want a dick now?"

Was there another story you heard on *RISK!* that inspired you to want to share this story?

I've been listening to *RISK!* on my commute to work for quite some time now, and every story evokes some sort of emotion within me. *RISK!* reminds me that I need to relax, enjoy, and learn from the experiences that life throws at me.

What do you hope comes across in this story?

I really wish I had been able to wait until after my mom had finished grieving the loss of her mother to tell her the news that I was transitioning, but it just didn't happen the way I had hoped. It wasn't ideal, but hey, that's life.

MOLOCH MASTERS

IN THE SHADOWS

I was thinking about a time when me and my dad bonded. We were watching the Dead or Alive video for "You Spin Me Round," and we got up and started dancing. My dad stopped me. "Do you see the way he shimmies?" he asked. "Let's shimmy the way he shimmies!" We started to shimmy, and it was especially fun, because my dad was typically so guarded.

My dad had this uncanny ability to put up walls around himself, like a magic force field that no one could get through. It was his way of dealing with the darkness of his parents. He was an escapist who read fantasy books like there was no tomorrow. When you tried to bring him back into the real world, he would always veer back into his own land. He was always there, but he was rarely really present.

I was a big fan of metal music. One of the recurring themes in an album I listened to a lot was "kill or be killed." People say that those kinds of lyrics make you violent, but I know that, in my case, I gravitated to them because violence was *already* within me. I inherited it. It is something that has been a part of my family for years.

I remember one of the worst times I let it get the best of me. I was living in Cuyahoga Falls, Ohio, and I had gotten to know this boy, Paul, a stereotypical dork with thick, black glasses. He was pale, a lot taller than me, and I was attracted to him. I liked him. I was an eight-year-old child, and I didn't know how to express my feelings for him, so I started to punch him. I didn't know why, but when I would hit him and I could see the pain register on his face, it felt very satisfying, like fireworks going off. One day, my grandparents were talking about how girls can't beat up boys, and I said, "I can beat up a boy, and I'll show you." They came along and stood across the street while I just hit and kicked this kid, over and over. My grandparents laughed and cheered, waving their arms like this was the best thing they'd ever seen.

Another time, my dad got really sick, and while he was weak and hurting, I was telling him he was a terrible dad. "How could you have said this?" I was asking about some minor, stupid thing he'd said.

He looked me right in the eye and said, "Some parents rape their children. I'm not perfect, but that kind of thing happens in other families."

I didn't know what to do or what to say—I was in complete shock. As time passed, I realized that he had been trying to tell me that he had been a victim of abuse.

If you were looking for darkness in my family, you didn't have to look far. I remember there was a microwave that had been my great-grandfather's, which we kept in a basement room after he passed away. One day, I opened it up, and this horrid stench hit me. It was thick, alive, deathly, so many things at once. I looked inside the microwave and saw brown splatters, mold, and flattened, furry parts on the bottom of the microwave.

I was horrified. I wasn't sure what I'd found. I took it to my dad, and he barely batted an eye.

"Yeah, that's your great-grandpa," he said. My great-grandfather got pleasure from harming smaller, weaker things. He'd been throwing rats in the microwave and watching them die for entertainment. I knew he could be nasty to people, but I couldn't understand how he could go from just being a jerk to everyone to killing small animals.

My mom didn't have that inner voice that was calling her to the dark side like my dad did, and like I have. Because of that, I related to my dad a lot more than I did to my mom, even though her kind nature made her easier to get along with. My dad could be very strange, but it was a strange I understood. I remember when *The Silence of the Lambs* came out, he would quote that movie over and over again. "So I ate his liver," he would say, "with a nice Chianti and some fava beans!" We would all quote it to each other. Among family members, he would sometimes bring up topics such as whether we would ever eat anyone. I would say, "I'd eat the people I hate!" because I was getting bullied, and it made me feel powerful to say that. It was hard to tell if he liked that answer, hard to read through his force field.

I learned when I was young that my dad's closet wasn't exactly a regular closet. There was a wall in it that didn't go all the way up to the ceiling, and if you climbed over that, there was a whole new room behind it, with shiny, wooden floors. The kids weren't allowed there, which we all knew, but of course, when you're a kid, and your parents are telling you not to do something, you do it.

One day, I went up there. There were books and pamphlets

and boxes of papers. I started to read everything that was stacked around the room. I remember finding a document, a little pamphlet with three staples in it and four illustrations. Every illustration was a different color.

The first illustration was of a woman jogging, and it said she wouldn't be good to eat because she doesn't have enough meat on her. Her flesh would be ropey and rough, and you might as well not even bother. The second illustration was in a different color, and it was of a bodybuilder. The pamphlet said that this guy would also be a waste of effort because his muscles are way too dense to eat. The next picture was of an obese man, and it said that he had too much excess fat on his body, and not enough edible material, so you would have to deal with too much waste product. Then, there was a picture of a regular guy, a little heavy in the middle, but by no means obese. Because of his sedentary lifestyle, it said, he would be the best person to eat. His muscles would be soft, and he had the right amount of fat to keep the meat moist without leaving you a ton of waste material to dispose of. The title of the pamphlet was "What Kind of Person Would Be the Best Meal."

I should have run away screaming. But part of me was fascinated. Part of me was laughing at it, like my grandparents watching me beat up the boy. And part of me was confused. My friends' parents were hiding porno magazines, but my dad was hiding articles like this one, and anatomy books.

I found myself attracted to the anatomy books. Up in that secret room, the first time I came upon an illustration of a man without skin, I gulped, feeling a tingle down my spine. I felt alive in a way I didn't ever remember feeling alive before.

My nerves came to life. It seemed like another form of porn, and I couldn't get enough of it.

If you live in a conservative Christian family, like we did, and something turns you on, you hide it. You don't talk about it, knowing that sex is very bad. The materials up in that room seemed sexy in a way I understood, because they were so hidden.

When I was a child, I didn't eat very much, and I hated ham. When my dad came to my bedroom one day and he said, "I cooked some ham. Would you like some?" I said "No, I don't like ham."

"Well, this isn't regular ham," he said. "This is the best ham that you're ever going to eat. And you'll be very sad if you don't try any." I told him I didn't care and he left. But later, he came back. He was holding this little, pink piece of meat in his palm, very light pink, with a strange, gossamer coating on one side.

When I looked at it, I knew it wasn't ham—the meat wasn't marbled with fat, and the color was wrong. There was just something not right about it. But I picked it up and I took a bite of it, my teeth cutting through the meat like I was biting into Play-Doh. I chewed, and my mouth flooded with saliva. I didn't taste the salty taste of ham, but something unlabeled in my brain. I looked at the meat, and I could see that where my teeth had cut through it, the fibers of the meat were compact, the texture almost like velvet.

My dad was staring at me intensely. "*Don't stare at it, just eat it!*" he blurted out. I ate the rest.

My dad went away, and I continued to think about this delicious meat. After some time, I went downstairs, looking to sneak some more. I didn't want him to have the satisfaction of knowing that I loved it. He spotted me in the kitchen and stopped me, blocking me from the oven.

I said that I wanted more ham, and he said, "There is no more ham." I went back up to my room, because when my dad puts that wall down, there's just no getting past it. "Why did he seem to be hiding something?" I wondered, "And what did I eat?" I went back to the alcove in my dad's closet, but all the magazines and anatomy books were gone.

My dad died in 1999 with fourteen tumors in his brain, one of them the size of a lemon. After his death, my mother would not allow any talk about anything he ever did that was bad. But I still needed to talk, and when I said, "Remember the time Dad…?" my mom would say, "It was because he had fourteen tumors in his brain."

But the truth was, my dad gave me that "ham" before those tumors had a chance to grow. I would love to blame it all on the tumors, but I can't. I know now that even though we may not be flawed equally, all of us are flawed. Refusing to talk about our secrets only lets our problems fester, until we can't help but act out.

I believe that my dad fed me human flesh, which makes him a cannibal, and it makes me a cannibal. He always wanted to go in his own direction, and I know he was haunted in many ways by what his family did to him. Sometimes, he went in the wrong direction. I don't want to deny that. I don't want to leave it all hidden in the shadows, because I forgive him, and I love him.

TAKING THE RISK!

A Q&A WITH MOLOCH MASTERS

How did you feel about the way people reacted when this story ran on the *RISK!* podcast?

There are some people who have said that there is no way my story is true. I wish it weren't true. I have been trying to erase these memories from my mind for decades. The memories won't wash away because they are hard-wired into my consciousness through taste, smell, sight, and touch. I wish I could say it's just a delusion or a lie because I don't want my dad to be a bad guy. I love my dad.

I have been trying to unburden myself from these memories for a long time. It feels awful to look at the pictures of missing people on websites. I feel like some of those faces have been burnt into my retinas. I know there is another side to this story: the side of the victim's family. If they are out there, I hope they have a chance to share their story. I don't want to hurt anyone, but I do want some answers. Most of all, I hope that they could forgive me. Doing the podcast made the burden of this information feel manageable. Having this story in a book might have the same effect.

WALTER ZIMMERMAN

ASKING AND TELLING

In May of 1967, I was a twenty-year-old enlistee in the United
States Air Force. I was a computer operator, and had just
been assigned a one-year tour of duty on the remote naval air
station at Keflavik, Iceland. Back in the United States, Aretha
Franklin was singing about some "Re-Re-Re-Re-Respect
(just a little bit)," and all three volumes of *The Lord of the
Rings* were finally available in paperback. And thousands of
miles away from all that, and from me, five hundred thousand
Americans in uniform were fighting in the jungles of Vietnam.

So there I was, in the doorway of my new barracks room
in Iceland—the barracks were more like college dorms, instead of the old, open bay barracks in the movies—and I was
jet-lagged, with my big duffel bag stuffed with uniforms, and
my cheap little green suitcase filled with art supplies. I was
watching my new roommates busily taping aluminum foil to
the inside of the windows. I thought, "This is never going to
pass inspection," but they told me that, in May, in Iceland,
the sun stops going below the horizon, and it's too bright at
night to be able to sleep. So I just shrugged my shoulders

and started to unpack my underwear and put it away in the military fashion.

But it turned out they weren't the only ones who were blocking things out at that moment. I had been in the Air Force for three years, and I learned that the sex games I had played with my high school buddies meant way more to me than they ever did to them. I was doing my best to hide the feelings I started having for other men in the service with me. And now, here I was, on a remote military station, with young marines and sailors and fellow airmen, all in the peak of health, with hormones at full blast. Some of these guys seemed to see right through me, propositioning me right and left. I wanted to take them up on it, but I was terrified. After all, we were living under the Uniform Code of Military Justice, and if you were even considered feminine, you were in trouble. I honestly believed that if an officer thought I was queer, he could take me out behind the barracks and shoot me in the head, no questions asked.

My fears weren't just paranoia. Shortly after I arrived in Iceland, we heard, from a fellow airman, about an event in Greenland, where two airmen had been found having sex with each other. One of them, rather than face disciplinary action, had walked off the end of a runway into the North Sea. His partner was sent to our station in Iceland, to be held temporarily, and then returned to the United States for a dishonorable discharge.

I still remember that man's waxen face when he arrived. He never met anybody's gaze. He ate the few meals he had there alone. I still feel guilty that I never said hello to him, but I was afraid of guilt by association.

That encounter struck enough fear in me to keep me isolated for a while, with my focus on my tasks as a computer operator, and my punch cards. Life would go on, I thought.

But the seasons changed, and the aluminum foil came down, and I really began to crave intimate contact with someone. One weekend, I was in the enlisted men's club, to get a cheeseburger and watch some television, and I saw a sailor, sitting at a table by himself, with some colored pencils and a piece of paper, working steadily away. I like to draw myself, so I thought, "This is interesting," and I went over and asked him what he was doing.

He looked up at me. He had thick, black, glistening hair, and bright, blue eyes, like an Alaskan husky. He had such an innocent but intelligent look on his face. "Oh, I'm drawing some pictures to send home to my mom in Quincy," he said. "I'm Mark." I was thunderstruck. So I just kind of plunked myself down and ate my cheeseburger and watched him draw. The other sailors there, and the marines, were getting drunk and ready to fight each other, like they always did on the weekends, so I suggested we might go back to my room where we could talk. It'd be more quiet. He said that would be okay.

We got there, and I lay down on my bunk, and he sat down on a chair at the foot of the bed. I don't really remember what we talked about, only that at some point we stopped talking and just started to stare at each other. Neither one of us flinched. We were just looking at each other openly, honestly, while the room filled with a kind of electricity I didn't understand.

Up to that point, I had never felt anything like that in my life. I didn't know what it meant. But it was palpable.

Then, I guess, somebody made a noise in the hall, and we both kind of woke up. He had to get back to his barracks, and I was left there to wonder about what had just happened.

Mark and I kept running into each other, and every time, we always ended up back in my room, with me on the bed, and him on the chair, staring at each other while the room filled with that mysterious energy that I couldn't comprehend.

Now, at about the same time in my tour, I was working in the office one day. It was lunchtime, so nobody else was there. I decided to get a drink of water, and when I went around the corner, there leaning against the wall, writhing as though in some kind of hypnotic trance, was a sailor in uniform, with his eyes sort of unfocused, and both his hands on his crotch, massaging the biggest erection I had ever seen, trapped in a pair of trousers.

I couldn't believe it. I mean, there was the Uniform Code of Military Justice, right on the wall, and here was this sailor, putting on an overt sexual display. I thought it was delightful. Finally, I had to pull myself away from this show, and got my drink at the water fountain. It took a long time to get back to my desk. And then I realized that I was still dying of thirst. So I went right back around the corner, and then I just stood there and watched. It was wonderful.

Eventually, he realized he had an audience. He pulled himself away from the wall, looked me right in the eye, and walked into the men's room. I followed him, like the best puppy in obedience school. He marched right up to the urinal and undid the buttons on his bell bottoms, and out sprang the plumpest, most beautiful dick I had ever seen. I mean, it was the dick Michelangelo would have sculpted if the Pope had given him permission.

And this guy knew it. He was fondling this thing, caressing it, giving it all the attention it wanted. I was dancing around like the floor was on fire. I didn't know what to do, but I wanted to do something.

Then he jerked his hips a bit and sprayed himself all over the urinal. I never knew I could be so jealous of a piece of porcelain. Then he seemed to calm down. He wiped himself off and stuffed himself back into his bell-bottoms. "Hey," he said. "My name's Steve. I'm gonna be in the showers at the base gym this Saturday at two. See ya there."

So at one fifty-five p.m., my clothes were checked into a little wire basket with a number on it, and I walked into this big white, steam-filled shower room. And there he was, naked, wet, soaping himself up and starting to get hard. In about a nanosecond, we were all over each other, wound around each other like jungle vines, twisting, rubbing against each other. No kissing, nothing above the neck. But still, it was terrific.

Then we heard a *pat, pat, pat*—some guy coming around the corner, no doubt there to take a legitimate shower. So we pulled apart. Steve stood on one end, and I stood on the other, each of us facing the wall and trying to hide our excitement.

The other guy finished up his shower, and then, *bam*, we were right up against each other again, grinding away. Then, *pat pat pat*, more bare feet, and another guy came in to take a shower.

"Let's go back to my room," Steve said. And in record time, we were dried, dressed, and across the base, up in his second-floor barracks room. I remember him reaching up to close a little hook and eye at the top of the door, even though it wasn't military issue. I guess folks in the navy understood that a man needs his privacy.

We stripped as fast as we could, and suddenly, I had that Michelangelo dick in my mouth. It was totally satisfying. I felt so authentic. I felt so...useful.

Then he pushed me away, and I wondered, "What? Am I doing something wrong?" But no—he wanted to return the favor. He went down on me. But he had a sort of strange attitude about it, almost resentful, like he was being forced to do something against his will. "That's strange," I thought, and I probably would have wondered about it more, but it felt so fabulous that I couldn't really think.

So we switched off, back and forth, giving each other as much pleasure as we possibly could. And then, at one point, it was my turn, and I knew he was about to go over the top, and I was doing everything I could to give him the best orgasm in his life. Then, once again, he pushed me back.

"Not in your mouth," he said. "I don't wanna live like that."

Then I watched him spurt all over a T-shirt on the bed. But I was shocked. I mean, he might as well have punched me in the face. But it was his room, and it was his dick. So I just sort of followed his example, but I was still in something of a daze—I mean, that orgasm was the whole reason I was there, because I was discovering that, for me, there is something almost sacred about that kind of male-to-male communication, that inimitable intimacy when two men share their essence. And besides, it's really just protein and fructose. I mean, I already knew that when I was thirteen.

So anyway, I got dressed and then I said I'd see him

around, and went back to my barracks. And two days later, I was in the big main chow hall, and there he was, with his tray of reconstituted scrambled eggs and his bad coffee. "Hey Steve," I said. "How are you?"

He looked right through me like I was made of ozone. He brushed past me and sat down at a table with some other sailors, with his back to me.

Now, at about the same time, my friend Mark—the sailor with the blue eyes and black hair and the pictures for his mom—was on leave. Maybe this is why the rejection from Steve hit me so hard. I plunged into a deep depression. I couldn't eat, I couldn't sleep, and one morning, I passed out in the latrine. So I went to the base doctor and told him all about my symptoms—except for the sex part, of course. And he sent me to the Air Force hospital in Wiesbaden, Germany, where I was told that all of my problems were existential. I was there for three weeks, before being sent back to Iceland.

When I got back, Steve was still there, still pretending he didn't know me. And blue-eyed, black-haired Mark had...disappeared. He was nowhere to be found. I went to all the places we used to hang out. I didn't really know where his barracks was, or where he worked, and I was afraid to ask. I couldn't afford to raise suspicions, remembering that icy Air Force runway in Greenland. So with what little wisdom I had at the time, I decided that our safety was more important than the mysterious power that filled my room, as we sat there staring at each other.

So, I finished my enlistment, got my honorable discharge and my GI Bill, and went to college. But those two little events in Iceland really made a difference in my life. I learned that, although having simple physical, sexual contact with a guy could be pretty gratifying, try as I might, it just wasn't enough for me. As much as I appreciated Steven's gorgeous dick, what I really wanted was that vibrational power in the room when I was with Mark—that sense of something incredible happening.

Now, I'm very happy to tell you, I have an extraordinary husband, and we've been together for over thirty years. We got married in California the *first* time it was legal. But I have to admit that despite everything I've gotten out of life, I still think about that room, and that powerful feeling I couldn't understand. And even though he seems to have disappeared from the face of the earth, I still think about blue-eyed Mark from Quincy, Massachusetts.

And when I do, there's just one thing I want to know. Mark—did you feel the same thing, too?

TAKING THE RISK!

A Q&A WITH WALTER ZIMMERMAN

You first told this story at a *RISK!* show in Brooklyn. How was that?

I think *RISK!* has the perfect audience—I could tell they were with me from word one. Their attention and energy improved my telling of it—my own story suddenly seemed more immediate to me, as if I were rediscovering it along with their hearing it for the first time. One man was in tears afterward! It was truly remarkable, sharing something so secret and even painful.

If a younger version of yourself told this story, how might you have done so?

I think it would depend on which "younger me" we were talking about—I've been through so many life changes! I've often thought that "Me, age 22" would cross the street to avoid "Me, age 39" with "Me, age 60" watching from a coffee shop, and shaking his head. I've always been my own roller-coaster ride, really.

MAKING THE
BEST OF IT

OMG

When I was a very young comedian, I got the opportunity to go on a college tour. This sounds a lot more interesting in concept than it was in real life. I thought I'd be performing in brightly lit theaters in front of eager young people, their fertile minds open to the most cutting-edge humor and elevated ideas, their wide eyes constantly on the lookout for the next hip, emerging talent.

That was not what the tour was at all.

Instead, it was more of an extended road trip to perform in the acrylic lounges of DeVry Institute buildings and regional university cafeterias at lunchtime, a trip in which no one amongst what I had previously envisoned to be my "audience" knew why there was an extremely tall Black woman screaming at the top of her lungs while they were trying to furtively consume their institutionally issued tater tots and fluorescent macaroni and cheese.

There were three of us on this tour, and we would all perform for ten minutes each. There was a game show element, too, which was a part of the draw of coming to our performance—if you stopped by casually to watch the show on your way to the library or your afternoon nap, or otherwise tolerated our halfhearted performance, you could, at the very least, win money for your troubles.

Here's how the game worked: an audience member had to last for one minute onstage with us, without laughing, giggling, or breaking a smile, as we performed with increasing, wheedling, desperation.

Amazingly, they were all very good at it.

Still, we, despite our abject inexperience and the wildly mixed reactions we got, kept skittering out there and doing our very level best. On the tour with me were an optimistic young Asian comedian, and a deeply jaded White guy. Despite our Rainbow Coalition bona fides, we had a hard time getting along. Part of the problem was our circumstances— we were riding around the country doing shitty college shows in a van that smelled like fetid dreams crushed under the heel of a college kid's Chuck Taylors. We were hungry and we were poor. And there was something else: a low-simmering rage circulating between the three of us, a rage coupled with simmering sexual frustration. I was a newly-wed, separated from my husband only months after our wedding day. The other two comedians were single men in their twenties. Together, we went about the daily task of stuffing the sexual tension and combative rage of a minimum-security prison yard into the stuffy nylon confines of a late-model rental van.

And still, we soldiered on, wielding our meager jokes like talismans against our waxing despair.

Fitfully, in halfhearted spurts of ambivalence, we worked our way across the continent, finally tumbling into the South. We were rightfully terrified, because we were driving dark

back roads at night in an unmarked and unremarkable rental
van as a Black woman and an Asian guy and a White guy who
had a suspiciously liberal Afro. Along these country roads,
neon crosses would periodically float up out of the inky dark.
Some of them looked as if they were on fire, which you can
imagine was not my ideal imagery. There was always a simmering, low-level terror in our vehicle. There was so much
murky apocrypha we'd heard about the South, some of it
based in reality, some of it heightened by our sense of unknown, that our shared fear of the unkown slowly began to
knit us together, like an unwanted, family-sized scarf.

There were, of course, a surfeit of Christian schools along
our Southern leg. Why anyone thought it was a good idea to
send stand-up comedians to Christian schools, I have no idea.
The very nature of our comedy—indeed, of *all* comedy—was
to offend somebody at some point. My goal was to offend
everyone, at all points. That was how I knew I'd done my job.

This was nothing less than a recipe for oozing disaster.

The general rules for the Christian schools were that we
could not curse, use sexual innuendo, dance, speak about
dancing, or do anything that implied dancing. These edicts
pretty much wiped out all of my material. I was a baby comic
with about ten minutes of material, and I was milking all of
my meager comedic powers just to hit that ten-minute re-
quirement. Most of my sets involved three minutes of wild-
eyed, sweaty vamping, followed by at least a full minute of
silent staring at the audience, trying to remember who and
where I was. My sets seemed experimental, when what I was
really doing was just trying to stay alive.

Slowly, though, we got into our rhythm, which meant

the shows were all consistently terrible. We would resort to asking the students what people made fun of at their particular college, in the hopes of exploiting pre-existing, low-hanging fruit. This worked...for the most part. At one particularly devout school, we tried to mock the cafeteria food, since that had previously proved to be something that students were eager to join in on. "The food here is lovely!" a "heckler" responded. "We love our food. We love our school." And they loved God and they loved long skirts, we later discovered—while we hated our lives and every single choice that had compounded to bring us to this insufferably miserable end.

Sometimes, as we muddled through the first part of the show, we would just decide to hang it up altogether and cut straight to the "not-laughing" contest. At that point, with the unwitting, yet immutably dour contestant onstage, we'd try to break them down with various psychological tools. These included, for one of the guys traveling with me, a reedy and uncomfortable striptease only performed on other men. That always worked at the Christian schools, owing to the thinly veiled homosexual over (and under) tones, which, I gather, was equal parts hilarious and painfully revealing. He would give a boy a lap dance, and that boy would inevitably collapse in a puddle, either fearing we were tainting his salvation, or terrified we were cracking open the door of his poorly constructed closet. This was not comedy. This was desperation on all fronts. We were all of us—audience members and comedians, the saved and the damned—trying desperately to keep it together.

There was one particular school with a very officious

school administrator in a supermarket suit, accented by what I remember vividly as a tie with cheery Disney cartoon characters on it—as if to declare he was a wholesome man through and through, and would beat you to a creamy pulp to prove it. This jerk dispensed his morality lecture through gritted teeth, the kind of smile you reserve for things you truly dislike, like unruly children or the neighbor's mangy rescue dog. "If you people break these rules," he told us after running through them cursorily, "we will not pay you, we will not feed you, and we will not give you a hotel room. Additionally, we will run you out of town on a rail."

On a rail! We weren't even sure what that meant. But we knew *he* knew what it meant.

I was paralyzed with fear that night, because one of my fellow comedians was incredibly undisciplined. Whether it was deliberate or unintentional, he seemed to have a complete lack of control over his own speech. He responded to verbal restrictions with operatic vulgarity. We all feared the worst—no food, no warmth, curling up on the cold floor of our metallic van to sleep, with only the embers of our burning dreams to keep us warm.

We started the show, and somehow, by some prayerful miracle, the better-behaved comedian was really good. He was a sweet guy, and he could play his comedy right up the middle. He won that judgmental audience over with his ingenuousness. So far, so good.

The second guy was on what could only be described as his best behavior (we all *really* wanted that hotel room). Although he didn't break the rules in any literal sense, the audience didn't like him. They could smell the ashen smoke of his

empty soul wafting out along the walls of the auditorium—
they knew he was *no good*. They were turning, and I could feel
it, like that tin-foil taste in the air right before an electrical
storm. When I finally stepped out onstage, following them
both, I was gripped with icy fear. All I could remember was
the seriousness in Cartoon Man's face when he told us, "Under no circumstances can you use the Lord's name in vain."
My forehead was a frosty plane of crystalline sweat.

I did my first joke. It didn't work. I did another joke. That
didn't work. And then the words tumbled from my lips—"Oh
my God"—and I realized I had blown it.

What followed was the most explosive series of Tourettes-
like impiety I'd ever delivered from my lips.

"Oh my God" I said. "Oh my God, oh my God, oh my
God, oh my God, oh my God, oh my God, oh my God, oh my
God, oh my God, oh my God, oh my God, oh my God, oh my
God, oh my God, oh my God, oh my God, oh my God, oh my
God, oh my God, oh my God, oh my God, oh my God, oh my
God, oh my God."

It felt like I'd said it a thousand times. Like hiccups within
an echo chamber of my own damnation.

I melted and folded in on myself, like a human black hole.
The faces in the audience morphed into the demon faces from
The Devil's Advocate, writhing and shaking in dismay. To
them, I was here to ruin us all, to suck this entire comedy congregation into a fiery hell.

"Get off the stage," they were yelling. "You're evil and we
hate you!" At least their heckles were clear and to the point.
You couldn't misconstrue where they were coming from.
They wanted us out. And out we went.

We didn't even finish the show. Abandoning the game-show portion of the evening, we fled.

But as we were making our way out of the theater, a few of the students came up to us and said, "Look, we're really sorry for the behavior of our classmates. We don't think that was right, or Christian. We would love to take you out to dinner."

That was great, because it was crystal clear we wouldn't be paid for the show, and we were absolutely starving. Blaspheming really works up an appetite. So we went to a submarine sandwich shop and ate together. Delightfully, the students were nice. Not at all judgmental.

But then (of course) what happened was that they commenced the process of proselytization. Even though they were quite lovely and reasonable about it, they were also totally oblivious to the fact that they were barking up the wrong three trees. We had a wonderful conversation about the concept of an absolute religion—the idea that only their version of Christianity would get you into heaven and that all other churches were evil manifestations of Satan. As I listened, I was trying to get through my sandwich as quickly as possible, so I could make my escape. Still, I *was* curious.

"So...what happens to an Eskimo," I wondered out loud, my mouth full of turkey, "or a dude in the Brazilian rain forest who never gets to have an opportunity to hear your particular version of things? Is that guy just expressly born to die and continue on to hell?" It seemed like the most ridiculous of theological propositions.

They consulted each other, then nodded. "Pretty much, yeah!" they said.

"Man," I thought. "This sandwich is great, but you guys are dicks."

We finished our sandwiches. I admired how civilized they were. It truly was something to see—their confidence that they had somehow won the game of this mortal plane, and would someday rocket up to the clouds while everybody else lingered down here, lamenting our poor choices and eventually burning in eternal hellfire, probably at a mall or while eating a vegan meal. It must be nice to live your life that way, I thought, to know with certainty that, despite the fact that three comedians tried to aggressively taint your salvation, you were impervious to their powers, and, more than that, you did your pious part and gave them some nice coloring books, along with a nice, healthy Christian sandwich, thus ensuring your path to paradise.

That certainty must have really felt good on the inside. To this day, I envy it. Because on the inside of me, I am absolutely riddled with self-doubt, and I want to eat bacon.

Satan probably wants me to eat bacon, too. He's gonna win.

TAKING THE RISK!

A Q&A WITH AISHA TYLER

Are there any little ways you bent accuracy to get at the emotional truth of this experience?

This story is basically true to life, but like all comedians, I have embellished wildly for effect. All comedic recountings have a bit of elasticity—metaphor, hyperbole, flourishes—but the emotional core of the story is accurate.

Was there anything you originally wanted to include in the story, but felt might be a whole other story?

No. If anything, I probably included more details than were necessary. I like texture.

Where do you fall on the spectrum of the "Some things are better left unsaid" and "Live without filters" philosophies?

Unfortunately, you cannot be an effective comedian and retain the typical brain-mouth barriers that most people employ to keep themselves from injuring themselves and others.

MELANIE HAMLETT

UNBREAKABLE

"Who's *that*?" I asked my friend, who was now my boss at this pizza shop.

He followed my gaze to one of our coworkers. "Jesse... why?"

"No reason."

He gave me one of those "Dude, don't you even think about it" looks, then rushed off.

I was *absolutely* thinking about "it." This guy was *hot*. I'm not so into the overgrown beard look, or the fact he was probably a decade younger than me, but those were minor details really. "Just look at those thick, tattooed forearms," I thought. They were bulging out of his sleeves as he kneaded that tender, white mass of dough, then gave it a good spank.

I was dead.

I really needed excitement in my life right then. I was 36, waiting tables in a ski town (yet again!), and broke. Totally winning at life. But, *whatever*, I thought. I was not planning on being there for good, just long enough to write and save some money. New Mexico had been a home base for me back in my twenties and now seemed like the perfect place to regroup during my transition from starving artist in New York City to starving artist in Los Angeles.

So I'd started working in New Mexico at this pizza shop, and within the first week, I could tell Jesse was into me, too. His eyes said, "I wanna fuck your brains out, girl," from under his PBR trucker hat while he did all kinds of foreplay on that dough. Soon after came the secret sexting. Then the hugs out back in the storage shed. This forbidden workplace romance shit was HOT.

Oddly enough, at this point in my life, after decades of mostly one-night stands peppered between insanely long periods of abstinence, I was actually ready and willing to try this thing they call a relationship. After "working on myself" like it was a second job, I finally respected and, dare I say, even loved myself, which is remarkable, given that I'd spent a couple decades destroying myself. What I really wanted at that point was something meaningful for once.

Just not with him.

I never once thought I should date Jesse, or even hook up with him, just to be clear. The guy wasn't relationship material and he practically sweated red flags.

But we spoke the same gypsy language. I was a minimalist who'd lived in my truck for five years all over America, one year in Europe, and another bouncing around South America. He'd lived out of a backpack on a *train* for ten years. A legit *hobo*.

So, he was fascinating, cracked me up, and laughed at all my jokes. Plus, he loved my stories on the *RISK!* podcast, which, I thought, meant he got me.

I managed to keep him at arm's length until, one night, our

dishwasher, Big D, got drunk, slammed into a tree, and shot out the window to his death. This devastated me for reasons I still don't understand. At his funeral, when D's mother broke down crying and fell into Jesse's arms, he petted her hair and cried with her. For a toxically masculine tomboy who couldn't access tears easily myself, this moment completely disarmed me. Now it wasn't just my loins. My heart was sucked in, too.

The next day, I woke up to a flat tire. But I was no damsel in distress. On the contrary, I wouldn't let men help me even when I probably should have. But with all the rust under my truck, I couldn't get the tire off. I should have called AAA. I called Jesse instead.

Watching him fix my tire was even hotter than watching him spank that dough ass. When he was done, I invited him into my house, which was a first.

For months already, I'd been watching two forces duke it out in my head. My intuition was all, "Girl, no. Bad idea!" But my ego was like, "Shut up, bitch! This shit's FUN." I'd even made ground rules. Months ago. No kissing or touching pink parts, hence the hugs.

See how much I didn't trust myself with this guy?

He sat in my big lounge chair, so I sat on the ottoman, a good three feet away. During a pause in conversation, he gave me this look, rolled my ottoman closer, and plopped me down on his lap. Which I loved.

"No kissing!" I shouted.

"Don't worry," he said while rubbing his nose across my face, ears, and neck.

I wasn't used to this foreplay stuff. Most dudes had basically used my vagina as their right hand, and weren't even slightly concerned with my orgasm. This sensual stuff was neat!

"Well, hello there," I thought, feeling his boner right under my ass.

He picked me up (so strong!), threw me on the bed, then took off my pants and shirt.

"NO KISSING!"

I told myself we weren't *technically* hooking up because our tongues and lips didn't touch. But now that I understand the power of oxytocin and its ability to literally make people drunk on hormones, my contortionist thinking makes more sense.

He caressed every single inch of my front side, minus that black triangle down yonder and these mosquito bites I call boobs. It was by far the most erotic experience of my life. Who knew that *not having sex* was hotter than actually having sex?

This insanity went on another two weeks before I let him eat my pussy and fuck me good. Unfortunately, he was amazing at both. I'd gotten close to an orgasm before, but never could let myself go. But with him, woo boy! This fireworks stuff was crazy!

Part of me still felt in total control of this thing somehow, but most of me knew I was totally fucked. Besides him not being mature/healthy enough for me, there was another, even bigger reason why this was a terrible idea. Over a month into our flirting, he'd mentioned offhandedly that his girlfriend was picking him up at work that night.

"*Girlfriend?*"

He didn't get why I was so pissed about this new information.

She wasn't *really* his girlfriend, he said. He was just living with her until he found his own place.

I forgot, at that moment, that he'd never owned his own place, and that mooching off of others was his thing. The very idea of being his side dish made me feel like a garbage person. But there I was, months later, watching his phone light up with texts from her every time he came over. He never understood why her texts upset me, either. That was red flag number 112—always playing the victim to avoid accountability.

He complained about the woman who wasn't really his girlfriend all the time. Her mom, too. (I'd learned he lived with his girlfriend *and* her parents.) I remember exactly where I was sitting when I heard my intuition try to bitch-slap me after getting a gaslight-ẏ text from him. *This is* not *the kind of guy you should date. You know that.* Run, girl, run.

Nope, my ego piped in. *I want this too much.* The ego will do anything to get what it wants and doesn't much care about consequences.

I thought a three-week climbing trip to Cali would restore my resolve in saying no to this romance/whatchamacallit. But before I left, I gave Jesse an ultimatum: "This is killing my self-esteem. And hurting your girlfriend. Pick one. You can't have us both." He'd never leave her.

Nearly three weeks later, while I was at the top of a climb in Joshua Tree, I got the text.

"just bought a hammock and moved out"

He'd called my bluff.

When I picked him up at work a few days later, he was

standing there with a backpack and banjo—all he owned. "I guess this means we're heading to my house," I said.

I set some ground rules. For starters, he couldn't stay with me every night. I've never shared my home with a man (or even dated one really), and he certainly wasn't going to be the first. He told me not to worry. He and two of our coworkers had moved into a van and were camping in it down by the river and I'm not even kidding. I slept in it one night (the guys stayed in a tent) and found it equal parts thrilling, hilarious, and sad. But I shrugged it off—how dare I judge? I had lived in a truck for years!

The rules, of course, dissolved quickly. Because I let them—we were having fun, and I got used to having him around all the time. On weekends, we'd go on road trips together and end up in the most bizarre, random places. Having traveled solo most my life, I was starting to see the perks of companionship.

The final nails in my love coffin were small. He held my hand in public, which no one ever had. He washed my hair when we would shower together and cupped my ear to shield it from water. How thoughtful! When I was driving, he'd lace his fingers through mine on the stick shift.

Much to my surprise, this shit actually made me fall in love. Yes, me!

The irony here was that I'd always fancied myself a pretty badass woman. I'd been a raft guide, ski instructor, wilderness guide, and rock climber. I'd lived in the back of my Toyota truck for years all over America and traveled the world alone. I'd just spent years working on film sets and doing comedy in NYC. People had always commented on how fearless I was, and I am on many levels. But what they didn't know was that, when it came to intimacy and relationships, I was a fucking coward. Always had been.

But there I was, at the age of 36, finally letting someone in.

The worst part about all this was that Jesse had been able to contain his rage and jealousy until this very moment. Once I was hooked, the lid came off. At work, he'd watch me from the kitchen window, then shoot off a text whenever a man came to the counter.

"What the hell did he want with you?"

"A BBQ chicken pizza."

I soon found myself tiptoeing around his anger. And doing things my feminist self never would. Like switching my silver ring to my wedding finger at work. Like downloading a tracking app on my phone so he wouldn't "worry" about me. Like letting him stay every day at my house, rent free, and driving him everywhere, like a goddamn soccer mom. None of this ever comes suddenly. Your freedom gets chipped away. You allow one concession after another in an attempt to manage their anger. I imagine this is what it's like to have a two-year-old. In fact, dating him made me realize I'd be an excellent mother. I even carried a goddamn diaper bag around with me full of things like a Kindle and snacks, to pacify baby Jesse.

And yet I never knew what irrational thing would set him off, which meant I could never relax. When I refused to lend him $150 so he could buy an ugly kilt at the Renaissance Fair, he threw a glass at the wall. "Uh-oh," I thought. "He's the kind of guy who throws stuff." A few days later, it was a chair.

Whether your partner actually hits you or not, these kinds of things are his way of telling you he wants to.

He started talking about getting married, which seemed to be all about possession for him. He said he wished I hadn't just gotten that IUD, either. "You'd never leave me if I knocked you up." I laughed. "Oh honey, I'd just abort it anyways. If you really wanted to trap me, you'd get me a dog."

Days later he came home with a puppy, which I found a new home for immediately.

The first time I tried to break up with him, he told me they'd find his body hanging from a tree with a note around his neck saying, "This is what happens when Melanie Hamlett loves you." Now, I knew this was a classic manipulation tactic. And yet this *was* the first man I'd ever loved, so...

The next time I tried to break up, he said, "I guess you don't mind if those videos go viral."

"What videos?"

"Nothing."

The next time he got blackout drunk, I broke into his phone. Sure enough, there were two videos of me giving him head. And three of his ex. I also found he had a new side dish he was cheating on me with. Karma, right?

I erased everything, then texted the new side dish. "Hey, this is Jesse's girlfriend. Just wanted you to know he's a lying asshole."

The next morning, I told him we were finished. Surprise! It didn't go over well. He threw my DVD player across the room at me. Then my TV, too, for good measure. I grabbed my phone and texted my friend Eric, the only guy who knew that Jesse's anger concerned me.

"Need help. Come over now."

"Who the *fuck* you texting?"

He wrestled it out of my hands, then pinned me down to the ground, like a wrestler. The self-defense class I'd taken long ago told me you're supposed to go for the face, but which part was escaping me. So, I guessed, and stuck my hand in his mouth. Don't ever do that! He bit down so hard I thought I was going to lose my fingers. He finally released his pit bull grip after I screamed and he heard the neighbor upstairs open her door and walk outside.

I brushed myself off slowly, then darted outside.

"You OK?" she said from the porch.

"No. I'm scared of him."

She got her boyfriend to take Jesse to work. Eric arrived shortly thereafter and took charge. "I just texted him," he told me, "and said all conversations go through me from now on." He then loaded Jesse's banjo and pack into his own truck and literally followed him around all day. Even to the bridge Jesse swore he'd jump from. Every woman needs a friend like Eric.

I should have blocked Jesse out of my life right then, but I just couldn't. His hysterical, unrelenting texts wavered between suicide threats, professions of love, pleas for forgiveness, and calling me a whore.

He wore me down until I took him back. Like so many of us, I couldn't forget who he was before he turned insane. It's the biggest mindfuck. Plus, we worked together and I was too embarrassed to tell my boss/friend about the drama I'd brought into his business. I was moving to LA soon and needed the money. I'd manage to get through these last months here.

So, after only a week, I took his ass back under new rules—no more throwing stuff or calling me a whore. A lot of good that did!

Two weeks later, he was sending those "You fucking that guy?" texts at work. He invited himself to my friend's wedding so he could monitor me. After he got blackout drunk, I took him to my friend's place, where he was house-sitting, and put on *Young Guns 2* until he passed out.

"Which is more dangerous," I wondered, "staying here, or going home?" It's truly shocking how codependent I could be. I chose to stay because I was more worried about him driving drunk to my house if he woke up than about what he'd do to me if I stayed.

At 3 a.m. I woke up to the bedroom door being thrown open.

"Why THE FUCK did you leave me out there, goddamit?"

Some people choose flight, others to fight. I play dead. Always have.

He crawled into bed and immediately tried to have sex. Too bad—I was pretending to be sound asleep! When he started going for my butt, I pretended to stir. "Whuh? No, zzzzzz…" It's amazing how peaceful I can seem when my adrenaline and heart rate are actually through the roof.

When he tried to stick the tip into my asshole, I said *fuck this sleepy time routine*, "woke up," pushed him off, and said, "No!" In what I can only describe as that voice in *Ghostbusters* when Zeus has possessed Sigourney Weaver, he said "YES."

"This is not going to end well," I thought.

He kept at me, trying to fuck my ass, which he knew was

a no-fly zone. "NO," I screamed several times. "YES," Zeus kept saying back. When I realized I would not win this battle, I screamed, "You're fucking RAPING ME!" But he didn't seem to mind. In fact, he seemed to take pleasure in the fight.

He rode me like one of those horses from *Young Guns 2*, grabbing wads of my hair like a mane, pulling the side of my cheek with his finger, like a fish on a hook. I was surprised at how calm I was. That's what people being traumatized tend to do—disassociate. Being in your body as it's being violated is *no bueno*. So you leave it for a while. And do other stuff, like make jokes. *And here I thought I was too old to get raped!* I heard in my mind. Laughing in the face of tragedy is how I've gotten through literally everything, so this was no different. Feeling dead inside comes later. When you're safe.

I told one of my friends the next day. "You've gotta get out of here!" she insisted, and started making plans for me. "No! This will be on *my* time line." You cannot force someone to leave a partner, or they will go back. Plus there's the whole not-wanting-to-die factor. When I'd stopped by the women's shelter for a little advice, they'd told me that the days before and after a woman leaves are when she's most likely to get murdered. Basically, you're fucked either way.

They told me to go to the police and file an incident report, so the rape would be on record and help prosecute him when (not if) it happened again. But when I tried to do that, the cops were such dicks. They said if I reported it, I would no longer have a say about whether they pressed charges. "But I LIVE with this man," I pleaded. "Do you have any idea what he'll do to me if he finds out I was here?" They said I didn't have a choice if I "claimed" I was raped. So I did what I had to. "Okay *fine*. I made it all up. *He never raped me*. I LIED."

By the very end, I was getting sick all the time. I developed this crazy throat infection, from silencing myself, no doubt, that landed me in the emergency room (but kept me from having to give BJs, whoo hoo!). Everyone commented on how tired I was all the time. Jesus, it's exhausting when your adrenals are shot. My body was falling apart. After the rape, I'd break out in hives whenever he came near me. My body was like "GET AWAY FROM THIS DUDE!" and yet I couldn't. I had to play it cool, and wait until I had my window.

The irony in all of this was that when I used to hitchhike around South America and Europe, and live in my truck, all solo, as a woman, people always said, "Aren't you afraid of getting raped or murdered?!" I'd always answer, "I think you watch too much *Law and Order: SVU*." The reality of being a woman in America is this—the only time I was raped and almost murdered was in the comfort of my home, by someone I fucking loved. These aren't just strangers doing this. It's usually the men we know, love, and trust most.

A few days before I was set to leave, my friend Annie flew down from Alaska to help get me out of New Mexico alive. I lied to Jesse, saying he could join me as soon as I got settled. He was intuitive, though, so he knew something was up. He insisted we have sex even more, which I was too afraid to say no to, but cried through anyways. "Gentle rape sure beats the violent kind," I thought. I'd hit my limit, though, by my last day in town, and pushed him off of me in the shower. Later that day, he tried to drive off a cliff with me in the car, *Thelma*

& Louise-style, minus the female empowerment and hand-holding.

Despite all of this, I was still worried more about him than about myself. I even called a friend and asked them to make sure he was okay after I left. That's how codependent I'd become by the end. I'd been so focused on him being okay (I was a diaper-bag totin' mom, after all!) that I'd abandoned myself entirely. I had nothing left.

Luckily, I had Annie, who loved me more than I loved myself, and who wasn't mad or disappointed in what I'd done. She understood why I loved him, but reminded me I had to love myself more. I had to. We all do. That was my mantra the whole drive to Los Angeles.

My first stop in LA was Planned Parenthood. I told the nice doctor I just wanted to make sure he hadn't broken my lady bits. While the cold duck lips were in me, holding my vagina open, she asked me more about him. "Did you guys live together?"

I laughed. Because it hit me now that the things I'd laughed off weren't actually funny. They were disturbing. "Only because he was HOMELESS," I said. In that moment, I remembered the time when I'd caught him eating dog food. "It's good!" he'd argued. "I used to eat it all the time when I rode the rails." When I'd asked him another time why I'd never seen him brush his teeth, he assured me he did out back...with his *index finger*. "You don't really need toothpaste—dirt's an abrasive."

He texted me for weeks after I left.

"I got shot last night thank you very much glad to know you have that kind of pull"

"What? I don't know anyone who would *shoot* you!"

I went all Nancy Drew, asking why he wasn't in a hospital then, if this was true.

"I sewed it up myself with a needle and dental floss"

When I realized I was still engaging with this crazy man, I knew I was sick. Despite hating him, I was still somehow addicted to this man. This drama. I even fantasized about seeing him one last time. This terrified me, so I got professional help. They convinced me to block him. Men like this don't take no easily, though, so he started a Twitter account for the sole purpose of tweeting about what a whore I was at me.

"Sounds like you enjoy sleeping around @melaniehamlett!"

Stuff like that. He even changed his profile picture to one of my pussy. I must have been asleep when he took it. Thankfully, I got the account taken down and didn't hear from him for a while. But then on Thanksgiving, a number I didn't recognize sent me a text.

"hey you don't know me but my name is jake you know my friend Jesse I just found him hanging from a tree"

Apparently "Jake" wanted to know where I lived so he could mail me Jesse's suicide letter (i.e., come murder me). At first, I was hysterical. Maybe this *was* what happens when Melanie Hamlett loves you! Then, I realized the text was in all lowercase with no punctuation. *Fucking Jesse.*

I tracked down one of his old exes on Facebook and asked her if he would ever leave me alone. She said he still sends her pics of his penis in her ass, six years later, and that the last time she'd seen him, the cops had dragged him away in handcuffs for breaking her ribs and trying to choke her to death. I sure lucked out. Jesse faking his own death meant he couldn't ever contact me again.

I was finally free of this sociopath.

I'd love to say it all ended there, but no. There was the PTSD. The shame of how insane *I* had been to stay. The hardest part of all of it was forgiving myself. Here I was, this proud feminist who dated a total fucking misogynist. The funny thing is, I used to be one of these assholes who shamed women like me. "Duh, you idiot," I'd thought when I heard the horror stories. "Just LEAVE."

But now I get it. There's love involved. And fear. And a ton of codependency. Usually, the woman shares children, money, friends, and a mortgage with her abuser. The way we talk about domestic abuse needs to change entirely. Not just so we don't call the women who date these men stupid, but also so we don't call the men themselves monsters. I find this name-calling both ignorant and cruel. I would never date a *monster*. I loved Jesse. We all love someone like him. They're our brothers, our husbands, our boyfriends, our coworkers, our teachers, our allies at marches, our friends. They're everywhere. At least one man in your life is doing this to a woman. You just don't know it yet.

They're not monsters. They're sick, and need help. Sure, most of them belong in jail. But then what? Jesse was a broken boy who'd watched his father try to kill his mother. Plus, he was poor. The odds were stacked against him. Regardless of what he did to me, I don't think prison is going to fix him.

I waited a year before I dated anyone because I didn't want to bring this trauma into a new relationship. But when I was finally ready, I had a higher standard than ever. I would find a way to keep my heart open, but to guard it, too.

As a result of listening to my intuition now, instead of telling it, *fuck off, this is fun!* I've only gone on dates with or had sex with awesome dudes. Some weren't ready for a relationship, and I conveniently ignored them telling me this, and I got my feelings hurt. I slept with one guy I really liked, and he ghosted me. Because I tried to push him into something he wasn't ready for. I cried for days over this dumb boy, until one day, I thought, "Yeah, but he didn't rape you or anything." True! He didn't. "What am I so upset about? I've survived worse. I'll be okay. I always am."

If I can bounce back from a goddamn rape and almost-murder, nothing can destroy me. I'm un-fucking-breakable at this point. Hear me roar.

TAKING THE RISK!

A Q&A WITH MELANIE HAMLETT

You were very engaged with the conversations this story inspired on our website and on social media. How did you feel about all the responses people had to your story?

I was touched by how many strangers reached out to me after this story came out. Some of them said I gave them hope, others that I made them feel less alone, and several that my story even inspired them to leave their current abusive relationships. I wrote back to every message I got because I know how lonely their situations are. I might very well have been the only person they were reaching out to. Even the chattiest of Kathies will either downplay it all, or become mute about her reality once she's in over her head. Biting our tongue becomes the default, and isolation is par for the course. Some are forced into that by the partner, but a lot of it is self-imposed out of fear, shame, denial, and concern for our loved ones. We become so fucking codependent and locked into this shit that we not only put our partner's needs above our own safety, but we convince ourselves that our family and friends shouldn't be burdened with more worry. So we lie by omission. Constantly. What if they don't believe us? Or what if they intervene and try to make us leave before we truly want to? There's no fucking winning in this situation. I've never felt so stuck in my life, and I was only bound by a job, love, and my addiction to him, not money or kids or marriage. Many women aren't that lucky.

This story inspired another person to share their story on *RISK!*, the episode called "The Monster and the Man." A man who went by the pseudonym "Larry Talbot" was so touched by the point you made about abusers not being "monsters" that he decided to share his own story on the podcast about having once been an abuser who went through a decade of therapy and medication to change his ways.

Getting that message from "Larry" was one of the most moving moments of my life. I will never hear from Jesse again, nor do I want to. Even if he changes, which I doubt he will, I never ever want him to resurface in my life. I cannot unsee him raping me, and I cannot unlearn being terrified of him. I don't even want to know which jail he's living in, or if he's alive or dead. But I'm not mad at him. My anger was poison that almost destroyed me.

I want abusers to get help and make changes. And yet, to be completely honest, I didn't think men like this *could* change. Knowing so many people, myself included, who were fucked up for so long, and changed dramatically, I'd wanted to think anyone could. But abusers? I was skeptical. Larry changed my mind on that. He still has some work to do. His shame, like that of most people who feel awful about their past, can be exhausting at times. But it was genuine, and that surprised me. His remorse for what he'd done freed me from feeling crazy. It's like he was a stand-in for Jesse. He said the things I wished Jesse had. And I was a stand-in for Larry's ex. Because I forgave Jesse, and refused to see him as a monster, Larry could let go of some of his own shame, and focus more on being better, instead of being consumed by shame. But in order to move beyond shame, you have to get help and face your shit. Larry did. Will other men? I fucking hope so.

HOOKERS 'N' BLOW

I'm coming home from doing comedy one night at two in the morning, my girlfriend out of town, and I pass a guy hanging out in front of my building, who says, "Want some coke?"

"No," I tell him. "I'm good—I'm coked. I'm all set with that."

Then a Latina woman comes up from behind him and asks, "You want a date?" I think the man must have been her pimp.

I look up at my bedroom window. "Well, I live here," I say, "so, what the hell. Yeah." It just seemed too convenient.

We go into the building, and she gets winded walking up the first flight of stairs. "How fucking high up is it?" she asks.

"It's just a couple more flights," I say.

When we're in my apartment, it's like the place is a shame palace now. There's someone in my head saying, "What the fuck is wrong with you?" I had never "consummated" anything with a hooker before.

But I ask her, "Well, what happens now?"

"Give me $40," she says. I give her $40. She says, "Why don't you lie down on the bed and take your pants off?" So I do.

She starts giving me head. Mind you, there are condoms sitting on the dresser but none on me. And my mind starts to run. "This isn't working out. This is fucking sad," I think. "Your girlfriend is out of town and you're having sex with a hooker you met outside your apartment at two in the morning." But, I think, maybe if she took her breasts out, that would quiet my thoughts.

"Will you take your top off?" I ask.

She says, "Ten more dollars." I put the $10 down, she takes her breasts out, and I put my hands on them while she's giving me head.

And we're going on like that, till she pauses to catch her breath for a moment, and she presses one of my hands into her breasts and says, "You feel a lump in there?"

I thought, "What kind of luck am I having with all this?" And I'm feeling her breast, and I'm horrified.

"Yeah," I say. "I think there is one in there."

"That's what I thought," she said. "I really got to get to the doctor."

So this is just not hot. Now I'm worrying about her future health. But, for whatever idiot reason, I want to finish this thing, so I try to focus as she goes on giving me head. Then the fucking phone rings, and it's my girlfriend. I let the answering machine pick up. "Hi, baby!" she says. "Just calling to check in, see what you're doing, and tell you I love you."

I'm listening to this with this hooker that probably has cancer who's blowing me in our bed. I'm thinking, "Oh my God. I am in the shame trenches."

Somehow, I manage to finish. There isn't much victory in it. It comes out more like, "Ohhh, God." I know, when I come, that I have far exceeded any horrible thing that I have ever done. And the woman gets up and tells me, "You know, usually, I work as a computer programmer."

I think, "It's a little late for that pretend-job shit." And she says, "Can I have these condoms?"

"Yeah, go ahead," I say.

"Can I have these cigarettes?"

"Yeah, take everything you want."

She left, and I immediately went into a panic. I have a syndrome in which I always think that I'm going to win the anti-lottery. So that began this meltdown, where I believed I was going to be the only guy that ever got AIDS from a blow job.

Years later, I bring up this story in therapy. And I realize that I hadn't said I wanted a date that night because I wanted to have sex with a hooker. I've never wanted to have sex with a hooker! But I do like panicking. I see now that if I'm not in some sense of panic, or worry, or dread, I don't know what to do with myself.

But also I realized how I was using choices like this in my relationship with my girlfriend. If I had things in my mind that made me feel guilty, things my girlfriend didn't know about, these things would make me want to behave like a halfway decent guy when I was with her. Knowing that, secretly, I was the biggest asshole that ever fucking lived made me act like a doting boyfriend. So, for a little while at least, in my secret state of contrition, I almost looked like a good guy.

TAKING THE RISK!

A Q&A WITH MARC MARON

This story was told at the very first *RISK!* show at Arlene's Grocery in August of '09. You gave us advice that night on running a podcast, in the midst of launching your own podcast, WTF. Would you have guessed that more than eight years later, both podcasts would still be going strong?

I'm generally surprised any of us make it another day, let alone eight years down the line.

In your work, it seems like you've always been able to shift gears from ridiculously funny moments to painful or brutally honest ones with ease. Were you always like that, or were you once more hesitant to get too real with stuff?

My impulse is to get too real. At some point I realized that bummed people out, so I learned how to ease it with the funny out of necessity, just so I'd have a few friends.

Now that your life is on more stable ground than it was back in the days of this story, are you somewhat grateful for the memories of a messier existence?

Not for the memories themselves, but yes, for getting through the events they represent, I am grateful.

CHAD DUNCAN

DOING GOOD

I don't know how, but for some reason, I was born with an innate ability to read people in seconds. I learned this in 1997, when I was a special education teacher. I could walk by classrooms and, through the narrow little window, I could spot a student who was in distress. I'd go inside and talk to the teacher and say, "Could I speak to this child outside?" When they would come out and they learned that they weren't in trouble, they opened up. And their stories were astonishing.

One student had just learned from a pregnancy test his girlfriend had taken that morning that he was about to be a father. Other students told me about when their mom's boyfriends had been put in jail. The worst stories were the ones when the boyfriend had gotten out of jail.

One night, I tried to describe to my wife, Jennifer, how I could look at people and immediately see if something was wrong. I was sitting on our sectional, trying to explain it in a metaphor: these kids were like Pig Pen from from the Charlie Brown cartoon—I could see they were covered in dust. The thing was, that the cloud around them wasn't dust. It was emotions.

"If you're so good at reading people," she said, "how come

you haven't noticed that I've been pissed off at you for the past two days?"

"I don't know, baby," I said. "Maybe this couch has some lead shielding, or the TV…"

She just gave me a wink. I knew she was pissed off at me, because she was wearing a certain pair of panties I'd always thought of as a signal flare that says, "It's not happening." I call them "Kryptonite panties" because there's no man of steel that night.

But with the students in the classroom, I began not just to be able to see what was wrong, but I started trying to help them regain the rest of their day. I could build them back up. Usually, when they confessed what was wrong, they were afraid their mom was going to get called, or they were going to be arrested. "You're alright," I would let them know. "You're with me. We're going to make it through this day."

Once I could see that the students were back in the swing of things and working on something, I would come up to them again and say, "You're doing good." It was those moments that truly filled my heart.

There was one day in February of 2011 when I was teaching Special Ed class. At one point, I reached into my pocket and pulled out my BlackBerry. I was looking at the screen, and it was smeared in this way that I'd never noticed before. I heard a scuffle, and looked back up and ran after two boys who were picking a fight.

But later that night, I pulled my phone back out of my pocket to figure out how the screen was smeared. I showed it to my wife. "My new BlackBerry—it's, it's messed up," I told her.

But Jennifer said it was just fine. She was so dismissive that I knew she hadn't really looked at it, and so I sat down next to her. "No, sweetheart, look. See this half of it? It's smeared."

"There's nothing wrong with your phone," she said. I just figured I must be suffering from some crazy allergies, and I decided to go to sleep.

When I woke up, there was this field of electricity, a lot like the static on a television set, only it was pulsating. I opened my eyes, and there was no difference from having them closed—everything around me was still perfectly dark. "This is a nightmare," I thought. "I need to wake up from this." I sat up, and I fumbled my way to the bathroom, flipping the light switch on and off. There was still no difference. "The light must be out," I thought. I went to the next room and flipped that light on and off, and there was no difference.

I shuffled back to Jennifer. "Something's wrong with my eyes," I told her.

We went to the eye doctor, who dilated my eyes and poked and prodded me. "I've seen three cases of this," he said. "Two were in med school, twenty-five years ago, and you're number three." He said he thought I had choroideremia, but I was going to need to talk to an expert.

"What about these flashes?" I asked. "When do they go away?"

He just shook his head. "I don't know enough about this," he said.

Jennifer and I went back home, and we called up my principal. She agreed that my teacher's assistants could teach my lesson plans, and do everything that involved sight. They wanted me to stay as an advisor, since I'd always been the one to see the problems and build those kids back up.

Jennifer took me to school the next day. My assistants brought the students in and they led the lecture. The students didn't seem to realize that I was blind.

Trying to sleep that night, I was haunted by the flashes pulsing at me. They pushed on my eyes, like I was being smothered by an electrical cloud.

For several weeks, we kept up this routine. Jennifer would take me to school. My TAs would teach the class and I would advise.

Then, a crisis happened: one of the students who was emotionally disturbed ended up throwing his desk. We got the students out of the room and tried to de-escalate the conflict as the TAs approached him. The next thing I knew, my TAs had restrained the child.

I guided him through it, and I was able to calm him down and restore stability. I was able to get him back.

Eventually, we got the other students back in and started doing the paperwork. "I couldn't believe," one of the TAs said, "that after he threw the desks over, he threw the chair at you."

He had thrown a chair at me? I was horrified. I thought, "If I can't make the classroom safe for myself, how can I make it safe for my students?"

That was the last day I taught.

The specialist who saw me agreed that I had choroideremia, which is genetic. "You're blind," he said, as if the finality of the statement might be some comfort.

"Thanks," I said.

We went back home. We had just moved into a new house that, at first, felt like a castle. Now, it was a blind man's prison, because we hadn't bought anything with my condition in mind. I couldn't use the microwave, whose buttons were totally flat. I couldn't walk alone down the porch stairs to the mailbox.

Soon, we had gotten one of those white canes for me, with which I started stabbing at the ground. I didn't know what you do with those things. We would go out in public, and that's when the disability really hit home. The waiter or waitress would look at Jennifer and ask, "What would he like?"

We would walk through a grocery store, and I'd stab at the ground. I would hear people talking, and then, all of a sudden they would be silent, staring. I would flash back to when I was a kid, mesmerized by the first time I ever saw a blind person let their cane lead them.

I spent most of my time home alone, not moving, waiting for Jennifer to return. I felt like gravity was sucking me down to the floor I couldn't see, and the whole room was spinning. My depression was so intense, it was like having had way too much to drink. Like I was on a roller coaster, all that blood rushing to my head, and everything hurt to move, and the only thing I knew to do was throw up. But it's depression. You can't throw up to get rid of it.

I was struggling, and I feared I was becoming a burden on Jennifer, who went off to work every day while I lay in bed at home. One day, I just shouted right out loud, "This is not the life I wanted! I don't want this for me!"

That was a moment of clarity. I realized that Jennifer was

still there. And even though I was stuck in my own body, unable to see her, she was still choosing me. She believed in me. I remember that when she came home that evening, I said, "Sweetheart, I'm going to be better. I'm going to stop crying. I'm going to go back to school and get a master's in social work." We decided to go out to dinner in public, and I used my cane. At the restaurant, the server asked my wife, "What would he like?" and I turned my head in his direction and said, "Reckon I'll have them french fried pertaters!"

We started venturing out more often. I got more comfortable with using my cane and the way it hit the obstacles in my path, showing me, implicitly, my way around them. I learned that my sense of humor helped me deal with some of the disturbances around me. One day, for instance, we were traveling, and while Jennifer was describing how I was going to walk ten feet to the men's room on my left, then hook a right at the end, a man walked past me, asking if I'd be needing a disabled toilet. "No," I said. "I need one that works!" I was so proud of myself.

Two years after I lost my sight, as I was working through that master's degree, I decided I ought to get a dog. I applied to this guide dog school, and they said they would match me with a dog. I thought, "The dog's going to match me? This dog's going to be high maintenance, socially awkward, and obsessed with my wife's boobies?" That was going to be weird!

They told me I had to give up my cane, now that I would rely on the dog. They said I shouldn't combine them, because they're such different modes of navigating. When you're using a cane, you let your own momentum carry you into whatever obstacle your cane hits, and then you get around it. But a dog follows your instinct and becomes your own momentum, guiding you forth, and stopping you.

Jennifer and I were on FaceTime when they introduced me to this one particular dog. His name was Perry. "He's beautiful," Jennifer said, and at first I wondered if she was just saying that. But it turned out, he was.

He was intense, they warned me. He was fiercely determined, a fast walker.

I went up to Michigan to pick him up, and they showed me how to talk to him. "It's okay," I found myself saying. "You're doing alright." Even when he would stop to sniff flowers, which he wasn't supposed to do, I would talk to him calmly. I would tell him, "It's alright," and give him a little tug away from the distraction.

I went from living in a prison to having a companion who held me accountable.

We began to walk for about an hour every day in my neighborhood. We both liked to check things out. There were obstacles—loose dogs and blocked driveways—and sometimes Perry didn't know the best way to proceed. He tried to figure out how to read me. I tried in turn to be enthusiastic and reassure him. "It's okay," I'd tell him when a dog barked. He would notice the dog, be jiggling in the harness, wanting to say hello. I'd say, "It's alright, it's okay!" and when he'd refocus, I'd say, "You're doing good."

It's been five years to the month since I lost my sight. Five years since the path that I'd been on for thirty-eight years seemed to disappear in front of me, my plans vanishing. The flashes are still with me, though, and so is Jennifer. My path is different. I'm not a teacher anymore, but a social worker.

And now, I have a companion with me for this lifelong trip. We come home from my job, and I put on my running shoes, and we go for a walk. In the night air, without any of the visual distractions I'd once been used to, there is an incredible intimacy. It will be just him and me and the sounds of the crickets; the mist starting to hit me as the air cools. I hear the scrape of my footsteps, and I hear Perry breathing. "It's okay," I tell him. "It's alright. You're doing good." I say it a lot, because I need to hear those words.

TAKING THE RISK!

A Q&A WITH CHAD DUNCAN

How do you think people reading your story in this book will experience it differently from those who saw you tell it live onstage in Dallas with Perry beside you?
The truth is, I forget that I am blind. I painted the portrait of myself in the beginning as sighted. I wanted the audience to know how valuable my sight was to what I did to give a sense of what the sudden loss of that dynamic ability was like. I sought to show the thoughts, emotions, and questions you experience when you dramatically lose a sense that gave you freedom, a career, and an identity.

How did you first get to know *RISK!* and reach out to us?
My screenreader listed *RISK!* as one of the top five best podcasts, and I was curious. People with visual disabilities enjoy listening to lots of podcasts. I was hooked by Ray Christian's story about the pigeons, "Comfortable in the Water." He crafted such a visual picture. Though I could no longer see, Ray offered such a rich vision of what his life was like. I was hooked, and as I listened to

other people's stories, it gave me hope that I could find my voice.

The rich, raw stories of *RISK!* made me thirst to experience what it would be like to tell my story the way they did. The podcast is a medium that a blind person can readily enjoy. We are all blind listeners, and we wait for the storyteller to complete the picture in our mind's eye.

I was so nervous when I wrote my story and sent it to *RISK!* that I neglected to include my contact information or where I lived.

PAUL F. TOMPKINS

WHO TALKS LIKE THAT?

I started doing stand-up comedy in Philadelphia, which was a great and difficult place to start. It was great in fact because of its difficulty. I had tough audiences—they would be vocal about it—and I felt that the comedy that I was doing was very smart. Like pearls before swine!

When I moved to Los Angeles, I fell in with a different kind of scene: "alternative comedy." This scene was dominated by the kind of stuff that I always *thought* I was doing, but I wasn't doing. So I began to aspire to do this other kind of more offbeat comedy, performing at this club called Largo, a venue that was half for hip musicians, and half for these alternative comedians.

At Largo, I was becoming one of the cool kids and getting an inflated sense of myself. "Finally," I thought, "I've gotten to the place where people *understand* me, and I'm performing for crowds that *deserve* my comedy."

I didn't realize I was in a bubble. At one point, a friend of mine, a musician, told me his band was playing a show on New Year's Eve, and he was wondering if I'd like to open for them. I was wary, since I'd been doing this long enough to know that there's something about the idea of comedy before music that makes people lose their minds. For some reason, music crowds can't handle it—comedy is the last thing they want to happen.

Still, I'd opened for this guy's band at Largo a number of times, and for some reason his fans seemed to have embraced me. So I figured it would be fine.

On New Year's Eve, before the show, my friend tells me everyone's going to dress up crazy.

"Well, how crazy is crazy?" I asked.

"Well, I'm gonna be wearing a space suit and angel wings," he said.

I said, "Okay!"

So I show up in a sort of modified ringmaster's costume with a top hat on. I thought, "This is gonna be fantastic, doing what I love with ridiculous friends."

My friend introduces me from an offstage mic, and the crowd goes crazy, though I'm sure it's the alcohol talking and not because they have any idea who I am.

I go out there onstage, wearing my crazy outfit, and five minutes in, everybody is loving everything that I am saying. They're laughing at setups, and cheering for stuff that's not even supposed to be funny. Then, in minute six, I sense that someone has flipped a switch, and the happy, welcoming, approving faces swiveled around to the backs of their heads. Now these mean, hateful faces locked into place, looking back at me.

"BOOOOOOO! Why are you *still* up there?" they said. "We have tolerated you for *five minutes*!"

I had endured my share of tough crowds in Philly, where people throw batteries at their professional sports teams, but I had never experienced anything like this. There was a wall of hate directed at me. People were saying, "Boo," "You suck," and "Get off the stage," those three things, almost like in a round. Like a "Row, Row, Row Your Boat" of hatred.

But I'm still doing my comedy! Acting like it's going to be fine. One guy, as if he was feeling confined by the insults that have been thrown at me so far, starts to get a little jazz with it. He yells at me, "YOU'RE A PIECE OF SHIT!" A human being said that to me! Keep in mind, I had not taken a detour from my set to commit some genocide onstage—I was still just telling some jokes.

I did not, unfortunately, win the crowd back with my witty rejoinder of, "Sir, if I didn't know any better, I'd swear you were trying to hurt my feelings."

"BOOOOOOOOO!" I hear. "WHO TALKS LIKE THAT?!"

Minute twelve is when the first ice cube hits me—*clink!*—right in the chest. It falls on the stage and immediately begins melting under the hot lights. Seconds later, another ice cube hits me from the other side of the room. That means that the second guy saw what the first guy did and thought, "Of course, ice! I'm holding a whole glass of it!"

All told, I would say about ten ice cubes hit me. I guess it was a small mercy that the ice-hurling idea came to these people so late in my set, and most people were drinking beer. One way or another, I make it all the way up to my fifteen minutes and I say, "Thank you, good night!" to a chorus of boos.

I get off the stage, and I am a little shaken. I sit down for a second at the bar to collect myself and review what just happened. Maybe my material isn't quite as bulletproof as I thought. Maybe I had some more growth to do as an artist.

Maybe I haven't been taking into account that some places are full of horrible people.

As I'm contemplating these things, people sitting in the audience start coming up to console me. "Heeeeeeeey, *I* thought you were funny." "Listen, don't quit, dude!" I never said I was gonna quit! Now they're starting to make me feel like maybe I should consider it! If I was gonna quit comedy, would I still be sitting here at the show? "Oh well, time for a career change, no reason I can't enjoy the rest of the show!" Then a few people start coming up to me, saying, "You know what? I admire you, because you stuck to your guns. You could have gone off at any time, but you stayed there, and you did your time."

That is when I realized…I could have gone off at any time! So many moments I could have walked off that stage, and no one would have blamed me at all! I let people throw things at me! Nobody would have batted an eye if I had walked off when the guy called me a piece of shit! People would have said, "Well, you heard what that guy said."

Then my musician friend goes out there. He says a couple mildly amusing things, which the audience thinks are hilarious.

Later on that night, when he's all done with the show, my musician friend says to me something that all my musician friends eventually say to me at one point or another. He says, "I could never do what you do." I told him what I always say to this. "You are goddamn right you couldn't! It's hard! Hard, you coward! You stand up there hiding behind your songs. Everybody claps for songs! You have to, because it's polite! No way could you do what I do. At the very least, if worse comes to worst, guitars deflect ice!"

TAKING THE RISK!

A Q&A WITH PAUL F. TOMPKINS

How does it feel that this story is adapted from a recording of you telling it for an audience that was loving you talking about another audience hating you?

It is extremely comforting. The reaction of the people hearing the story was reassuring proof that the reaction of the audience in the story was not normal.

Have you ever tried telling a not-at-all funny story onstage before?

Not completely. In my stand-up I've told stories about serious subjects, including the death of my mother, but I can't stay too serious for too long. And I've never found myself in a position to be sharing anything completely candid without the context of humor. I can't say that I have been consciously avoiding being in such a situation, but I wouldn't put it past my subconscious.

RAY CHRISTIAN

COMFORTABLE IN THE WATER

I was comfortable in the water—for a Black kid who grew up in the urban ghetto called Church Hill in Richmond, Virginia, anyway. I was comfortable in the water because I like to swim. In fact, when I was eleven years old, I was the first Black Boy Scout to win the Mile Swim Badge. I was comfortable in the water, in part because of all I had survived— I had damn near drowned in the pool, in the lake, and in the James River.

I spent a lot of time in the James River in particular because I loved to fish, and I was always looking for that special honey hole, sometimes making my way out to these little islands that existed in the middle of the river. I must have slipped and busted my ass a couple dozen times swimming out to them. I've been taken away by the current, stuck on logjams, and gotten my ass cut up by branches. All those close calls helped me get confident in my ability to swim.

Church Hill wasn't the kind of place where most people would venture out into the river. It was a place where the nighttime lullaby was the sound of passing freight trains, the wail of sirens, the sound of an occasional guy on the street going, "What up, motherfucker?"

It was a city where hundreds of abandoned dogs and cats roamed the streets aimlessly. It was nothing to see a dead dog or cat on your sidewalk, on the curb, or in an alley, swollen and bloated with maggots. That was hard for me to see, since I loved animals. I loved animals so much that if I found a wounded dog or a wounded cat or a bird with a broken wing, I brought them home and tried to nurse them back to health. But of all the animals I got a chance to collect, I loved pigeons the most.

There was something like a pigeon culture in Church Hill—boys who raised pigeons and fed them. One day, when I was about twelve, I learned there was a much bigger pigeon culture in a nearby area called Fulton, the one place in Richmond that was worse than Church Hill.

If Church Hill was a toilet bowl, then Fulton was like the stain at the bottom of the bowl. Fulton was the kind of place with a constant smell of mold in the air because it flooded every three to five years. The place where people were abandoning all those dogs and cats and cars and trash. And an occasional dead body.

The boys who played with pigeons there were an odd bunch. One of the three main characters was named Roger. He was about fifteen years old—a guy with gaps in his teeth who was prone to slobber a lot. Roger was interested in all things criminal and all things sexual. He used to brag to me about having raped an old woman, having molested little schoolgirls, having forced anal sex on small boys, and I was so young I was just kind of dumbfounded by all that. Then there was Ralph, this chubby, dark-skinned guy, who hung on Roger's every word. Roger would fart. Ralph would say it was music. The third was Mikey, a kid who was shaving in middle school because he'd been held back so many times. Mikey spoke funny. If you said something to him about food, for instance, he might respond, "Motherfucking food want fucking hungry as a motherfucker, man!" But I once saw Mikey strangle a kid to unconsciousness for his milk money. You didn't mess with these guys.

But, like me, they loved the birds. We called the pigeons we played with "rollers." Homing pigeons fly for distance and time and speed. But when we threw ours up into the air, we could make them flip. They could tumble over and over through the air, almost all the way to the ground. To get them to do that, we would start screaming and hollering and slapping our hands, and the birds would flip, flip, flip, flip, flip, and in those moments, I never felt like I had so many friends in my damn life. I was part of the group, and I never had been so damn happy.

But being friends with these guys came with a price, and that price was you had to accept everything that they wanted to put upon you. Some of the games they liked to play involved grabbing each other around the ass and humping on each other. Especially on the littler guys. I remember Roger doing this to me a couple of times, and saying to me one day, "Hey, Ray. You ever been fucked in the ass?" I said, "Hell, no." Then I started noticing I was getting way too much damn attention from this guy. I remember one particular incident when we were all standing outside of an abandoned building, and Roger and Ralph took one of the smaller boys inside. We all stood outside, and somehow we seemed to know why.

We could hear the sounds of slapping skin, and the

smaller boy saying, "Uh-uh, no, uh-oh." We looked around at dogs stalking down the street, in search of a distraction. We pretended like we didn't understand what was happening. When Roger and Ralph came out of the building, they were smiling, and gave each other a high five. The boy was crying, though not loudly. Nobody in the group said anything.

Later, there was an incident where we went into a old abandoned factory building, looking for pigeons, and as I was working my way up into the rafters, in the hollowness of the building, I heard them talking about me down below. "We're gonna fuck his ass today," Roger said. "One of you guys get by that door. One of you guys get by the other door."

As soon as I'd heard that, I snuck out a window in the back, and I waited outside. I don't know why I stayed there. But about thirty minutes later, Roger came out and he was pissed. "Goddammit, Ray!" he said. "Your ass would have been fucked! You are one lucky fucking dude." I tried to laugh.

One day, the boys asked me, "Hey, Ray! Do you know the best place on the river to go fishing?"

"Hell, yes!" I was glad to hear that. Finally, they had taken their minds off my booty and were talking about something I could relate to.

So we went down to the river, and I was guiding them, excitedly saying, "Yeah! There's an old, abandoned dock over there, and there's some habitat over there where you can catch a lot of bass!" I was just walking and talking, wading into the water just a bit, till I noticed that no one was saying a word to me. I turned around, and Roger had his erect penis in his hand. He was reaching toward me. He said, "Get your fucking ass out the water, boy."

I said, "No. Uh-uh…" and I started backing into the water. Then Ralph chimes in, "Oh yeah. Get your ass out of the water, Ray!"

I heard one of them say, "Man, his ass is scared, leave him alone."

But Roger said, "Oh no. He's gonna get fucked. Get out of the water, boy."

He was reaching out for me, but I could tell that he didn't wanna get wet. So I kept backing up deeper into the water. The whole time, I was thinking to myself, "I didn't want this! All I wanted was to play with pigeons. I didn't wanna be fucked or killed. All I wanted was friends!"

But now they were all coming toward me. I went further and further back into the water, and suddenly, the current took me. And when they saw me get swept away, everybody took off and started running.

The current carried me swiftly, as I was struggling to stay as close to the bank as I could. Branches in the riverbed were hitting me, slapping me, cutting me, and the boulders were cracking my knees. I went about a quarter mile down the river before I finally managed to grab onto a branch, and pull myself up on the bank. I was dirty, tired, and cold. But mostly, I was scared. Every time I would hear so much as a crackle of a branch, I trembled. I didn't wanna die. For a half hour, I was just petrified, standing there waiting, wondering if these guys were going to rape or kill me.

After about a half hour, I didn't hear anything else, so I

crawled out of that dirty riverbank and made my away across the lot, back up to Church Hill, into the neighborhood.

In the next couple days, I got word that the pigeon guys thought I was dead. But when they found out that I wasn't, they wanted to kill me. So as for Fulton, I never went back there anymore.

But on my way back home that day, a homeless guy saw me and started yelling at me, "Hey, boy. What are you doing wet?! You look like shit, you know! What the hell were you doing in the water?"

I was just happy to be alive. I said, "Man, I'm comfortable in the water."

TAKING THE RISK!

A Q&A WITH RAY CHRISTIAN

What was it like going from thinking "I could share some stories on some storytelling shows" to actually doing it?

It was a long road of pitching stories and getting rejections at first. No show wanted my stories until I found *RISK!* I started just hoping I could get a written version of my story out. The idea of telling my story onstage was scary. Telling personal stories onstage in front of an audience is so emotional.

What has storytelling meant to you since then?

Storytelling has given me an opportunity to share parts of my unusual life with people who might never have come in contact with someone from my background and perspective otherwise. We need more of that in this country.

AFTERWORD

It's said that the children's TV host Mr. Rogers kept a note in his wallet that a social worker once gave to him, saying, "Frankly, there isn't anyone you couldn't learn to love once you've heard their story." If that's the case, we need to get a lot more stories heard. By the time this book hits the shelves, we'll have featured 1,200 stories on the *RISK!* podcast—and narrowing those down to our favorite few dozen to include in this book was tremendously hard!—but there remain so many more great stories to be shared. While you're reading this, someone might have just wound up homeless, or been resuscitated on a hospital gurney, or looked back at the rest of us for the first time from the International Space Station, all of them living through a potential future *RISK!* story.

I hope these stories make you consider the times in your life where you cared the most about what would happen next, the days when you felt especially surprised or thrilled or wounded, the nights you faced a test you never envisioned. Feel the tingle you felt in your guts at those moments. Hear the words you were surprised to find coming out of your mouth. Try telling a close friend about it. Don't be afraid to share the memories that embarrass you. Instead, tell them how those memories changed you. Consider visiting us at the Submissions page at www.risk-show.com. There, we offer all kinds of tips on how to prepare your story for our show, and if you dare to share it, we'll be happy to help you work on your story as well.

If I have learned one thing while hosting this life-changing podcast, it's that I'm most satisfied when I live boldly, share my secrets, and help others to share theirs.

ACKNOWLEDGMENTS

One of the many things I've learned from *RISK!* is that asking for help is a huge part of success. There are so many people who have helped make *RISK!* what it is. Among them are Michael Ian Black, the guy who prodded me to "take a risk" and start telling my own true stories onstage, and Margot Leitman and Giulia Rozzi, who gave me my first chance to do that at their delightful *Stripped Stories* show at the old UCB Chelsea. Michelle Walson, who directed shows that I loved at The PIT, also played a big role in getting *RISK!* off the ground, producing the first live shows of *RISK!* in New York, and the first episodes of the podcast. She continues to coach the storytellers for our New York and LA shows, lending storytellers her amazing ear and insightful edits. The arts organization The Field, in New York, also supported us in the early days, and one of my dearest friends, the brilliant Jan Warner, helped us move beyond maxing out my credit cards to turn *RISK!* into a business. The brilliant Chris Castiglione helped us to develop our organization on the business side alongside Phil Murphy in the early years.

There are so many talented folks who helped *RISK!* with the audio production early on, including Tim Meehan, Nick Montalbano, Andy Kroner, Jeff Mercel, Cal Rifkin, David

Crabb, and especially Mike Cades, who edited our first episode while working for almost nothing, which was exactly what the whole show's budget was. Ellis & Park and Stuckey and Murray provided fun and clever music at our live shows in the early days.

From the wider podcasting world, we're so grateful to have received such crucial advice from Marc Maron, Brendan McDonald, Jesse Thorn, Seth Lind, Thomas Hillard, and the amazingly helpful Rob Walch at Libsyn. We are lucky as well to have had great artists such as Jessie Glass, Stefan Lawrence, and René Martinez create artwork for the show that helped our personality as a brand shine through. John Sondericker and the band Wormburner came up with our opening theme song for the show.

David Owen created one of the greatest comedy festivals in America and gave us our first out-of-town gig at San Francisco Sketchfest in 2011.

JC Cassis took the helm as the business director of *RISK!* in 2011 and managed the Herculean task of building a functioning machine from all our then-disparate parts. She and I meet every morning on Skype to go over the business of the show, and we consistently behave ridiculously while hacking away at it all. Without JC, I myself would barely function and *RISK!* would never have lasted and grown. She made a monumental contribution toward the completion of this book as well, managing all the communications between our agent, editor, legal team, and storytellers; assembling the various parts of the manuscript; keeping track of an insane amount of information; and making sure we crossed all our t's and dotted all our i's.

We enjoyed being a part of the Maximum Fun podcast network for the years that we were there and loved meeting lots of new friends and fans in that community.

Through most every year in which we've been in operation, Jeff Barr's contribution to the show has been massive. He took over the helm as episode editor around 2011 and has been sewing the episodes together, editing radio-style stories and creating crazy audio interstitials for us ever since. John LaSala and Marty Garcia have become essential assistant audio editors, making raw storytelling come to cinematic life.

A lot of interns have been a tremendous help to us—among them, Nina Mozes, Charlie Bruce, J. Paul Gale, Daniel Nguyen, Duke Eisenhower, Adam Weinrib, Zack Bornstein, Will Ruehle, and Henry Epp. I assume that by the time they are reading this, they will all be millionaires.

A few other people have offered invaluable help with different aspects of running the podcast and show. Sheila Kenny, with her company Right On!, has managed PR for the show phenomenally and become a dear friend. Alana Crow and Paul Hazen have provided meticulous help with our legal considerations. Jocelyn Conn and Jeremy Wein have provided wonderful help when it comes to casting. Gary Levitt, Zac McKeever, and Dave Paolucci have recorded most of our NYC and LA shows, bringing countless stories to the podcast. Matt Anderson, Jesse Gold, and Conor Lynch have provided lots of professional help with video work. Anytime we need help with our websites, Ethan James is there to save us. Josh Lindgren helped us start touring to so many more cities than before through his work at Billions, and he has a splendid beard. Lynda Balsama helped us find and shape many absolutely unforgettable stories. Cyndi Freeman and Brad Lawrence have carved out integral roles on the team, especially in helping our storytellers prepare for the tour shows and in engaging our fans on social media. They have helped make *RISK!* what it is today.

The producing and hosting of the LA show was first in the hands of the wonderful Matteson Perry. Then Beowulf Jones took over that role and has been the heart and soul of the show out there ever since. The brilliant Pete Holmes and Kumail Nanjiani previously hosted our LA show and were positively excellent.

The Story Studio helps many of our storytellers hone their stories, and it wouldn't be possible without a few key people. Shelle Jordan, who consistently provides invaluable administrative assistance for *RISK!* and The Story Studio, is one of them. David Steele ran The Story Studio's social media with great dedication for years. The Story Studio teachers themselves are, of course, integral and cannot be beat. There's Amy Salloway in Minneapolis; Beowulf Jones, Giulia Rozzi, and David Crabb in Los Angeles; and Cyndi Freeman, Dawn Fraser, Julia Whitehouse, Mel Dockery, Gail Thomas, and Brad Lawrence in New York. If you take a workshop with any one of them, you're in for a real treat.

Many other storytelling shows have been helpful to us along the way. Though there are too many to list them all, Bawdy Storytelling, created by our dear friend Dixie De La Tour; Spark London, with Dave Pickering and Joanna Yates; Story District in DC, created by Amy Saidman; and First Person Arts in Philadelphia, run by Jamie Brunson, have all been big inspirations and great friends to us. The Mystery

Box in Portland, hosted by Eric Scheur and Reba Sparrow, has provided lots of stories we've featured on the podcast.

Liz Parker, our super-supportive literary agent, was essential for making this book possible. Our book editor, David Lamb, as well as our publicist, Marisol Salaman, and marketer, Michael Barrs at Hachette Books, were phenomenal.

We are blessed with supporters across a few different platforms that, together, make *RISK!* possible. Midroll has introduced us to so many great advertisers for the podcast, and all of our sponsors have been essential for keeping *RISK!* running. Our students at the Story Studio continue to inspire us with their courage and creativity. And our Patreon supporters are an invaluable aid in helping us make the show all it can be.

We are most deeply indebted to all the storytellers who have ever pitched us their stories and all the storytellers who have appeared on the show. They are the lifeblood of this work.

Finally, there are the fans. Every day, we are so thankful for those who are listening and reacting to our stories. You are the people who make *RISK!* an irreplaceable part of the storytelling landscape.

ABOUT THE EDITOR

KEVIN ALLISON is the host and creator of the *RISK!* podcast. He created the storytelling school The Story Studio, where professionals from all fields learn how to craft compelling stories and engage audiences effectively. Kevin is a member of the sketch comedy group The State, whose nineties MTV show remains a cult classic. He lives in Brooklyn with his cat, Donky.

CONTRIBUTOR BIOS

AMES BECKERMAN is a photographer, stand-up comic, actor, activist, proud trans man, and ice cream enthusiast. He is indebted to his partner, Sorcha Murnane, for, among many other things, helping him write his story, "Like Mother, Like Me." You can check out his most recent endeavor, *The Being Project: A Multi-Dimensional View of Trans Lives,* on Instagram (@TheBeingProject), and view his photography at www.amesbeckerman.com and on Instagram at @amesbeckerman.

MICHAEL IAN BLACK is an actor, a writer, and a comedian. He lives in the wilds of Connecticut with his wife and two children.

MICHELE CARLO has told stories across the U.S., including at *RISK!*'s live shows and on its podcast, at the Moth's GrandSlams and Mainstage in NYC, on NPR, and on the PBS World Channel TV series *Stories from the Stage.* She is also the author of the NYC-based memoir, *Fish Out of Agua,* and hosts the *Fish Out of Agua* podcast on PodOmatic and iTunes. For more about Michele: www.michelecarlo .com.

JC CASSIS is a multitalented artist from New York City, and the producer of the *RISK!* podcast. She has toured the United States as a musician and helped to build *RISK!* from a DIY project to a thriving independent business. But most important, she is a mom to her rescue chihuahua mix, Mrs. Pippington, who is the best dog ever. Learn more at JCCassis.com.

RAYMOND (RAY) CHRISTIAN grew up in poverty in the city of Richmond, Virginia, during the 1960s and 1970s. He joined the Army at seventeen and served as an infantryman and a paratrooper. A combat veteran who earned the Bronze Star, he retired at thirty-eight. He is a doctor of education and an adjunct professor at Appalachian State University. He resides in a remote, mountainous, and rural area of North Carolina with his family and animals. Find Ray's storytelling and African American history podcast, *What's Ray Saying*, at WhatsRaySaying.com.

TOM COLEMAN is a native of Acadia Parish, Louisiana. He is a thirty-eight-year newspaperman working under the flags of the *New York Times*, *Dallas Morning News*, and Louisiana State Newspapers. Coleman's avocations include art, music, and professional storytelling, weaving tales from his Cajun upbringing and heritage. He and his wife, Pamela, have seven children, six grandchildren, and a cat, Jolie, who allows them to live in her home in Lafayette, Louisiana. You can learn more about Coleman's work at www.coleman360.com.

POLLO CORRAL is a regular guy (no superpowers) who has messed up a lot in life. Many years ago, he hit rock bottom so bad that he almost lost his life. Almost twenty years later, he's sharing a story that's all about second chances, hope, and unconditional love, not only from his earthly father but also from his Heavenly Father. You're invited to sit in the ashes and enjoy the theme of redemption, which is laced throughout. Pollo has a pretty wife and two cool kids. They're living the dream, breath by breath.

DAVID CRABB is a writer, an actor, a Moth host, and a storyteller in Los Angeles. His solo show, *Bad Kid*, was named a *New York Times* Critics' Pick. The memoir adaptation of the show was released in 2015. David has lectured on and taught storytelling in the U.S., Australia, and Canada with Kevin Allison's The Story Studio, The Moth, The People's Improv Theatre, and the Upright Citizens Brigade.

From Burleson, Texas, CHAD DUNCAN is a loving husband, a knowledgeable and dedicated social worker, a tea connoisseur, a world traveler, and a dog lover. Chad's experience with struggle, his amazing compassion for his clients, and his sense of humor pave the way for him to make a real impact on his clients' lives. Every day is an adventure for Chad; he makes sure every day is an adventure for those who encounter his light.

KYLE GEST is the producer of his own storytelling podcast, *The Lapse*, at thelapse.org. Since his appearance on

RISK!, Kyle has grown into an accomplished writer and sound designer with a flair for filmic, audio-rich postproduction. If he has any advice, it's this: The worse the experience, the better the anecdote.

KITTY HAILEY is a professional investigator from Philadelphia. Storytelling has become an outlet that allows her to reflect upon those experiences and share some of those tales. In her profession, she has become known for writing about ethics. This venue allows her to talk about her own life while shielding the confidentiality of her clients. The "John" stories are about her husband, who was afflicted with Frontal Temporal Dementia. Together, they made the best of his remaining years. The "John" stories are a tribute to this wonderful man. Kitty can be reached via her website: www.kittyhailey.com.

MELANIE HAMLETT is a comedian, storyteller, and writer based out of LA, Spain, and who knows where else. She's won the Moth multiple times, has had stories featured on eight episodes of the *RISK!* podcast, and performs around NYC, LA, and now, Europe. She's represented by her literary agent, Scott Mendel, and writes for the *Washington Post*, the *Guardian*, *Glamour*, *Playboy*, The Huffington Post, and elsewhere. To see pics and stories from her travels and adventures, visit her website: melaniehamlett.com.

A. J. JACOBS is the author of four *New York Times* bestsellers, including *The Year of Living Biblically* and *Drop Dead Healthy*.

JJ is an entrepreneur with over a decade of experience in corporate and public finance. He has master's degrees in government and business.

NIMISHA LADVA is a storyteller, writer, and solo performer. Her stories have been broadcast on NPR's *Newsworks* and *CommonSpace* programs, and featured on *RISK!* and other podcasts. Her writing has been published in the U.S. and the UK, including in the *Crab Orchard Review*, *Stand*, *Connecticut Review*, and theguardian.com. Her solo performance play, *Uninvited Girl: An Immigrant Story*, was put on by the Women in Theater Festival, hosted by Project Y Theater.

After growing up in a small town in Vermont, MARCY LANGLOIS has found herself living an outdoorsy, active life in Colorado. In the midst of rediscovering herself, she met her wife, Tracey, and her daughter, Brianna, who have been by her side while Marcy has led a life of recovery and sobriety. Mortgage banking has brought her success, and time with her dogs, meditation, reading, hiking, and biking bring her joy on her time off.

ROY LAZORWITZ is a New Jersey native who studied screenwriting in college. After New York got the best of him, he moved to Austin, Texas, where he studied and taught sketch comedy. He loves his parents and regrets ever lying to the ones he loves. If he could be remembered for anything it would be that he tried to do his best and that he's the world's most discreet pro wrestling fan.

Best known as TS MADISON, Madison Hinton branded herself, initially, as an adult film star and producer. Today, she converts social media views into a lucrative business with revenue streams from YouTube, Facebook, and sponsors for the massive online show *The Queens Supreme Court*. The platform that she built for herself caught the eye of Hollywood producer Lee Daniels, which resulted in a deal with FOX as host of the *Star* after show.

MARC MARON is a stand-up comic. His podcast, *WTF with Marc Maron*, has become a worldwide phenomenon. He currently stars in the Netflix original series *GLOW*. His critically acclaimed series, *Maron*, aired on IFC. Marc has performed guest-starring roles in the series *Girls*, *Louie*, and Joe Swanberg's *Easy*. He has released several stand-up specials and albums. His most recent special, *Marc Maron: Too Real*, was released in 2017 and is currently streaming on Netflix.

MOLOCH MASTERS was born in Canton, Ohio. Her family moved eight times before she was in high school. She had to say goodbye to her closest friends over and over again. Her family had plenty of skeletons in their closet. To overcome darkness and loneliness, she turned to writing and art. She is the author of five novels and is currently working on her sixth. She lives in South Carolina with her Siamese cat, Twitch.

MAX likens himself to a cat with nine lives. He's burned through about half of them and hopefully has a few left. But he's come full circle and is a proud husband and father of two boys and considers himself an All-American working-class hero. He's been around the block quite a few times and danced with the devil, but ultimately, he's become a force for good in this wild world of ours. And whatever he does, he lives that life to the max.

MORGAN has been a stand-up storyteller for ten years and was in KQED's StoryCorps OutLoud's first live show in San Francisco. She has performed at the *RISK!* live show in NYC and LA, and at Bed Post Confessions in Austin, Texas. She got her San Francisco storytelling start with Bawdy Storytelling, studied with David Ford at the Marsh, and has a one-woman show titled, *Hold Still I Want to Tell You a Story*. She produces a monthly variety show in San Francisco called *Tuesday's Child* on Wednesday that's been running for over three years. And, of course, she plays numerous pee-in-the-corner bars all over San Francisco.

HANNA BROOKS OLSEN is a writer living in Seattle. Her work has appeared in the *Nation*, the *Atlantic*, the *Establishment*, *Pacific Standard*, *GOOD Magazine*, *Fast Company*, and the *Democracy Journal*.

JIM PADAR is a retired Chicago homicide detective, an author, and a storyteller. He is a four-time Moth Story Slam winner. Jim is also coauthor of *On Being a Cop*, fifty-three memoirs chronicling the experiences of himself and his son, who is also a Chicago police officer. The book is currently in its second printing. More of his stories can be found on his website, www.OnBeingaCop.com.

JONAH RAY (RODRIGUES) was born and raised on the island of Oahu in the state of Hawaii. Playing in punk bands since the age of thirteen, Jonah always had a desire to perform. So, in 2001, he moved to Los Angeles to act, write, and perform stand-up comedy. In the seventeen years since then, he's released two stand-up EPs, taped a Comedy Central special, co-hosted the hit podcast *The Nerdist*, and co-hosted and created *The Meltdown w/Jonah and Kumail*, a stand-up show that ran for three seasons on Comedy Central. He is currently the lead in the Netflix revival of *Mystery Science Theater 3000*.

CHRISTOPHER RYAN hosts his own popular podcast called Tangentially Speaking. He is also the coauthor (with his wife, Cacilda Jethá) of the *New York Times* bestseller, *Sex at Dawn*. His next book, *Civilized to Death*, is expected in late 2018.

DAN SAVAGE has been writing "Savage Love," a syndicated sex-advice column, for more than twenty-five years. He also hosts *The Savage Lovecast*, a sex-and-relationship-advice podcast. He's the best-selling author of seven books and has contributed to numerous publications. He lives in Seattle.

JAN SCOTT-FRAZIER is a director, a producer, a public speaker, a storyteller, a multimedia artist, an art/creativity educator, a translator, a Japanese animation industry veteran, and an invited guest speaker at more than three hundred anime, sci-fi, and comics conventions. She worked in the anime industry in Japan for fourteen years and had her own studio in Bangkok. Jan has written textbooks, magazine articles, technical manuals, and screenplays, and translated manga. She founded the nonprofit Voices For, and produced two albums for them.

TRACEY SEGARRA launched her career in NYC as a reporter and an editor for local newspapers and national wire services, interviewing assorted politicians, celebrities, and criminals. But now all she wants to do is tell stories to strangers about her own life. She has appeared on the *RISK!* live show and podcast, and *The Moth Radio Hour* on NPR, and hosts her own Long Island–based storytelling show, *Now You're Talking!* Find her at traceysegarra.com.

LILI TAYLOR works in film, stage, and TV. She serves on the board of National Audubon and American Bird Association.

JESSE THORN is the host and producer of *Bullseye* and *Jordan, Jesse, Go!*, and the co-host and producer of *Judge John Hodgman*. He's also the proprietor of MaximumFun.org, where he oversees a network of more than two dozen podcasts, along with video and other content production. A native of San Francisco's Mission District, Jesse lives in Los Angeles with his wife, podcaster and author Theresa Thorn, three children, and two dogs.

PAUL F. TOMPKINS is from Philadelphia and resides in Los Angeles. He is a comedian, a writer, an actor, and a podcaster. For a full list of Mr. Tompkins's stage, television, and film credits, ask your teacher or a policeman.

TORI is an artist and writer in the Boston area. Her writing has appeared in various literary magazines and her artwork has been displayed throughout the city. She has two degrees from that college that churns out famous comedians and is currently working on a personal essay collection.

AISHA TYLER is an award-winning director, actor, comedian, *New York Times* bestselling author, podcaster, and activist. She is the former Emmy-winning cohost of CBS's *The Talk*; voice of superspy Lana Kane on FX's Emmy-winning *Archer*; host of the CW improv juggernaut *Whose Line Is It Anyway?*; creator, producer, and host of the hit podcast *Girl on Guy*; and series regular on the long-running CBS hit *Criminal Minds*. Her feature-length directorial debut, *AXIS*, won the Outstanding Achievement in Feature Filmmaking award at the Newport Beach Film Festival. A San Francisco native, Tyler holds a degree in government from Dartmouth College. She is a bourbon, video-game, and hard-rock fan; a snowboarder and sci-fi obsessive; and confounding to all who know her.

MOLLENA LEE WILLIAMS-HAAS is a native New Yorker who has lived in Los Angeles and San Francisco before returning home. She has been a performer since the age of five, an acknowledged member of the BDSM community since 1996, twice a Leather titleholder, an award-winning short-filmmaker and author, and the wife and consensual property of Austrian composer Georg Friedrich Haas. Georg and she are the subjects of the 2018 documentary, *The Artist and the Pervert*.

Born in Montgomery, Alabama, WALTER ZIMMER-
MAN and his family moved eleven times before his high
school graduation in western Pennsylvania. After four years
in the U.S. Air Force, Walter earned a BS degree at Penn
State, focusing in art and theater. Walter recorded many full-
length books on tape, later earning an MFA in glassblowing
from Rochester Institute of Technology. He was a college
glass professor for seven years. He and his husband live in
South Orange, New Jersey.

PERMISSIONS

"Ham and Samurai" by Kevin Allison. Copyright © 2018 by Kevin Allison.

"Like Mother, Like Me" by Ames Beckerman. Copyright © 2018 by Ames Beckerman.

"The Ring of Fire" by Michael Ian Black. Copyright © 2018 by Michael Ian Black.

Michele Carlo, "The Gift," first published in *Fish Out of Agua: My Life on Neither Side of the (Subway) Tracks* (New York: Citadel, 2010). Copyright © 2010 by Michele Carlo. Reprinted by permission of the author.

"The Downward Spiral" by JC Cassis. Copyright © 2018 by JC Cassis.

"Comfortable in the Water" by Raymond Christian. Copyright © 2018 by Raymond Christian.

"Chasing the Sunset" by Tom Coleman. Copyright © 2018 by Tom Coleman.

"Redemption" by Pollo Corral. Copyright © 2018 by Pollo Corral.

"Every Day Is Halloween" by David Crabb. Copyright © 2018 by David Crabb.

"Doing Good" by Chad Duncan. Copyright © 2018 by Chad Duncan.

"Dylan" by Kyle Gest. Copyright © 2018 by Kyle Gest.